The Colonial Documentary Film in South and South-East Asia

The Colonial Documentary Film in South and South-East Asia

Edited by Ian Aitken and
Camille Deprez

EDINBURGH
University Press

Edinburgh University Press is one of the leading university presses in the UK. We publish academic books and journals in our selected subject areas across the humanities and social sciences, combining cutting-edge scholarship with high editorial and production values to produce academic works of lasting importance. For more information visit our website: edinburghuniversitypress.com

© editorial matter and organisation Ian Aitken and Camille Deprez, 2017
© the chapters their several authors, 2017

Edinburgh University Press Ltd
The Tun – Holyrood Road
12 (2f) Jackson's Entry
Edinburgh EH8 8PJ

Typeset in 11/13 Adobe Sabon by
IDSUK (DataConnection) Ltd

A CIP record for this book is available from the British Library

ISBN 978 1 4744 0720 5 (hardback)
ISBN 978 1 4744 0721 2 (webready PDF)
ISBN 978 1 4744 0722 9 (epub)

The right of the contributors to be identified as authors of this work has been asserted in accordance with the Copyright, Designs and Patents Act 1988 and the Copyright and Related Rights Regulations 2003 (SI No. 2498).

Contents

List of Figures   vii
List of Abbreviations   ix

    Introduction   1
    Ian Aitken and Camille Deprez

Part I   Issues of Colonialism, Late Colonialism and Independence
1. The People's Action Party Government of Singapore
   and *Berita Singapura*   29
   Ian Aitken
2. *Merdeka for Malaya*: Imagining Independence across
   the British Empire   45
   Tom Rice
3. The Language of Counterinsurgency in Malaya:
   Dialectical Soundscapes of Salvage and Warfare   63
   Peter J. Bloom
4. Figures of Empire: American Documentaries in
   the Philippines   79
   José B. Capino

Part II   Missionary Films and Christian Evangelism
5. Two Films and a Coronation: The Containment of
   Islam in Flores in the 1920s   107
   Sandeep Ray
6. Paradoxical Legacies: Colonial Missionary Films,
   Corporate Philanthropy in South Asia and the
   Griersonian Documentary Tradition   128
   Annamaria Motrescu-Mayes

7. Conversion, Salvation and the 'Civilising Mission': Christian Missions and Documentary Film in India (1900–60)   148
   Emma Sandon

Part III Documentary Representations: Projections, Idealised and Imaginary Images

8. Screening the Revolution in Rural Vietnam: Guerrilla Cinema Across the Mekong Delta   171
   Thong Win
9. *Ho Chi Minh in France*: An Early Independence Newsreel   186
   Dean Wilson
10. Archives of the Planet: French Elitist Representations of Colonial India   205
    Camille Deprez
11. 'Sufficient Dramatic or Adventure Interest': Authenticity, Reality and Violence in Pre-War Animal Documentaries from South-East Asia   223
    Timothy P. Barnard

Notes on the Contributors   236
Index   239

Figures

4.1	*In Old and New Manila with Burton Holmes*, juxtaposition of a horse carriage in the foreground and a soda fountain in the background	84
4.2	*In Old and New Manila with Burton Holmes*, juxtaposition of a motorised lawn mower in the foreground with the medieval-style ramparts in the background	85
4.3	A leprosy patient uses his hand to close his mouth, apparently with instructions from someone off-screen, in *Leprosy*	88
4.4	The legacy of American rule is highlighted in this float for a parade celebrating the liberation of the Philippines in the Second World War	95
4.5	A montage of shots depicts the perils of a communist takeover in the Philippines in *This Is My Home*	98
5.1.	Advertisements for *Flores Film* and *Ben-Hur*, 1928	113
5.2.	Father Simon Buis in staged contemplation in *Flores Film*, 1926	114
5.3 and 5.4	Missionaries braving the mountainous and riverine terrain of Flores in *Flores Film*, 1926	115
5.5	Killing a Komodo dragon in *Flores Film*, 1926	116
5.6 and 5.7	Stills from *Flores Film*, 1926: natives in Flores learn how to make a Christian prayer cross; Bishop Verstraelen blesses new converts	118
5.8	Poster for *Ria Rago* screening at the Polytechnic Cinema Theatre in February 1931	120

5.9	Father Simon Buis and the newly appointed Raja Baroek, *De Katholieke Missiën*, 1931	124
6.1	*Saint Joseph's Missionary Society Collection*, India, 1928–32	134
6.2	*Lemon Grove*, India, 2013	136
6.3	*Saint Joseph's Missionary Society Collection*, India, 1928–32	139
6.4	*Saint Joseph's Missionary Society Collection*, India, 1928–32	143
6.5	*Lemon Grove*, India, 2013	144
7.1	*Salvation Army Work in India, Burma and Ceylon*	153
7.2	Lakshini at school learning Bible stories	156
7.3	Liladhar, the convert Brahmin, now evangelist	163
8.1	Map of the Mekong Delta's three guerrilla war zones and their notable film screenings	174
8.2	The crowd gathers around the screen to watch *The Battle of Mcc Hoa* at the Đồng Tháp Mười screening on 24 December 1948	178
9.1	Mai Trung Thu, June 1946	195
10.1	Portrait picture of Jagatjit Singh Bahadur, Maharaja of Kapurthala	207

Abbreviations

APC	American–Philippine Company
BECM	British Empire and Commonwealth Museum
BFI	British Film Institute
CAOM	Centre d'Archives d'Outre-Mer
CFU	Colonial Film Unit
CMS	Church Missionary Society
COI	Central Office of Information
CoS	Church of Scotland
DRV	Democratic Republic of Vietnam
EIS	Emergency Information Services
EMB	Empire Marketing Board
GCFU	Gold Coast Film Unit
HKBU	Hong Kong Baptist University
HSBC	Hong Kong Shangai Bank Corporation
ICP	Indonesian Communist Party
IJA	Imperial Japanese Army
LMS	London Missionary Society
MFC	Missionary Film Committee
MFU	Malayan Film Unit
MMS	Methodist Missionary Society
MoI	Ministry of Information
MPAJA	Malayan People's Anti-Japanese Army
NARA	National Archives and Records Adminstration
NAS	National Archives of Singapore
ONS	*Ouvriers non spécialisés*
PAP	People's Action Party (Singapore)
RTM	Radio Television Malaysia
SA	Salvation Army

SVD	Societas Verbi Divini
UMNO	United Malay National Organisation
USIA	United States Information Agency
WMMS	Wesleyan Methodist Missionary Society

Introduction

Ian Aitken and Camille Deprez

THE SOUTH AND SOUTH-EAST ASIA DOCUMENTARY FILM RESEARCH PROGRAMME AND WEBSITE

This new anthology is, in part, associated with research activities related to the South and South-East Asia Documentary Film Research programme, founded by Professor Ian Aitken and Dr Camille Deprez at the Academy of Film of Hong Kong Baptist University in June 2013. This research programme draws upon ongoing Hong Kong government-funded research projects;[1] a number of Hong Kong Baptist University-granted projects on British and French colonial documentary film in Asia; and three international conferences held at Hong Kong Baptist University in 2009, 2012 and 2013 respectively. In May 2015, the new South and South-East Asia Documentary Film Research website was also launched in collaboration with the Hong Kong Baptist University Library.[2] This new online platform has been designed to hold and disseminate primary and secondary research materials – including texts, images, video and audio files – pertaining to the subject of documentary film in South and South-East Asia and covering the colonial, late colonial and post-colonial periods.

The notion of the 'archive' traditionally refers to the physical location where primary and mostly unique source documents of historical, evidentiary or cultural significance are kept. A film archive more specifically collects, preserves, restores and also shares. The digital archive presented in the website just referred to collects, electronically processes, preserves and disseminates primary and secondary research materials pertaining to the documentary film in colonial and post-colonial South and South-East Asia using web and database archiving techniques. In its initial phase of development, this website contained over 3,000 electronically processed pages of official documents relating to the use of official films in South-East Asia, including Hong Kong, written between 1945 and 1973. The majority of these documents was written by government officials and reveals the process of colonial withdrawal from the region, as well as the role played by the official film in that disengagement. As such, these documents offer insight into the region at the end of much of the British Empire. This database is one of the outcomes of the afore-mentioned government-funded research projects on the use of official films in Hong Kong, Singapore and Malaya over this period, carried out by Ian Aitken. As a result of the digitalisation process, these primary materials can now be cross-referenced in a number of ways using web search and retrieval tools that facilitate the open access and sharing of information worldwide. Related to the wider developing field of 'digital humanities', the website, which is now available online, marks a major achievement in the advancement of academic research, as scholars are now able to freely access this archival material and contribute to further developments in the area of colonial, late colonial and post-colonial film studies in the South-East Asian region. A whole new set of materials on this topic, which includes an additional 2,500 pages, as well as 3,000 pages of primary documents pertaining to Camille Deprez's government-funded research project on the history of the documentary film in India between 1948 and 1975, will also be analysed and digitalised over the academic year 2015–16.

This open-source online digital archive constitutes a major aspect of this research programme and its co-founders seek to enhance its scholarly impact by compiling this present anthology on the colonial documentary film in South and South-East Asia. Six speakers from the conferences held in January 2012 and August 2013 have contributed to this volume. These contributions have supplied new research findings on issues of colonialism and documentary film, some of which have already appeared in publications in scholarly journals and books (Aitken 2012, 2015; Aitken and Ingham 2014; Deprez 2013, 2014; Rice 2013, and others). This anthology brings these and other research findings together, to constitute the first book-length study of its kind.

GEOGRAPHICAL SCOPE AND TIME FRAME

Colonial film studies constitute a growing area of scholarly research activity worldwide. Up to this date, scholars have studied issues of colonial and imperial film mainly from an international perspective (Cowans 2015; Sherzer 1996; and others); within national contexts (Aitken and Ingham 2014; Basket 2008; Blanchard et al. 2015; Cooper 2001;

Deprez 2013; Di Carmine 2011; Furhmann 2015; Hargreaves 2005; Norindr 1996; Rice 2013; Slavin 2001; Woods 2001; and others); or from the point of view of the colonised and their negotiations with the colonisers (Chowdhury 2000; Jaikumar 2006; Raju 2012; Sarkar 2009; and others). Others have focused their interest on the African continent (Burns 2002; Landau and Kaspin 2002; Larkin 2008; Reynolds 2015; Smyth 1983, 1988; and others), but there has been comparatively less focus on colonial Asia. In terms of South-East Asia, a number of works have appeared that cover the development of colonial public relations and propaganda policy, including Carruthers (1999), Lashmar and Oliver (1998), Taylor (1999) and others. This work, however, focuses only tangentially on the official film. Similarly in the South Asian context, publications on public relations policy and propaganda address power struggles in the press (Israel 1994), in revolutionary pamphlets (Sanyal 2014) or in the fiction film during colonial or late colonial times (Chowdhury 2000; Kaur and Mazarella 2009, and others); seldom examine the official documentary film. Literature on French colonial public relations focuses mainly on the empire at large (Aldrich 2002; Chafer and Sackur 2002; Daughton and White 2012; Thomas 2005), and when scholars more specifically address the situation in Asia, they concentrate mainly on Indochina, where the French held their strongest colonial positions (Cooper 2001; Ha 2014; Robson and Yee 2015). Yet, here again, apart from Murray-Levine (2010), and to a lesser extent Bloom (2008), studies addressing the official film remain scarce.

Hence, this anthology is the first to focus primarily on the use of the official and colonial documentary film in the South and South-East Asian regions. The area covered here ranges from the South Asian subcontinent in the West; Singapore, Malaysia, Indonesia and the Philippines in the South; to Indochina and Hong Kong in the east. This collection of essays therefore encompasses diverse geographical and historical contexts, which are nevertheless all connected to issues of colonial occupation, including the British rule in India, Hong Kong, Singapore and Malaya; the French colonial presence in India and Indochina; the Dutch occupation of Indonesia; the Japanese intervention in French-colonised Vietnam; and US influence in Indonesia and the Philippines. Some territories, such as Burma, are not covered in this volume, and this is mainly because they have not been studied sufficiently yet, and/or because no contributors could be identified who were willing or able to write on them. Hopefully, this lack will be rectified by other scholars in the future. Given that the colonial era and its relation to the official film varied in terms of time period across the South and South-East Asian regions, chapters in this anthology also cover various time frames, spanning from the 1900s to the 1960s, and encompassing colonial rule, the transition of territories into decolonisation and national independence, and the early period of independence.

DEFINING THE COLONIAL DOCUMENTARY FILM

Although a number of relative y recent publications focus on the documentary film during the colonial era (Aitken 2012, 2015; Aitken and Ingram 2014; Amad 2008; Bloom 2008; Creed and Hoorn 2011; Druick and Williams 2014; Grieveson and MacCabe 2011a, 2011b; Murray-Levine 2010; Rice 2013; Stollery 2000, 2011; and others), it remains the case that most scholars continue to prioritise the fiction film and other forms of popular culture, such as music, postcards, colonial expositions, popular fiction, advertising, comic books and so on (Blanchard et al. 2015; Blanchard et al. 2008; Ezra 2000; McKinney 2013; Robson and Yee 2005; and others). The field of colonial documentary film studies is therefore a developing one, and this brings with it problems of definition, in part also because forms and practices of documentary film vary according to specific historical and geographical contexts. As a result, this volume covers a range of types of documentary film, including newsreels, amateur films; missionary, philanthropic, nature, educational, informational and promotional films; official, public relations, sponsored and propaganda films; and also travelogues; and this is a range of material that also points to the eclectic practices, discourses and styles involved here. This heterogeneity also corresponds to the vibrant period of transition from pioneering proto-documentary film practices to more standardised film production methods, as well as the early appropriation of the film medium in different ways by colonised populations. Additionally, this diversity reflects the varying – and often conflicting – forces at work, including the official political and military mandates of the colonisers, the strengthening of industrial and commercial ties with the colonised based on principles of either 'free trade' or imperial preference (both of which deployed advantage to the metropolitan colonising centres), and the Christian mission of moral uplift and conversion of supposedly 'backward' populations (Aldrich 2002; Conklin 1997; Girardet 1986, and others).

The films analysed in this volume also stem from various documentary film traditions. In terms of Britain, small British companies shot films in the colonies from almost the beginning of cinema. So, for example, companies such as Hepworth and the Warwick Trading Company made short 'scenic' films such as *Hong Kong Circular Panorama*

(Warwick Trading Company, 1900) up to and during the First World War. Many of these companies, however, did not survive the economic circumstances generated by the war, and the tradition of the simple, scenic British documentary film also more or less came to an end during the war. Later, from the 1930s onwards, the British tradition of the film units developed within the British documentary film movement, with the Empire Marketing Board Film Unit (EMBFU) making films such as *The Song of Ceylon* (Basil Wright, 1934). From 1930 onwards, official film units such as the EMBFU were established in various colonised and decolonised countries, and, by the mid-1950s, over twenty such were in existence. In the Dominions (from the mid-1950s, the 'Commonwealth realms'), such as Canada, New Zealand and Australia, these became extensive units, while in smaller colonies such as Hong Kong they were more limited in size and scope. One film unit of British origin in the area, the Malayan Film Unit (MFU) (1946–57), also continued as a local post-colonial unit after Malaya gained independence in 1957.

In British South-East Asia there were two film units. The abovementioned MFU was established by members of the British documentary film movement in 1946 and continued on a modest scale up to 1950, when it began a process of transformation into a major enterprise against the backdrop of the Malayan Emergency (1948–60): the British struggle against communist insurgents in Malaya. The other film unit was the Hong Kong Film Unit (HKFU) which was established in 1959 and continued making films up to 1973. In Singapore, although there was no specific film unit, there were some limited production centres linked to the British Foreign, Colonial and Commonwealth Relations Offices; and also to the Shell oil company. In addition to film production, British documentary films were also distributed to and screened in British South-East Asia from 1945 onwards. The main organisation involved here was the Central Office of Information (COI). Between 1945 and 1952, the COI made films through its Crown Film Unit, which was disbanded in 1952. After that the Films Division of the COI continued making films and commissioned others, and these films then reached British South-East Asia. Prior to the independence of Malaya and Singapore, colonial governments in these territories played a role in supporting official film activities, including distribution and exhibition. After independence, and the departure of colonial governments, that role was taken up by agencies such as the British Information Services, the United Kingdom Information Services and the British Council. These organisations built up extensive libraries of British documentary films, made by the Crown Film Unit and others, which were then borrowed and screened in schools, colleges and via mobile units. These films played an important role in building up a sense of identity between newly decolonised territories and Britain.

In British India, the British Ministry of Information (MoI) established the Information Films of India, the Indian News Parade and the Army Film Center in 1943, at a time when the British government knew that the independence of India was inevitable. These units produced propaganda newsreels and documentaries to promote the war effort on Indian territory, but, additionally, up to the closing down of these units in 1946, some films also attempted to spread the pro-colonial message that the eventual handover would not be obtained by Indian nationalists but had been planned and offered by the British themselves (Deprez 2013: 150). A section of Indian nationalists accused these film units of forcing the Indian people to participate in an unwanted war, and the controversy that ensued from this even led the colonial Indian Legislative Assembly to cut the budgetary grant of Information Films of India and the Indian News Parade in 1946. This effectively brought their operations to an end (Deprez 2013: 151). These three colonial British film units did, however, prepare the foundation for the creation of the state-sponsored Films Division of India in 1948, one year after independence was declared on 15 August 1947.

A distinction between the 'Colonial Office' and 'Griersonian' traditions of the British official film was also of importance here (Aitken 2012). The Griersonian tradition, or, to put it another way, the tradition that related to the British documentary film movement, tended to find a home in the Dominions and larger colonies such as Malaya. However, the Griersonian tradition was also at odds with what has been referred to as a 'Colonial Office' tradition of British official film-making, which was the dominant force in Africa, the Caribbean, and, in South-East Asia, in Malaya (after 1952), Singapore and Hong Kong; although a Griersonian influence did creep into Hong Kong in the final years of the Hong Kong Film Unit, from 1970 to 1973 (Aitken 2012). The location of these traditions was also linked to the changing configuration of the British Empire. As the empire contracted and colonies disappeared, the British Colonial Office lost much of its power. A small number of small – often island – colonies did, however, remain closely linked to the Colonial Office and its officials. In South-East Asia, this was the case with Hong Kong. The difference between these Colonial Office and Griersonian traditions also had consequences for the types of films produced, with those emanating from the Colonial Office tradition being far less progressively inclined than those stemming from the more pro-democratic and egalitarian Griersonian tradition. Films in the Colonial Office tradition, often produced through the

Office's own film unit – the Colonial Film Unit CFU) (1939–55) – but also through government film units or offices based throughout the colonies, were also far simpler than those made within the Griersonian tradition, and stemmed from forms of pre-Second World War 'educational' film-making, often related to health education, which emerged in British colonies such as Nigeria, India, Malaya and Hong Kong. The tensions created when these two traditions collided, as they did in Singapore, Malaya and Hong Kong, would have an impact and created different sorts of legacies, as will be covered in the chapter on *Berita Singapura* (Chapter 1) and elsewhere in this anthology.

In addition to the British tradition of official film-making, there was also a French intervention in which four principal private companies, Pathé Frères, Gaumont, Éclair and Éclipse, all based in the French metropole, were involved in making affordable, easy-to-film and highly profitable productions. Contrary to the preconception that France did not make a significant contribution to documentary film-making prior to the interwar years, from the introduction of the cinematograph by the Lumière brothers in 1895, French film pioneers began shooting a succession of single shots (views) that were supposed to reproduce the act of looking and observing, rather than telling and arguing (Monsaingeon 2004: 247–52). Soon organised into sequences and later into series of sequences, these views demonstrated the early urge to classify, make an inventory of and document the 'real' world. In 1904, Pathé created the term *actualités* (or 'topicals' in English) to describe scenes of what was considered to be of international and general interest. This term was limited to its literal meaning (topical) and did not yet refer to notions of information – in the sense of newsreels – or authenticity. This kind of topical production ended in 1908 with the introduction of the Pathé Journal or *Premier journal vivant de l'Univers/First Living Newspaper of the Universe* (Baj and Lenk 2004: 268).

Commercial topicals, travelogues and exploration films were also often not distinguishable in subject matter and style from early films shot by anthropologists: all depicted indigenous art forms, ceremonial life and pre-industrial activity, and favoured long and medium shots in order to maintain a safe distance between the film-maker and the subject, so as to avoid – it was hoped – influencing that which was being filmed. According to one scholar, in order to represent people and situations as they might appear in real life, these naturalistic films used more camera movement than any other genre in early cinema (including pans and tracking shots), and opted for a form of rough continuity editing technique that made the films comparable to a series of 'snapshots in a photo album' (Abel 2005: 221–2). From the 1920s onwards, these fragmented series of 'views' were then slowly transformed into more systematically organised assemblages of filmed 'facts', as in *Voyage au Congo/Voyage in the Congo* (Marc Allégret, 1927), which depicted, among other activities, the specific phases of rubber cultivation in French and Belgian Equatorial Africa. Simultaneously, a greater visual experimentation with and narrative construction of 'real' events, people and places gradually developed (Deprez 2014), as illustrated in the variety of sub-categories of documentary film covered in this anthology.

French *cinéma colonial*/colonial cinema emerged at the peak of French colonial expansion in the interwar years with the popular success of the fiction film *L'Atlantide* (Jacques Feyder, 1921). Shot on location in Algeria, this film relocated the myth of the Atlantis to the Sahara desert and represented the colonial endeavour as an exotic and romantic experience. From this period through to the Second World War and until the end of the French Empire in the early 1960s, documentary films mostly reflected France's determination to maintain its imperial territories and exalted the French colonial enterprise, despite rising anti-colonial rebellions in the colonies and continuing French disengagement from the colonies, as in Vietnam.[3] As a result, publications have tended to focus on this official colonial standpoint (Blanchard et al. 2015; Bloom 2008; Norindr 1996; Pinoteau 2003; Slavin 2001). The few scholars who have focused on how the fiction film played out tensions between metropolitan and settlers' interests, as well as between colonial conservatives and reformers, have also mainly done so in order to place emphasis on and explicate official colonial policy and the French sense of civilisational and racial superiority that was predominant at the time (Benali 1998; Ezra 2000; Rony 1996; Slavin 2001). Albert Sarraut, Governor General of Indochina (1911–14 and 1917–19) and Minister of the Colonies in 1932 and 1933 – among other governmental positions held – was the main initiator of French colonial policy in the interwar period. In favour of the promotion of the colonies at all levels (yet first and foremost at the economic level), he contributed to the establishment of the Comité de Propagange Colonial par le Film/Colonial Film Committee in 1928, which was commissioned to produce films for the 1931 Colonial Exhibition in Paris and to develop an official documentary film-making policy. Sarraut envisioned film as a tool to make the colonies better known to France and vice-versa, and more generally used film as an instrument to preserve French colonial interests across the empire (Bloom 2008: 127–8). In terms of film style, the production of French colonial documentaries also occurred against a larger context of thriving debate over documentary film theory and practice in France, including for instance the contributions of Louis Delluc and Jean Epstein, which emphasised the manipulation of reality through visual effects, and, building on the legacy of French impressionist cinema of the 1920s, advocated the use of 'impressionistic delineations of the urban or rural environment', indeterminate narrative structures and fluid camerawork and montage (Aitken 2001: 72–3). A previously mentioned, French colonial documentary films developed in parallel with geographic/anthropological expeditions and an ethnographic cinema, as in the films of Jules-Félix Régnault, which have sometimes been criticised in more recent scholarship (Rony 1996: 147–8) for their Western-oriented representation of the indigenous. At the time, the separation between scientific research and entertainment films was not clearly drawn, and one consequence of this was that the camera became, in some respects, intentionally or unintentionally, a new means of exercising Western superiority and control over indigenous subjects (Rony 1996).

Also part of official policy of educational cinema that could serve both in the colonies and in metropolitan France, French documentary films spread the officially senctioned message of a humanising economic expansion linked to French republican values, interests and priorities. The educational and colonial enterprises were thus closely intertwined. The documentary film was, therefore, increasingly used in the colonies in order to better superintend indigenous people, whereas commercial cinema was regarded as frivolous and immoral and as unsuited to that task by conservative segments of French society. Shown primarily in Indochina and in Algeria, educational film programmes also aimed at thwarting the influence of the French Catholic Church by publicising secular educational values (Bloom 2008: 127–52; Murray-Levine 2010: 63–9, 120–8). As with Britain, France also justified the use of documentary film propaganda as a strategic tool against communism. For example, the documentary films produced by the Service Cinématographique des Armées/French Military Film Services during the First Indochina War (1946–54), such as *La Bataille du Tonkin/The Battle of the Tonkin*, produced in 1952, aimed to convince an indifferent French opinion of the necessity for the war, while also promoting the notion of a successful process of indigenous pacification and emancipation, carried out in close relationship with the French authorities, and conforming to the French model of modern development (Pinoteau 2003: 56, 60), including the strategy of carrying out a 'civilising mission' and 'assimilation' (aiming at colonised populations into greater integration of French culture and society) in the colonies. As a result of this approach, most colonial films excluded the expression of anti-colonial sentiments and protests and avoided issues of colonial misconduct (such as corruption), colonial segregation, or progress towards self-determination. Yet, these films also reveal – more or less intentionally – how the French intelligentsia and political class were torn between anxieties relating to France being overthrown in the colonies, and confidence in the just jurisdiction of French colonial sovereignty. During the 1950s, rising anti-colonial movements throughout the French colonial empire, including the communist independence movement led by Ho Chi Minh in Vietnam, generated anti-colonial sentiment in France. It was also under the influence of sentiment related to decolonisation and self-determination that French visual anthropologist Jean Rouch[4] began to instil more participation and self-reflexivity in the ethnographic film, yet with limited impact on the scientific academy. Likewise, the French New Wave film-makers broke away from the spirit of pro-colonial cinema and openly criticised the impact of French colonialism on foreign societies and cultures. Thus a film such as *Les Statues Meurent Aussi/Statues Also Die* (Chris Marker and Alain Resnais, 1953) used the documentary essay form to address the highly topical concern of decolonisation. Although such a film demonstrated a certain shift of mindset among the young generation of French people, it, like others, was nevertheless heavily censored by the government and did not reach a wide French audience.

The Dutch tradition of colonial documentary film-making is perhaps a lesser known tradition compared to the British and French. Yet, although comparative records do not exist, the highest number of non-fiction films made by any colonial government was, in all probability, produced by the Dutch in the East Indies – the colonial geopolitical construct now called Indonesia. On 24 April 1912, a brief announcement appeared in the newspaper *Nieuwe Rotterdamsche Courant*: 'To a Captain in the Ordnance Survey in the Netherland East Indies, J. C. Lamster . . . our union [the Colonial Institute] makes available funds for making cinematographic and photographic images for a term of one year or less as necessary'.[5] This signalled the start of the process that would document several decades of the Dutch presence in the East Indies and their efforts at bringing modernity to their colony, as well as some of the darker consequences of these actions, such as the exploitation of labourers on large-scale agricultural production systems. The beginning of active, voluminous film-making had a social as well as a political purpose.

The Colonial Institute (Vereeniging Koloniaal Institute) was established in 1910 and aimed to collect data and disseminate knowledge about the colonies. The Institute saw in making films a promising way of providing visual evidence of the state of the colony, as well as a means to persuade civilians in the Netherlands to take pride in the socio-economic development of the East Indies. It was in the early discussions of the Colonial Institute that the novel notion of using film as a tool to create informational programmes was developed. The issues covered in these short films included a wide range of topics – agriculture, healthcare, urban planning, infrastructure, arts and crafts and transmigration, among others. After employing two film-makers, J. C. Lamster and L. P. H. de Bussy, who made several dozen films, the Colonial Institute withdrew from active film production in 1922 when companies with more vested commercial interests began to dominate the field. The Institute did, however, continue to screen and promote the films that were subsequently backed by private corporations and made under the banner of large production houses like Polygoon and Haghefilm. The vast majority of the screenings were held in the Netherlands and hardly any films from this entire collection were shown in the colony.

The Colonial Institute was a private foundation and lacked the organisational backing for large-scale commercial dissemination of their films. Lamster and De Bussy, the two film-makers the Colonial Institute employed directly, were not professionals. Lamster was a captain in the army and De Bussy an agricultural scientist. They did, nonetheless, produce an impressive and important body of work under trying conditions. The Institute had a specific policy of not showing their films commercially as they were deemed 'educational'. Still, their outreach was significant. The Annual Report of the Colonial Institute from 1918 records that there were 63 requests for film screenings in which 314 individual titles were shown at the Colonial Institute or at educational institutions that borrowed their films (Van Dijk et al. 2010: 57).

The next director to embark in film-making in the colony had a very different profile from that of Lamster or De Bussy. Willy Mullens was the most famous documentary film-maker in the Netherlands in the 1920s. In 1899, along with his brother Bernardus Albert, Mullens had founded one of the earliest Dutch film production companies, Alberts Frères. In 1914, he went on to start a second company, Haghefilm, which eventually surpassed the original family company in reach and reputation. With the decline of Colonial Institute productions, Mullens saw an opportunity in the Netherlands East Indies and arrived there in 1924. Given his favourable reputation, it was not difficult for Mullens to raise substantial sums of money for his new venture. Mullens was a maverick, a self-promoting showman who once blasted himself out of a canon as a human canon ball at a fair. But, as importantly, he was also politically astute and highly regarded in the Dutch media. In 1917, he made a two-and-a-half-hour documentary, called *Holland Neutraal: Leger en Vloot/Holland Neutral: The Army and Fleet* (Willy

Mullens, 1917), espousing Dutch neutrality – while subtly indicating the need for a strong army reserve – which attracted a mass audience and won him a coveted reputation with, amongst others, the royal family. Benefiting from his professional reputation, Mullens received several more contracts to film in the East Indies. On the eve of his second departure in 1926, he announced on radio the astounding number of backers for his work – the Department of Colonial Affairs and Education, Baron Baud's companies, Senembah, the Deli Batavia, the Tobacco Bureau, the Association for Rubber Cultivation, Dordtsche, the South Preanger Rubber Company and the Indies Rubber Society – all entities with commercial interests in the Netherlands East Indies. By the time he returned to The Hague in 1927, Mullens had filmed a staggering thirty-four kilometres of footage (Hogenkamp 1988: 21).

Just as Willy Mullens had come to the Indies to make documentaries subsidised by private corporations, other professional film-makers followed suit. Perhaps the most remarkable of these would be Isidor Arras Ochse, who came to the colony in 1925 as a cameraman for Nederlands-Indische Filmmaatschappij. Ochse came to the Indies expressly to compete with Mullens, and brought with him the best available equipment. *The Straits Times*, the long-standing Singaporean English-language newspaper, heralded his arrival with much optimism. In the candid words of its correspondent, who had little regard for the quality of prior Dutch propaganda films:

> It is hoped, however, that this time a little more attention will be given to the daily lives of the people, European as well as native, as all previous films of the Netherlands Indies are conspicuous by their lack of this, and are, accordingly, rather dull. (*Straits Times* 1925: 10)

Over the next two years, Ochse would make a series of high-quality non-fiction films. Vincent Monnikendam, the director of *Mother Dao*, the famous documentary film re-edited in 1995 from colonial footage shot between 1912 and 1932, remarked: 'Without any doubt the best cameraman by that time [mid-twenties] was I. A. Ochse. He was the only one who moved with his tripod and camera near the people. He seemed the only one who had respect for the indigenous people.'[6] The last major entity that contributed to Dutch colonial film-making in the 1920s was a religious group called the Societas Verbi Divini (SVD). Its collaborations with the Dutch colonial government to promote evangelical awareness about and conversion of autochthonous groups in Eastern Indonesia are detailed in Chapter 5 of this volume. The dynamic priest-turned-film-maker, Father Simon Buis, who continued the efforts initiated by cameraman Willy Rach, went on to blend non-fiction coverage into re-enactments and scripted constructions, giving rise to a new wave of hybrid film-making in the colony.

The feverish production of Dutch colonial non-fiction propagandistic films, totaling several hundred, came to an almost complete halt by 1930 due to a saturation of the limited range of themes available and a reduction in resources caused by the Great Depression. The next phase of colonial documentary film production took place in the mid-1940s during the Japanese interregnum when the Japanese government co-opted the fledgling Indonesian film industry and set up a branch of the Japan Film Corporation in Jakarta to produce a series of propaganda films. After their expulsion following the Second World War, American and Australian news corporations would continue to film in-depth news segments (more akin to documentaries than newsreels) on Dutch attempts to reclaim their colony right up to 1949, when Holland recognised Indonesia as an independent nation.

American films made in South and South-East Asia constitute the last significant colonial documentary film tradition covered in this anthology. During the colonial occupation of the Philippines by the United States from 1899 to 1946 government entities and private organisations made what would later be defined as documentary films to serve a wide variety of purposes. In the first years of American imperium, commercial motion picture firms such as the Edison Manufacturing Company restaged scenes from the Spanish–American War of 1898 and captured scenic views of the islands, the natives and the new colonial population (Del Mundo 1998: 29–30). These films were part of a fledgling trade in documentary images and narratives about the colonial experience. Such representations included oversized books of pictures and travel writing, life-like stereopticon views (also known as magic lantern), exotic pulp fiction, variety shows and melodramas. In the 1910s, when the first bills for Philippine independence were placed before Congress, three notable figures incorporated lengthy film screenings into their lectures about the colony (Capino 2002) in debating the case for and against independence. E. Burton Holmes popularised the American travelogue, Dean C. Worcester was former Secretary of the Interior in the Philippines, and Clarence B. Miller was a Republican Congressman from Minnesota. Their films stressed the contrast between the 'primitive' way of life of the tribal Filipinos and the modern habits and technologies introduced by the Americans. While Holmes demurred from taking a side on the politics of independence, Miller and Worcester advocated the retention of the colony. Holmes's Philippine films were later repackaged for theatrical exhibition and, in the 1920s, for use in classroom instruction (*Moving Picture World* 2016: 81; *Indianapolis Star* 1922: A1). These films then joined a growing number of privately made educational films about the Philippines that were produced across the colonial period, reaching a peak of output in the 1970s, long after independence had been achieved.

Simultaneously, as indicated by archival holdings, the US military began using motion pictures to document its operations in the Philippines. Deocampo points out that the US Army produced a compilation film called *Military Activities in the Philippine Islands, 1917–1930* (director unknown, c. 1936) (Deocampo 2011: 143). Some years earlier, the same outfit made *Greetings to the Washington Corral of the Military Order of the Carabao from General Emilio Aguinaldo* (director unknown, c. 1929) as part of its 'pictorial history files'. Aguinaldo led two anti-colonial wars, first against the Spanish (who occupied the Philippines from 1521 to 1898) and later against the Americans (who declared their intention to annex the Philippines in 1898). The film records a series of events commemorating American colonial history in the Philippines but its inter-titles make no references to the conflicts that defined those events. Apart from leaving out the gist of Aguinaldo's speech (the 'greetings' cited in the title) and the fact that he was President of the First Philippine Republic, the inter-titles also say nothing about the Philippine–American War (1899–1902), whose veterans comprised the Military Order of the Carabao and who included Aguinaldo .

With the outbreak of the Second World War, the US Signal Corps and the Office of War Information shot propaganda films, newsreels, training films and footage of actual battles and wartime events in and around the Philippines. Because US armed forces retained military bases in the Philippines until the early 1990s, film production continued in the next five decades after the war, in the form of orientation pictures and documentaries of military activities. Apart from the military films, the US government's largest and most sustained effort at documentary filmmaking in the Philippines occurred after decolonisation, beginning in the early 1950s and extending into the next decade. At the height of the Cold War, the ex-colony served as a key site and audience for anti-communist propaganda. The United States Information Agency and its predecessors recruited leading directors from Philippine movie studios such as LVN Pictures to make public relations (read: propaganda) films aimed at the Philippines and other nations of the 'free world'. Although closely supervised by US bureaucrats, these Cold War efforts sustained a novel enterprise in transnational and post-colonial documentary film-making.

THE ENCOUNTER BETWEEN COLONIALISM AND DOCUMENTARY CINEMA

Emanating from public or private funding sources; inspired by various film styles and traditions; reflecting official, professional or amateur viewpoints; circulating in both theatrical and non-theatrical venues in cities and in more remote areas (through mobile vans, screenings organised by missionaries etc.); in the colonies or in metropolitan centres; colonial documentary films, usually unintentionally, sometimes reveal ambiguity, inconsistency, and other contradictions associated with the colonial enterprise. Based on in-depth case studies, this anthology aims to disentangle these complexities. Important publications in the field of colonial film studies have already examined the encounter between cinema and the colonial enterprise, including the role played by cinema in the control, organisation and governance of colonial empires. This anthology addresses this literature, including work that covers issues of colonial policy (Bloom 2008; Jaikumar 2006; MacKenzie 1988; Norindr 1996; Smyth 1988; Woods 2001; and others); colonial relationships and networks (Aitken 2015; Aitken and Ingham 2014; Cooper 2001; Druick and Williams 2014; Grieveson and MacCabe 2011a, 2011b; Landau and Kaspin 2002; Murray-Levine 2010; Rice 2013; Stollery 2000, 2011; and others); identity formation (Burns 2002; Chowdhury 2000; Deprez 2013; Raju 2012; and others) and nationalism (Dissanayake 1994; Gillroy 2004; Murray-Levine 2010; Sarkar 2009; Yoo 2013; and others). The anthology additionally revisits the discourse of the 'civilising mission', wherein some European intellectuals and politicians believed that European, Western culture was superior to other cultures and as such was expected to lead supposedly backward populations onto the path of technical progress, scientific reason and 'appropriate' values (Conklin 1997; Creed and Hoorn 2011; Daughton 2008, and others). These beliefs were also related to notions of exoticism, Orientalism and cultural control (Assayag 2001; Berstein and Studlar 1997; Clifford 1988; Evans 1991; Kennedy-Karpat 2013; Lowe 1991; Norindr 1996; Said 1979; Stollery 2000; and others), and these notions are also addressed in this anthology.

Compared to existing studies, contributions in this anthology also focus on under-researched or little-known films, film-makers and film traditions; and, in doing so, also emphasise interstitial significations in relevant issues pertaining to academic debates on colonialism and colonial documentary film studies. Some of these issues include the specific ways in which films reveal incongruities within reformist and more conservative colonial discourses; within discourses of interventionism in and disengagement from colonial territories; and within gestures of acceptance of, cooperation with and opposition to colonial authorities. Contributions within this anthology not only cover the documentary film sector generally, including the production, distribution and exhibition of films in colonial territories and metropolitan centres, but also the debates that were taking place at an institutional level in colonial centres in response to specific international and local contexts. The anthology, therefore, aims to embrace the full spectrum of colonial documentary film, including the perspectives and interests of the colonisers and colonised and the complex sets of interactions that existed between colonisers and colonised in the South and South-East Asian regions. On the latter, Ian Aitken has recently (2015) described how the British government adapted the role and management of its diverse overseas information services in South-East Asia – and more particularly in Malaya and Singapore – to the local context, a context that included demands for independence after the Second World War and the actual process of decolonisation in the 1950s and 1960s. This study showed that strategies, some of which involved the production and distribution of official films, were not fixed but evolved according to the prevailing circumstances. In the case of Malaya and Singapore, Aitken argues that such strategies, although aimed at maintaining the British influence in the region after the colonies reached independence, should not be understood as constituting a form of 'neo-colonisation', but rather as a 'late colonial metropolitan strategic disengagement' based on 'a rhetoric of consociation (2015: 48).

Elsewhere in his recent publications, Aitken has also demonstrated that in Hong Kong, as in other places under British control in South-East Asia, colonial documentary films frequently combined the colonial agenda with elements of local culture and identity. Such elements were, thereby, accommodated within the colonial framework rather than suppressed by it (Aitken and Ingham 2014: 35). This anthology further elaborates on these strategies by exploring the ways in which official films produced in or about South and South-East Asia reveal the intricate relations linking colonial offices with indigenous film industries; colonial authorities with local elites; and colonial, imperialist and missionary agencies with native populations. Despite the existence of undeniable differences between these parties, less evident connections also occurred as a result of both colonial plans of control and local strategies of resistance, as, for example, and in terms of control, the relationship that developed between heads of Indian princely states and representatives of the British colonial regime in colonial

India. Yet, as chapters of this anthology demonstrate, instances of direct and substantial cooperation between colonial and local elites, such as the one just referred to, were mainly restricted to the more superficial realm of sociocultural prestige, and rarely touched on the more apposite domain of real political and economic power. Some scholars, including, for example, Bipal Chandra, have also argued that imperialist and indigenous elites did not rule colonised peoples in the same manner, and that, in addition, the pre-colonial authority – however oppressive it may have been – also remained as an organic part of each indigenous society. Chandra also argues that indigenous elites sometimes played a role in the anti-colonial struggle (Chandra 1999: 14). A close analysis of such complexities in specific colonial contexts in South and South-East Asia constitutes a major contribution of this anthology.

Under such colonial circumstances, the issues mentioned above are explored in this anthology against historical contexts that reflected imperial and indigenous realities as well as imagined nationalist and post-colonial projections. This anthology further demonstrates that the films under scrutiny here pursued various objectives, including well-understood objectives related to the promotion of imperial interests in the colonies and in the home countries, war propaganda and military activities, or evangelism; but also less well-understood objectives related to the reinforcement of colonial state policy, the upholding of the pre-colonial sociopolitical status quo during colonial times, and even, intentionally or unintentionally, resistance against colonial regimes. These films also reveal the importance of particular environments in shaping practices in colonial territories, the consolidation of the European influence in former colonies, and the elaborate understandings of the colonial enterprise developed by both imperial and indigenous parties. Furthermore, in exploring these issues not only from the dominant perspective of the colonisers, but also from the lesser-known viewpoints of the colonised and others present in the colonies (including such as visiting film-makers and explorers), the anthology confronts the colonial heritage at large. According to Lee Grieveson, 'across these differing filmic forms, there emerged a set of related formal practices and tropes, belying any simple separation of the real and the imaginary' (Grieveson and MacCabe 2011a: 3). Elaborating on this argument concerning the real and imaginary as continuum, this new anthology shows that documentary films contributed to the construction of an imaginary space where imagined or idealised representations of the colonial endeavour and relations with indigenous populations were shaped. The anthology does, however, also assess the disparities between this imaginary space and the reality on the ground, both in the colonies and in metropolitan centres.

Writing from a wide range of historical perspectives, contributors to the anthology also shed new light on historical, theoretical and empirical issues pertaining to the documentary film, in order to better comprehend the significant transformations of the form in colonial, late colonial and immediate post-colonial and postcolonial times in South and South-East Asia. In doing so, this anthology addresses an important gap in the global understanding of documentary discourses, practices, uses and styles. The anthology also contributes to the assessment of the Griersonian legacy in the region. In their recent co-edited volume, Druick and Williams demonstrate that Grierson's ideas were 'mobilised by a variety of groups and constituents, from governments and industry to film-makers and cultural nationalists' in a number of countries and regions around the world, and Druick and Williams assemble details on how 'such forces were aggregated and sustained'. Druick and Williams's book describes a number of attempts to employ a Griersonian approach in order 'to cope with the realities of modernity', both inside and outside the British sphere of influence, and also reveals how the 'creative treatment of actuality' usually if not always took place in compromised conditions of one sort or another often related to official sponsorship (Druick and Williams 2014: 5–6). In Druick and Williams's *The Grierson Effect*, Ian Aitken also sets out what Griersonian incursion occurred and endured in Malaya, Singapore and Hong Kong, and identifies a clear opposition between the more propagandistic work of the CFU and the poetic and liberal stance of the Griersonian documentary; while Camille Deprez shows how the Films Division of India appropriated Grierson's notions of integration and consensus to fit the social context of national heterogeneity in a newly independent India. Both chapters emphasise the complex and contested legacy of the Griersonian tradition.

Building upon this critical examination of the many forms of the 'Grierson effect', the anthology presented here not only analyses under-researched films made in or about South and South-East Asia that were influenced by John Grierson and the British documentary film movement, but also pays attention to other important film traditions, such as French colonial and Hollywood cinemas. This anthology also demonstrates the various ways in which high levels of aesthetic creativity can be found in these films despite the limitations and constraints provided by the potentially unpropitious contexts of sponsorship, colonialism, nationalism, war, revolutionary conflict and struggles for independence. Finally, the originality of this volume rests upon the fact that it is based upon recent and first-hand primary archival research conducted in various national and film archives in Europe (Britain, France and the Netherlands) and Asia (India, Malaysia, the Philippines, Singapore and Vietnam). The under-researched primary documents under scrutiny here include minutes, memoranda, policy papers and letters written by government officials, private film companies, missionaries, travellers and explorers. Additionally, rare and under-researched films also provide an evidentiary base for the anthology. In terms of methodology, contributors to the book provide various templates on how to use archival materials to understand the complexity of colonial discourses and relations between the colonisers and the colonised; and also the variegated practices, uses and styles of the documentary film employed by both colonial authorities and colonial subjects.

REASSESSING CURRENT UNDERSTANDINGS OF THE COLONIAL DOCUMENTARY FILM

Based upon in-depth essays written by international authorities in the field and cutting-edge doctoral projects, this anthology is the first to encompass different periods, national contexts, subject matter and style in order to address important and also relatively little-known issues relating to colonial documentary film in the South and South-East Asian regions. This anthology is divided into three main thematic sections, each of which crosses national or geographical boundaries. The first section addresses issues of colonialism, late colonialism and independence. Here, contributors look at the ways in which official films were used in order to serve the interests of the former and present colonisers and new post-colonial elites against the context of decolonisation, and how these films also reveal limits and contradictions in such strategic attempts. In his chapter on the Singaporean official newsreel series *Berita Singapura* (1963–9), Ian Aitken explores how this film series embodied and propagated the ideas of the Singapore People's Action Party (PAP), and those of the Party's leader, Lee Kuan Yew. Aitken provides an outline of the political context involving Britain, Malaya and Singapore that led to the ascendancy of the PAP, and also relates the films of *Berita Singapura* to particular key PAP policies, such as on housing and education. Aitken also shows how the films presented the authoritarian-capitalist agenda of the PAP within a visual rhetoric of 'modernisation', and describes tensions that arose between the film producers, who were European expatriates, and the authoritarian and interventionist PAP leadership. In his chapter on '*Merdeka for Malaya*: Imagining Independence Across the British Empire', Tom Rice explores how this film produced by the MFU in 1957 portrays Malaya's path to independence. Through this case study, Rice brings relevant nuances to the accepted discourse of change between the colonial and post-colonial periods. He demonstrates that both the film and the film infrastructure reveal a continued British influence, although they also validate the transition to an independent state. In his argument, the process of independence as it is recorded on film remains mainly idealised and conceals tensions for the sake of the project of imagining the new nation. Focusing on the period of the Malayan Emergency (1948–60), Peter Bloom further elaborates on the process of decolonisation in this region and the complex relationships between the coloniser and the colonised it entailed. In his chapter, he analyses how the mobilisation of official documentary film, radio language and sound effects created a critical site in authenticating the legitimacy of the British-led campaign against the communist insurgency, and the extent to which it also contributed to Cold War realignments during the post-war era.

Farther east, the US also developed empire-building strategies in the Philippines. In his chapter, J. E. Capino demonstrates how a variety of official and private documentary films were deployed to serve American imperialist interests while also documenting the Filipinos' daily life under direct US imperial rule (1898–1946), and over the post-independence period. This contribution highlights the specific filmic elements employed to both acknowledge and belie US imperialism in the Philippines, and demonstrates how specific documentary forms were influenced by the history of American imperialism in the region and, reciprocally, how non-fiction forms also forged significant aspects of imperialism.

The second section of this anthology investigates missionary films in South and South-East Asia and the complex issue of Christian evangelism in the region. This section demonstrates that such propagandistic films supported the project of a 'civilising mission' embedded in a long tradition of imperial culture while also presenting early yet still significant documentary and ethnographic material. The films studied also reveal paradoxes that place the conventional view of colonialism as a monolithic exploitative mode of interaction with the colonised into question. In his chapter, Sandeep Ray explores two films shot in 1926 in the under-studied region of Flores in Eastern Indonesia, by a Dutch Catholic priest turned film-maker. In addition to setting out the more predictable propaganda deployed by these evangelical films in a local context of fierce confrontation between Catholics and

Muslims to gain religious control over the native population of Flores, and against the larger background of Dutch colonial expansion, Ray also argues that this single surviving visual record of the events that took place provides a unique source of insight into the modes of evangelism deployed in the area, as well as into details of local customs and mores. Adopting a different approach, yet in a similar vein, Annamaria Motrescu-Mayes investigates the paradoxical legacies of British imperial culture based on a comparative study of a missionary film shot in India in the late 1920s to early 1930s by the Fathers of the Saint Joseph's Missionary Society and a 2013 Hong Kong and Shanghai Bank Corporation television advertisement. Her study illuminates the documentary and anthropological merit of the early missionary film, despite its larger propagandist function. By looking into the heritage of John Grierson's principles of social and cultural engagement, she more unexpectedly demonstrates that the 1920s' film resists the stereotypification of race and colonised people that predominated at the time, whereas the 2013 commercial tends to perpetuate that. Emma Sandon further explores documentaries produced by English and Scottish Christian missions in India in order to highlight similarities and differences in the definition of a 'civilising mission' adopted by these missions. While, for example, some focused on the means of reaching salvation, others believed in the use of education to both bring about social development and instil Christian values.

Finally, the third and last section of this anthology analyses documentary representations of the colonies and emphasises the limits of authenticity in early documentary film-making, as both the film-makers and audiences remained subjected to the influence of their personal experiences and orientations, and also of the mainstream colonial culture of the 1920s to the 1950s in which they lived (whether they accepted or opposed that culture). Here, contributors highlight the ways in which documentary projections shaped imagined or idealised representations of the colonisers, the colonised, and the relationship between the two. In doing so, the four chapters presented here show discrepancies between these visual representations and the actual situation in the colonies and in the colonial or imperialist centres. In his chapter on guerrilla film-making and exhibition in colonised Vietnam, Thong Win explores how such underground documentary practices informed Vietnamese communist ideology and established support for the revolutionary cause in rural areas of the Mekong Delta in South Vietnam during the First Indochina War against France (1946–54), and after 1948. Win unravels the ways in which these alternative film practices dictated by the Viet Minh in Hanoi established a counter-model to

French colonial film-making and policy in Vietnam, and how they were also aimed at unifying the diversified regions of the country into an idealised coherent pro-revolutionary entity. Dean Wilson continues the investigation of colonial Vietnam by focusing on the film *Ho Chi Minh in France* (Mai Thu, 1946). This documentary was produced by two Vietnamese émigrés living in France and combined three short newsreels about nationalist political leader Ho Chi Minh's visit to France on the eve of the First Indochina War, a war that eventually led to the withdrawal of French colonisers from Vietnam in 1954. By presenting the social and historical context in which the film was produced, Wilson demonstrates how this first indigenous attempt in documentary film-making created a strong visual and ideological connection between political leader Ho and the Vietnamese, projected the possibility of an independent Vietnam to the Vietnamese audience, and thus served the project of decolonisation and independence. In 'Archives of the Planet: Elitist Representations of Colonial India', Camille Deprez investigates films sponsored by French patron of the arts Albert Kahn and shot in the princely states of India in the late 1920s. She demonstrates that, at the peak of French colonialism, this idealist project of intercultural understanding and cooperation was supported by strong associations with carefully selected members of the Indian elite, and that this led to a staged and compromised representation of India. She also argues that the films eventually overestimated the power of the traditional sociopolitical order of India in relation to that of the British colonisers and of other rising forces of decolonisation in the country. In the final chapter of this anthology, Timothy Barnard explores issues of authenticity and the close relations that always existed between documentary and narrative cinema. Focusing on American films about Komodo dragons shot in Borneo in the 1920s and 1930s, he presents animal documentaries as a popular site in which Western film-makers showcased supposedly realistic images of animals that ironically led to exotic and fantastic film depictions of those and other animals. He also argues that these films created a space where Western (American) desires, cultural tensions and anxieties about the perceived savagery and violence outside of Western civilisation could be projected.

ACKNOWLEDGEMENTS

We would like to thank José F. Capino and Sandeep Ray for respectively providing draft sections on the history of the colonial documentary film in the Philippines and Indonesia for this introduction.

NOTES

1. 'The colonial Film Units of Hong Kong, Singapore and Malaysia, and the influence of the British official film', 'Hong Kong documentary film', 'The documentary film series in Hong Kong', 'A study of the Singaporean colonial film series *Berita Singapura*', 'The television documentary films of ATV and TVB' and 'The documentary film in India (1948–75)'.
2. For more information on this research website, visit: http://digital.lib.hkbu.edu.hk/documentary-film/, last accessed on 30 April 2016.
3. See Chapters 8 and 9.
4. Visual anthropology is a branch of social anthropology pertaining to the study and production of ethnographic photography, film and, since the mid-1990s, the new media. Jean Rouch contributed to the development of this branch in French universities from the late 1950s onwards.
5. *Nieuwe Rotterdamsche Courant*, 24 April 1912, p. 2.
6. Vincent Monnikendam, personal electronic mail communication dated 17 December 2013.

REFERENCES

Abel, Richard (2005), *Encyclopedia of Early Cinema*, London: Routledge.
Aitken, Ian (2001), *European Film Theory and Cinema: A Critical Introduction*, Edinburgh: Edinburgh University Press.
Aitken, Ian (2012), 'The development of official film-making in Hong Kong', *Historical Journal of Film, Radio and Television*, 2: 4, 589–609.
Aitken, Ian and Ingham, Michael (2014), *Hong Kong Documentary Film*, Edinburgh: Edinburgh University Press.
Aitken, Ian (2015), 'British governmental institutions, the Regional Information Office in Singapore and the use of the official film in Malaya and Singapore, 1948–1961', *Historical Journal of Film, Radio and Television*, 35: 1, 27–52.
Aldrich, Robert (2002), 'Imperial *Mise en Valeur* and *Mise en Scène*: recent works on French colonialism', *Historical Journal*, 45: 4, 917–36.
Amad, Paula (2008), *Counter-archive: Film, the Everyday, and Albert Kahn's Archives de la Planète*, New York: Columbia University Press.
Assayag, Jackie (1999), *L'Inde fabuleuse, Le charme discret de l'exotisme français (xviie–xxe siècle)*, Paris: Éditions Kimé.
Baj, Jeannine and Lenk, Sabine (2004), 'Le premier journal vivant de l'Univers!, Le Pathé Journal, 1909–1913', in M. Marie and L. Le Forestier (eds), *La firme Pathé*, Paris: Association française de recherche sur l'histoire du cinéma, pp. 263–73.
Basket, Michael (2008), *Attractive Empire: Transnational Film Culture in Imperial Japan*, Hawaii: University of Hawaii Press.
Benali, Abdelkader (1998), *Le cinéma colonial au Maghreb: L'imaginaire en trompe-l'œil*, Paris: Le Cerf.
Bernstein, Matthew and Studlar, Gaylyn (eds) (1997), *Visions of the East: Orientalism in Film*, Piscataway, NJ: Rutgers University Press.

Blanchard, Pascal, Bancel, Nicolas and Lemaire, Sandrine (eds) (2008), *Culture coloniale en France, De la révolution française à nos jours*, Paris: CNRS Éditions.

Blanchard, Pascal, Bancel, Nicolas, Lemaire, Sandrine and Thomas, Dominic (eds) (2015), *Colonial Culture in France since the Revolution*, Bloomington: Indiana University Press.

Bloom, Peter (2008), *French Colonial Documentary: Mythologies of Humanitarianism*, Minneapolis: University of Minnesota Press.

Burns, James (2002), *Flickering Shadows: Cinema and Identity in Colonial Zimbabwe*, Ohio: Ohio University Research in International Studies.

Capino, J. B. T. (2002), Cinema and the Spectacle of Colonialism: American Documentary Film and (Post)Colonial Philippines, 1898–1989, dissertation, Northwestern University (unpublished).

Carruthers, Susan L. (1999), *The Media at War: Communication and Conflict in the Twentieth Century*, New York/London: Palgrave Macmillan.

Chafer, Tony and Sackur, Amanda (eds) (2002), *Promoting the Colonial Idea: Propaganda and Visions of Empire in France*, London/New York: Palgrave Macmillan.

Chandra, Bipan (1999), *Essays on Colonialism*, London/New Delhi: Orient Longman.

Chowdhury, Prem (2000), *Colonial India and the Making of Empire Cinema: Image, Ideology and Identity*, Manchester: Manchester University Press.

Clifford, James (1988), 'On Orientalism', in *The Predicament of Culture: Twentieth-Century Ethnography, Literature, and Art*, Cambridge: Cambridge University Press, pp. 255–76.

Conklin, Alice L. (1997), *A Mission to Civilize: The Republican Idea of Empire in France and West Africa, 1895–1930*, Stanford: Stanford University Press.

Cooper, Nicola (2001), *France in Indochina: Colonial Encounters*, London/New York: Bloomsbury Academic.

Cowans, Jon (2015), *Empire Films and the Crisis of Colonialism, 1946–1959*, Baltimore: Johns Hopkins University Press.

Creed, Barbara, and Hoorn, Jeanette (2011), 'Memory and history: early film, Colonialism and the French civilising mission in Indochina', in *French History and Civilization: Papers from the George Rudé Seminar 4*, 201–12.

Daughton, James P. (2008), *An Empire Divided: Religion, Republicanism, and the Making of French Colonialism, 1880–1914*, Oxford/New York: Oxford University Press.

Daughton, James P. and White, Owen (eds) (2012), *In God's Empire: French Missionaries and the Modern World*, Oxford/New York: Oxford University Press.

Del Mundo, C. A. (1998), *Native Resistance: Philippine Cinema and Colonialism : 1898–1941*, Manila: De La Salle University Press.

Deocampo, N. (2011), *Film: American Influences on Philippine Cinema*, Mandaluyong City: Anvil Publishing.

Deprez, Camille (2013), 'The Films Division of India, 1948–1964: the early days and the influence of the British documentary film tradition', *Film History*, 25: 3, 149–73.

Deprez, Camille (2014), 'Colonial discourse and documentary film at the margins: the case of *Delhi grande ville de l'Inde supérieure* and *Dans l'État du Cachemire*, two early Pathé Frères films shot in India', *Studies in European Cinema*, 11: 1, 26–39.

Di Carmine, Roberta (2011), *Italy Meets Africa: Colonial Discourses in Italian Cinema*, Bern: Peter Lang Publishing.

Dissanayake, Wimal (ed.) (1994), *Colonialism and Nationalism in Asian Cinema*, Minneapolis: Indiana University Press.

Druick, Zoë and Williams, Deane (eds) (2014), *The Grierson Effect: Tracing Documentary's International Movement*, London/New York: BFI/Palgrave Macmillan.
Evans, Martin (ed.) (1991), *Empire and Culture: The French Experience, 1830–1940*, New York: Palgrave Macmillan.
Ezra, Elizabeth (2000), *The Colonial Unconscious: Race and Culture in Interwar France*, Ithaca: Cornell University Press.
Furhmann, Wolfgang (2015), *Imperial Projections: Screening the German Colonies*, New York/Oxford: Berghahn Books.
Gillroy, Paul (2004), *After Empire: Melancholia or Convivial Culture?*, London: Routledge.
Girardet, Raoul (1986), *L'idée coloniale en France de 1871 à 1962*, Paris: Hachette.
Grieveson, Lee and MacCabe, Colin (eds) (2011a), *Film and the End of Empire*, London/New York: BFI Palgrave Macmillan.
Grieveson, Lee and MacCabe, Colin (eds) (2011b), *Empire and Film*, London/New York: BFI Palgrave Macmillan.
Ha, Marie-Paule (2014), *French Women and the Empire: The Case of Indochina*, Oxford/New York: Oxford University Press.
Hargreaves, Alec (ed.) (2005), *Memory, Empire, and Postcolonialism: Legacies of French Colonialism*, Lanham: Lexington Books.
Hogenkamp, Bert (1988), *De Nederlandse documentaire film 1920–1940*, Amsterdam/Utrecht: Stichting Film En Wetenschap.
Indianapolis Star (1922), 'From Filmland', 12 February.
Israel, Milton (1994), *Communications and Power: Propaganda and the Press in the Indian National Struggle, 1920–1947*, Cambridge: Cambridge University Press.
Jaikumar, Priya (2006), *Cinema at the End of Empire: A Politics of Transition in Britain and India*, Durham, NC: Duke University Press.
Kaur, Raminder and Mazarella, William (eds) (2009), *Censorship in South Asia: Cultural Regulation from Sedition to Seduction*, Bloomington: Indiana University Press.
Kennedy-Karpat, Colleen (2013), *Rogues, Romance, and Exoticism in French Cinema of the 1930s*, Plymouth: Fairleigh Dickinson University Press.
Landau, Paul and Kaspin, Deborah (eds) (2002), *Images and Empires: Visuality in Colonial and Postcolonial Africa*, Oakland: University of California Press.
Larkin, Brian (2008), *Signal and Noise: Media, Infrastructure, and Urban Culture in Nigeria*, Durham, NC: Duke University Press.
Lashmar, Paul and Oliver, James (1998), *Britain's Secret Propaganda War*, Stroud: Sutton.
Lowe, Lisa (1991), *Critical Terrains: French and British Orientalisms*, London: Cornell University Press.
MacKenzie, John (1988), *Propaganda and Empire: Manipulations of British Public Opinion 1880–1960*, Manchester: Manchester University Press.
McKinney, Marc (2013), *The Colonial Heritage of French Comics*, Liverpool: Liverpool University Press.
Monsaingeon, Églantine (2004), 'Les catalogues Pathé de 1900 à 1907: Un registre de consignes de lecture', in M. Marie and L. Le Forestier (eds), *La firme Pathé*, Paris: Association française de recherche sur l'histoire du cinéma, pp. 247–52.
Moving Picture World (1916), 'Paramount program: releases for the week of May 1 include more novelties and educational subjects', 29 April.
Murray-Levine, Alison (2010), *Framing the Nation: Documentary Film in Interwar France*, London/New York: Bloomsbury.

Norindr, Panivong (1996), *Phantasmatic Indochina: French Colonial Ideology in Architecture, Film and Literature*, Durham, NC: Duke University Press.

Pinoteau, Pascal (2003), 'Propagande cinématographique et décolonisation: L'exemple français (1949–1958)', *Vingtième Siècle, Revue d'histoire*, 80: October–December, 55–69.

Raju, Zakir Hossain (2012), 'Indigenization of cinema in (Post)Colonial South Asia: from transnational to vernacular public spheres', *Comparative Studies of South Asia, Africa and the Middle East*, 32: 3, 611–21.

Reynolds, Glenn (2015), *Colonial Cinema in Africa: Origins, Images, Audiences*, Jefferson: McFarland.

Rice, Tom (2013), 'Distant voices of Malaya, still colonial lives', *Journal of British Cinema and Television*, 10: 3, 430–51.

Robson, Kathree and Yee, Jennifer (eds) (2005), *France and Indochina: Cultural Representations*, Lanham: Lexington Books.

Rony, Tobing, F. (1996), *The Third Eye: Race, Cinema and the Ethnographic Spectacle*, Durham, NC: Duke University Press.

Said, Edward W. (1979), *Orientalism*, London: Vintage books.

Sanyal, Shukla (2014), *Revolutionary Pamphlets, Propaganda and Political Culture in Colonial Bengal*, Cambridge: Cambridge University Press.

Sarkar, Bhaskar (2009), *Mourning the Nation: Indian Cinema in the Wake of Partition*, Durham, NC: Duke University Press.

Sherzer, Dina (ed.) (1996), *Cinema, Colonialism, Postcolonialism: Perspectives from the French and Francophone World*, Austin: University of Texas Press.

Slavin, David (2001), *Colonial Cinema and Imperial France, 1919–1939: White Blind Spots, Male Fantasies, Settler Myths*, Baltimore: Johns Hopkins University Press.

Smyth, Rosaleen (1983), 'The Central African Film Unit's images of Empire, 1948–1963', *Historical Journal of Film, Radio and Television*, 3: 2, 131–47.

Smyth, Rosaleen (1988), 'The British Colonial Film Unit and sub-Saharan Africa, 1939–1945', *Historical Journal of Film, Radio and Television*, 8: 3, 285–98.

Stollery, Martin (2000), *Alternative Empires: European Modernist Cinemas and Cultures of Imperialism*, Exeter: University of Exeter Press.

Stollery, Martin (2011), 'From storm over Asia to dawn over Africa: transnationalism and imperialism in British intellectual film culture of the late 1920s and 1930s', *Transnational Cinemas*, 2: 1, 93–111.

Straits Times (1925), The week in Java', 4 July.

Taylor, Philip (1999), *British Propaganda in the Twentieth Century: Selling Democracy*, Edinburgh: Edinburgh University Press.

Thomas, Martin (2005), *The French Empire Between the Wars: Imperialism, Politics and Society*, Manchester: Manchester University Press.

Van Dijk, Janekke, Jaap de Jonge, and Nico de Klerk (2010), *J. C. Lamster, An Early Dutch Filmmaker in the Netherland East Indies*, Amsterdam: Kit Publishers.

Woods, Philip (2001), 'From Shaw to Shantaram: the Film Advisory Board and the making of British propaganda films in India, 1940–1943', *Historical Journal of Film, Radio and Television*, 21: 3, 293–308.

Yoo, Hyon Joo (2013), *Cinema at the Crossroads: Nation and the Subject in East Asian Cinema*, Lanham: Lexington Books.

PART I

Issues of Colonialism, Late Colonialism and Independence

CHAPTER 1

The People's Action Party Government of Singapore and *Berita Singapura*

Ian Aitken

This chapter will present a historical account of the 1960s Singaporean official film series *Berita Singapura* (1963–9). *Berita Singapura* emerged out of the context of British decolonisation in South-East Asia, Singapore's independence from Britain from 1959 onwards, and the territory's entry into and eventual expulsion from the Federation of Malaysia. Above all, however, *Berita Singapura* was the creation of and articulated the vision of the Singapore People's Action Party (PAP) and its leader, the ubiquitous Lee Kuan Yew; who also appeared in many *Berita Singapura* films. Because it would not be possible to understand *Berita Singapura* outside these contexts, the approach adopted in this chapter will be to first provide the reader with a synopsis of them, and particularly of the policies of the PAP, before outlining the genesis, constitution and overall configuration of *Berita Singapura*, and then arriving at conclusions concerning this film series. This approach will enable a detailed overview of *Berita Singapura* to be presented in relation to context. Given this approach and focus on the determining contexts and overall configuration of the series, however, and also given limitations of space, it will not be possible to engage in intensive textual analysis of particular films. This may be inopportune. Analysis of similar films is, however, carried out elsewhere in this anthology. The author also believes that what is of particular importance about this series is how it emerged out of and articulated the policies of the PAP, and this will therefore be the principal focus of this chapter.

THE PEOPLE'S ACTION PARTY (PAP)

As part of the process of colonial withdrawal from governance in Singapore, the first general election to be held in the city occurred in April 1955. No single party won sufficient seats to gain power. In 1959 a second general election was held, in which the PAP won a landslide victory, with the party leader, Lee Kuan Yew, becoming the first Prime Minister of Singapore. At the time, the PAP believed that a merger with Malaya was necessary for political reasons and that the antiquated Singaporean economy would also develop through being linked to the larger – and wealthy – Malayan economy. As the PAP Finance Minister, Goh Keng Swee, put it, 'whatever we do, major changes in our economy are only possible if Singapore and the Federation are integrated as one economy. The political reason for merger has a strong economic basis' (Turnbull 1989: 267). The PAP was not a united party in 1959 and was divided between two ideologically different groupings (Tan Tai Yong 2008: 39). Prime Minister Lee and a number of his moderate, British-educated senior colleagues were committed to the development of a capitalist and constitutionally democratic Singapore within the context of integration with Malaya. However, a rival faction within the party was pro-communist, and intent on the establishment of a more socialist and/or communist Singapore, and also Malaya. As the radical left both inside and outside the PAP stirred up anti-colonial sentiment in Singapore, the still evident and substantial colonial presence in the city-state also made Lee's political position increasingly tenuous, as he was accused of procrastinating over independence. His response was to further emphasise the future alliance with post-colonial Malaya. Lee did not want full independence for Singapore, as he felt this might lead to eventual communist control of the city, and possibly economic collapse; and this was why he stressed the necessity of the link to Malaya.

Eventually, and despite extensive misgivings, the Malayan leadership also came to the conclusion that, if they did not facilitate the integration of Singapore into Malaya the city might fall to communism. The change of heart on the part of the Malayan government came in 1961 when it appeared that the PAP government might fall following a by-election at which party opinion swung sharply to the pro-Chinese left. The British State of Singapore Act of 1958 had established a transitional constitution up to 1963, when it was envisaged that new elections would be held and Singapore would achieve independence. Now, fearing that Singapore might achieve such independence as a communist state, and that a 'second Cuba' might appear on its doorstep, the Malayan leadership, backed by Britain, came to the 'reluctant conclusion' that Singapore must be integrated into Malaya (Turnbull 1989: 270). A referendum was then held to that end in September 1962 in which 71 per cent of the electorate voted for a merger. Following that, the Malaysia Agreement was concluded in July 1963, with the formation of Malaysia scheduled to come into being on 31 August 1963. Singapore, along with Sarawak and North Borneo, joined Malaya to form the Federation of Malaysia. Under the terms of the Agreement, Singapore joined Malaysia with special rights to determine and govern its own internal affairs, though matters of defence, external affairs and security were under the provenance of the Malaysian central government in Kuala Lumpur. For a variety of reasons, some related to attempts made by the two territories to preserve and extend their own authority and others related to growing ethnic tensions between Malays in Malaya and the Chinese majority in Singapore, tensions between Malaya and Singapore escalated after 1963, until, in 1965, the Malaysian Parliament voted to expel Singapore from Malaysia. Singapore then gained full independence as the Republic of Singapore on 9 August 1965. The PAP formed the government, with Lee Kuan Yew as Prime Minister, a post he held until 1990. After 1965, Singapore concentrated on trying to heal the breach with Malaysia, while also consolidating relations with Britain, Australia, New Zealand, and, eventually, the USA, against the context of the anti-communist Cold War. Evidence of these relations can be found in many of the films of *Berita Singapura*.

PAP POLICIES

Lee and other senior officials in the PAP argued that Western-style liberal democracy, based on the multi-party state and the presence of a credible political opposition to the extant government, was inappropriate for Singapore because rival political parties, and the possibility of governmental change, would increase social instability within the city (Mauzy et al. 2002: 6). Liberal democracy was therefore rejected by the PAP because it implied regime change, and the PAP had no intention of handing over power once they had attained it. Lee himself intended to establish himself as the unequivocal leader of Singapore, then surround himself with a governing elite that might be replenished from time to time but would never be ousted from power (Barr 2014: 4–5). What Lee and the PAP also wanted was to inaugurate what has been described as a form of 'authoritarian capitalism' in Singapore, which combined a corporate-capitalist economy with political centralisation. Here, an immovable 'public authority' would broker deals with and allocate contracts to corporate-capitalist entities, but only if those entities allied themselves with the interest and policies of the public authority. According to the PAP, such arrangements would ensure both political and social stability, and economic growth However, the quid pro quo here, in terms of civil society, was that political opposition to the regime and an independent media which might sustain such opposition must be suppressed (Lingle 1996: 39–40).

The PAP came to power in 1959 on a platform that included an Asian–Malayan orientation; an antipathy towards Western-style liberal democracy, freedom of expression and political pluralism; the necessity of elite government; and the promise of social stability and economic development stemming from such elite and immovable government. As the Minister of Culture, Sinnathamby Rajaratnam, put it, 'the people are more interested in what is good government than in having an opposition'. Speaking in 1962, Lee himself asserted that the flaw with democracy was that it vested too much power in the uneducated, rather than in a competent elite; while, in 1965, the Minister for Finance, Goh Keng Swee, argued that the 'central authority' should be virtually 'irremovable' (Margolin 2010: 318). The PAP intended to remain that 'authority', and was prepared to subdue all opposition by whatever means necessary to achieve that end. When the PAP came to power in 1959 the priority – apart from that of staying in power – was to deal with the problems of unemployment, poor housing, an ethnically fragmented education system and the antiquated nature of the entrepôt-based economy – the latter a legacy of over-dependence on Singapore as a deep-water port by the colonial government. By the mid-1960s these issues had also become more pressing, as the separation from Malaysia, rapid growth in population and negative economic growth increased social tensions. Britain's decision in 1967 to withdraw from its military base in Singapore by 1968 by itself eventually reduced Singapore's gross domestic product by nearly 20 per cent (Mauzy and Milne 2002: 66). In the face of these difficulties, the PAP believed that Singapore economy and society had to be modernised *rapidly*. Such rapid modernisation, it was assumed, would reorient Singaporeans towards a modern, capitalist way of life, and also attract foreign investors and multinational companies to the city at a greater speed and in greater numbers (Mauzy and Milne 2002: 4). However, along with this economic development also went a necessity for intervention in terms of social welfare reform, as both poverty and archaic forms of discrimination had to be eliminated or at least reduced; and so the PAP introduced a number of important social welfare measures in areas such as health and women's rights, with, for example, its Women's Charter introduced in 1962 (Turnbull 1989: 276). These progressive measures would be promoted as a sign of benevolent governance in the films of *Berita Singapura*.

One of the most important issues facing the PAP when it came to power was the housing situation, with insufficient supply, generally poor-quality housing, and extensive slums spread across the city centre. In order to rectify this, the PAP embarked upon a substantial programme of housing construction, which, it was expected, would also increase employment substantially through the rapid expansion of the construction industry. The policy was also to be one of increasing home ownership as well as renting, partly as a means of countering itinerant aspects of Singapore society and in the process also securing a long-term basis of popularity for the PAP (Mauzy and Milne 2002: 90). In effect, the PAP policy on housing amounted to a massive project of social engineering that was intended to create the conditions for the growth of a modern economy and labour force. The PAP had, additionally, always been sensitive to the charge that the Chinese majority in the city might overwhelm the minority Malay and Tamil communities. The housing policy therefore became based on the premise that communities would retain their autonomy by living side by side. However, and despite this gesticulation towards cultural pluralism, the government's over-arching intention was to create a modern labour force that was unified at a technical and professional level. Differences would be preserved here, but out of necessity rather than altruism, and that which was important in order to ensure modernisation would also be sited across such differences. This comes out particularly strongly in *Berita Singapura* in films made on the housing situation, so that a film such as *A New Look at Housing* emphasises the homogeneity and correspondence of the buildings, rather than any sort of community-based miscellany.

If social engineering involving relocation of the population and the construction of a massive housing programme was a precondition for the creation of a modern economy, so too was mass education, and, housing apart, spending on education also proved to be the largest item in overall social-development spending over the 1960–6 period (Margolin 2010: 311). This was not education for its own erudite sake though. Lee and the PAP viewed the education system as a means of social control and regulation, instilling the preferred values into the population. Mass education could help provide a disciplined, technically trained labour force, and also play a role in creating a sense of national identity among an ethnically fractured population (Mauzy and Milne 2002: 103). When the PAP came to power in 1959, it inherited an education system with its media of instruction separated along lines of race and language. The schools were ethnically segregated, and their standards, syllabi and certificates varied and were in the four main languages of Singapore (English, Malay, Tamil and Chinese). The PAP then initiated a standardisation of this at various levels, although the parity afforded to the four main languages under the colonial Education Ordinance of 1957 remained, in order to sustain a sense of multiracialism, and provide a mother-tongue education for the four main language communities which fended off protest from those communities (Turnbull 1989: 260). The PAP also initiated a major programme of school construction, building schools at the rate of one a month and, in the process, dramatically increasing educational opportunities for girls (Mauzy and Milne 2002: 103). As far as the PAP was concerned, schools, whether for boys or girls, were 'the most efficient tool towards the transformation of society and the unification of the nation', and so the PAP ensured that the policies and outlook of the party in relation to this permeated such schools (Margolin 2010: 303). We can see this process of socialisation occurring very clearly in a film such as *Sang Nila Utama Secondary School* (1967). Here, education is directly linked to the service of obedient citizenship, as we see the disciplined regimentation of the students, a regimentation that also becomes more literal in scenes that show female police cadets marching in front of the students, as part of the preparation for the time they will eventually spend in the army undertaking National Service.

In addition to housing and education, another PAP priority area was race relations. Since colonial times there had been a deep cleavage between English-educated and Chinese-educated Chinese in Singapore, and these language and educational differences resulted in sometimes sharp divisions in cultural and political orientation. In general, the English-educated Chinese predominated in positions of power and status, while the Chinese-educated tended to be blue-collar and mass-based, and also politically more pro-communist. Aside from these intra-Chinese separations, during the colonial period different ethnic groups often also lived in separate areas, spoke their own languages, and practised their own religions, rituals and ways of life in a manner that has been described as 'living side-by-side but separately' (Mauzy and Milne 2002: 100). While seeking racial integration as part of the modernisation programme, the PAP was concerned not to give the impression that these racial and cultural differences would be entirely erased. Thus, the official policy was one of multiracialism and denial of any attempt to produce a homogenous citizenry. As one PAP official put it, 'our ideal has never been a melting pot' (Mauzy and Milne 2002: 101). But this actually went against the project of building a modern economy and unified nation, so integrative measures were in fact gradually introduced, including the promotion of English, and the introduction of national military service (Mauzy and Milne 2002: 101). In addition, overly emphatic expressions of ethnic identity were also 'summarily crushed', including such demonstrations of Chinese ethnicity, partly because these could create focal points around which a Chinese opposition to the PAP regime might consolidate (Barr 2014: 66). All of the above – apart from, obviously, the overt suppression of ethnic identity – are articulated in the films of *Berita Singapura*.

THE GENESIS OF *BERITA SINGAPURA*

Berita Singapura (*Singapore News*) was produced by Cathay Film Services, the documentary film branch of the Cathay Organisation film company, one of the largest such companies in the region at the time. Both were based in Singapore, and so it made sense for the Singapore government to approach them. In 1960, Cathay Film Services was commissioned by the PAP government to produce a series of films called *People's Singapore*. These films acted as the overt mouthpiece of the government and did not attempt to conceal that fact. Inevitably, the films were compromised by this, and their effectiveness prejudiced. It also seems that *People's Singapore* was meant more for international rather than local audiences, as the series' producer, Tom Hodge (see later), mentioned that the series was sent to the 'Central Office of Information, London, where it was shown to British and international newsreel and TV companies'.[1] In contrast to this propagandist and international profile, *Berita Singapura* was commissioned in 1962 in order to target the home audience (Hodge, in fact, complained that money was not available to send *Berita Singapura* to London, as had been the case with *People's Singapore*),[2] and provide a greater semblance of impartiality to Singaporean official film-making. From the outset, the films attempted to give the impression that they were more autonomous than *People's Singapore*. For example, an initial idea to call the series *Berita Malaysia* was dropped because 'it has too much of a tang of propaganda about it [in 1963, the formation of Malaysia was a hot political issue] and would tend to defeat the very purpose that the films should not be too obviously propaganda'.[3] Similarly, all reference to the source of the series in the Ministry of Culture was occluded and 'the only accreditation will be that of Cathay Films'.[4] The principal task of *Berita Singapura* was to promote the policies of the PAP and at the same time appear to be doing so relatively autonomously, and/or impartially. It remains unclear, because there is no evidence on the matter available, as to what extent *Berita Singapura* was actually perceived to be independent by the Singaporean public, but the fact that it was fairly obviously the direct successor to *People's Singapore*, which Hodge protested had been allowed to 'die' prematurely so that it could come into being, might have counted against such a perception.[5]

The first contract for *Berita Singapura* was signed with Cathay Film Services on 13 December 1962 and the first film was completed shortly after, on 4 January 1963. The last film in the series was completed in October 1969. Cathay Film Services produced two of these films per month, releasing them fortnightly. The series was shown on TV Singapura, the PAP-controlled and only television service in Singapore; and, during the period of time when Singapore was part of Malaysia (1963–5), on Malaysia Televysion, the Malaysian central government-controlled and only television service in Malaya. The series was also distributed to cinemas in Singapore, the Malaysian Federation and Borneo. The New Zealand film director Noni Wright, who had worked with John Grierson and the British documentary film movement during the 1930s, was the producer and director of the series until her premature death in an air crash accident on 20 June 1964.[6] After that, a Toh Weng Kai took over as producer for the remainder of the series.[7] Each film in the *Berita Singapura* series – essentially a newsreel series – ran from six to twelve minutes and was also usually divided into three to four segments dealing with different topics. The films were also made in four different language versions: Malay, Mandarin, Tamil and English, with some also made in Cantonese and Hokkien.[8]

The Head of Cathay Film Services during this period was Tom Hodge. Hodge had been associated with official film-making since the early 1940s. He worked at the Ministry of Information (MoI) in London between 1939 and 1942 making instructional official films. From 1942 to 1943, he worked for the MoI in their Chicago office, and, between 1944 and December 1951, was Director of Films and Publications at the British Information Service in New York (Aitken 2012: 598). In December 1951, he was appointed in Singapore as Film Advisor to the Commissioner General's Office in Singapore, with a remit to 'co-ordinate and enlarge British film activities' against the context of the deteriorating military situation in the region (Aitken 2012: 598). However, in August 1952, only nine months after taking up the Singapore position, Hodge was appointed to the combined posts of Director Films Division Malaya and Film Advisor to the Malayan Film Unit (MFU), taking up those posts in September of that year. Hodge was given a remit and power enough to ensure that the official film played a more effective role in shaping 'the information services of this country into a single more effective weapon against communism' (Aitken 2015: 38). Between September 1952 and July 1957, when he left in order to join Cathay Film Services in Singapore, Hodge oversaw a considerable expansion in the activities of the MFU, and turned it into an effective propaganda organisation (Aitken 2015: 38).

Unlike Noni Wright, not only did Hodge have no connection with the Griersonian tradition,[9] he was also openly hostile to it. Unlike film-makers within the Griersonian tradition, he preferred to make limited and direct official public relations films. Writing in 1957, as he left the MFU, he argued that under his watch he had instilled in the 'communal mind' of its film-makers two key questions: 'What do you want to convey?', and 'What do you want people to feel?' (Aitken 2012: 600). This was also the same pragmatic approach that he brought to the production of *Berita Singapura* – an approach which overwhelmed any 'Griersonian' orientation that Wright might have introduced. In his initial proposal to the Singapore government, Hodge also argued that *Berita Singapura* should be a compilation news magazine series, rather than a collection of individual news films, which would cover:

> almost anything that happens in Singapore which can be used to illustrate Government's policies and show Government's concern for the people's well-being ... The aim and object of the series is that the audience will accept them as news ... without the films being considered Government propaganda.[10]

But if *Berita Singapura* was 'news', it was hardly impartial news, and Hodge's 'object' may not have been realised in the end as a consequence of that.

Prime Minister Lee Kuan Yew himself intervened directly to initiate the commission of *Berita Singapura* and award Cathay Film Services an initial one-year contract, beginning on January 1963, by personally meeting Tom Hodge over the matter.[11] Hodge claimed that Lee 'gave me his personal authority to proceed at once' with the series.[12] However, it also seems that, from the outset, there were concerns among government officials about out-sourcing the series to a commercial company run by expatriates rather than producing it from within the government. For example, Lee Kong Chong, a member of the Film Sub-Committee within the Ministry of Culture, argued that it was a problem that *Berita Singapura* was 'produced by a European woman' (Noni Wright),[13] and that:

> The way she produced the English version may be suitable for English picture-goers but not necessarily suitable for the other three languages. To copy everything from the English version and give it to the Chinese people is just like asking them to swallow the English food. They may not be able to digest it.[14]

Chong generally complained about the attitude of both Hodge and Wright, referring to Hodge as 'a European' out of touch with the local media, and defensively asserting that Wright had accused him of 'not being cooperative'.[15] Chong also suggested that '*Berita Singapura* would be better produced by *Television Singapura*', which was Singapore government-controlled,[16] and argued that television was simply better than film because it was able to report with greater immediacy and that 'by the time we see this item on *Berita Singapura* it has lost its impact and meaning already'.[17] Chong concluded that he could 'see no point in continuing production of *Berita Singapura* by Cathay Film Services'.[18] However, despite such opposition, a second contract with Cathay for *Berita Singapura* was approved with, apparently, Lee Kuan Yew's support for the series proving crucial. Hodge, for example, claimed that 'Last night, I met the Prime Minister who told me we should continue to make the *Berita Singapura* films after our contract ends on November 15th [1963]'.[19] Thereafter, the series was contracted out to Cathay until 1969, when it closed.

As mentioned, the *Berita Singapura* series was produced and directed by Noni Wright until her death in 1964, and thereafter by Toh Weng Kai. No information is available concerning who else may have been involved in filming the series, as cameraman, for example; and the only credits that appear on the films are for Cathay Film Services. The series consists of eighty-six films, which are available for viewing at the National Archives of Singapore (NAS).[20] The first sections of most of these films have been digitalised and are available for viewing online on the NAS website. The eighty-six films also divide into 216 sections, which can in turn be classed under the following twelve tentative categories:[21] (1) relations with other countries, (2) Singapore/Malaysia nationality and unity issues, (3) government administration, (4) social welfare, (5) city development, (6) public utilities/facilities, (7) housing, (8) traffic, (9) education, (10) economic development, (11) leisure activities and (12) local customs and traditions. The topics covered in *Berita Singapura* are mostly about Singapore internal affairs. More than half of the film sections (125) are about government policy (social welfare, public facilities, housing, and so on); and just under one-quarter (sixty-five) are related to leisure and cultural activities.

A look at the number of film sections in each category also gives a clearer picture of the central concerns of *Berita Singapura*. The 'relations with other countries' category consists of around ten film sections with the main countries concerned being Australia and New Zealand, featuring in films such as *New Zealand, Friendly Ally* (1965). This reflected the concern to build a relationship within the Commonwealth with Australia and New Zealand following

Singapore's expulsion from Malaysia, and in response to the perceived threat to Singapore posed by Indonesia and the Philippines, a threat apparent in a film such as *The Infantry Regiment* (1963), which refers to an incursion into Singapore by Indonesian armed units (Indonesia and the Philippines were opposed to the inclusion of Singapore within Malaysia, fearing that the city would become a centre for communist-Chinese influence in the region). The 'Singapore/Malaysia unity' category consists of around sixteen films, all made prior to 1965, and concern topics such as military training, the confrontation with Indonesia and a celebration of the formation of Malaysia. Films here include *Australia and Malaysia* (1963) and *Singapore's Help to Malaysia* (1963). The 'government administration' category covers some fourteen films and focuses on the activities of government ministers and the Legislative Assembly. One of these, for example, celebrates the anniversary of the founding of the PAP. Interestingly, six of these fourteen films, including *Police Women* (1963) and *New Police Recruits* (undated), focus on the role of the police, thus giving a high priority to the importance of effective internal law enforcement: one of the key concerns of the PAP. The 'social welfare' category contains around nineteen film sections, and that relatively large number is also predictable given the PAP focus on social development. These films have no particular focus, but cover a wide range of topics, from support for the blind to medical issues such as the control of tuberculosis, as in *Singapore Anti-Tuberculosis Association* (1963). Up to seven of these films also focus on the needs of children, including *Care of Abandoned Children* (undated), suggesting that the protection of vulnerable children may have been a particular problem at the time. Two of these films, for example, concern abandoned children. The 'city development' category consists of some twenty film sections covering various aspects of the city development, including the building of the important Jurong industrial complex, in which the Singapore government invested heavily, and which was intended to attract multinational corporations into Singapore. Two films were made on Jurong, one of which was titled the *Miracle of Jurong* (undated). Two films, *Maintaining Cleanliness* (1965) and *Cleaning up Operation* (undated), also concern the need for improved hygiene and cleanliness within the city. A related category here is also that of 'economic development', with some thirty-three films focusing on the development of Singapore as a site of industrial production, both small- and large-scale. This reflected the PAP policy of turning Singapore's economy away from a dependence on entrepôt trade to a light and heavy manufacturing economy. Films here include *Potato Chips Factory* (1964), *Perfume Factory* (1968) and *Making Candles* (undated).

In contrast to the above, another category of films relate more to social (though not specifically social welfare), public and cultural issues: for example, films falling into the tentative category of 'public utilities and facilities', which explore public rather than economic aspects of the development of Singapore. The theme of national identity is also present here, with a number of these films focusing on 'national' forums, such as the building of a National Library and a National Stadium. One of these films, *National Day* (1963), celebrates Singapore's achievement of self-governance. The category of films on 'traffic' issues cuts across both the last two categories in focusing on developments in public transport, including the building of new railway lines and the easing of traffic congestion in Singapore's narrow and congested city-centre streets. However, the major subject covered in this category is the development of the main Singapore airport, in films such as *Forging Closer Ties* (undated). It is perhaps understandable, however, given that one of the aims of *Berita Singapura* was, according to the series' producer, Tom Hodge, to 'portray almost anything that happened in Singapore', that the major category of films in the series should deal with a multitude of 'lifestyle' stories. Around sixty-five such films fall into this category, including *Singing Trio* (undated, on pop music), making it by far the largest category of films in the *Berita Singapura* series. There also seems to be an emphasis on the health benefits of sport, with up to twenty-seven of these films, including *International Athletics Competition* (1965), dedicated to the coverage of various sporting events.

As mentioned previously, two of the most important PAP policies related to housing and education; however, and perhaps surprisingly, only relatively few *Berita Singapura* films fall into these categories. Only six film sections as such fall into the category of housing: *Celebration of New Housing* (1963), *A New Look at Housing* (1967), and *Visiting New Flats*, *Rebuilding Houses*, *New Development* and *Housing Week* (all undated); while nine films fall into the category of education: *Singapore's Help to Malaysia* (1963), *Ngee Ann College* (1964), *Sang Nila Utama Secondary School* (1968), and *Vocational School*, *New University Chancellor*, *Secondary School*, *Advance with Science*, *New Schools* and *New Town Secondary School* (all undated). While this is a relatively small amount compared to the lifestyle category just considered, it should be borne in mind that it would have been impossible for *Berita Singapura* to secure a large ongoing audience if it were a heavy news magazine overloaded with serious subjects. The bulk of films made were, therefore, necessarily lifestyle films.

CONCLUSIONS: *BERITA SINGAPURA* — DISTRACTION, UNITY AND THE ENGINEERING OF CONSENT

During the 1960s and, it could be argued, up to the present day, the Singaporean PAP government succeeded in establishing an authoritarian-capitalist one-party state in Singapore. This involved massive schemes of social engineering in fields such as housing and education development, but it also involved what has been referred to as the 'engineering of consent' (see Bernarys 1955). Various means were used towards this end in Singapore during the 1960s, including the suppression of political opposition, the use of the legal and police systems, control of the media, censorship and the deployment of pro-regime public-relations material such as *Berita Singapura*. None of this can be said to amount to what the philosopher Jürgen Habermas has described as an ideal 'public sphere' of free communication within civil society. In his book *The Structural Transformation of the Public Sphere*, Habermas also warns that one of the threats to the formation and reproduction of an ideal public sphere is the increasing preponderance of 'lifestyle/human interest' material within the public sphere, which, he argues, provides a combination of 'entertainment and "advice"... which ... could have been invented for the purpose of public relations serving the cause of the status quo' (Habermas 1993: 175). With this in mind, it could be argued that one of the principle functions of *Berita Singapura* was not an informational but a distractive and manipulative one in the above sense, as is made clear by the great number of 'lifestyle' films made within the series. As a consequence of this 'lifestyle/human interest' distractive orientation, the films made on political matters in the series are also rarely informative or critical, and mainly focus on the personalities involved, the most prominent being Lee Kuan Yew, as in the 1964 film *Prime Minister Lee Kuan Yew in Brussels and London*. If one of the chief functions of the *Berita Singapura* films was to distract attention away from pressing circumstances, another was to emphasise the underlying unity of the nation. According to government policy, such unity was supposed to be established on a foundation of multiculturalism and multiracialism. However, the *Berita Singapura* films do not show this, and instead emphasise the overall unity of the nation as a modern nation that looked outwards with an international economic orientation, and was largely devoid of internal cultural and racial difference and division.

The rhetoric in the *Berita Singapura* films is always positive and straightforward, and rarely poses problems without then detailing solutions to them, even proclaiming that the housing problem has been solved (although it had not been). Technically, the films are also simply made. The fact that they are also so short, and presented in segments, also places limitations on their ability to deal in depth with any subject, and, indeed they are designed not to do so. *Berita Singapura* also straddled two key but potentially contradictory aspects of PAP ideology: ensuring government control of information and inviting corporate capitalist concerns into the city, in this case the Cathay Organisation. However, by 1970 the PAP preferred government control of information to relying on an external corporate source for such control and the contract for *Berita Singapura* was not renewed. The role played by the series was then taken up by the state broadcaster, Television Singapura, which had been directly controlled by the PAP since its inauguration in 1963.

Finally, although *Berita Singapura* was, without doubt, a creature of the PAP and controlled by the PAP, it remains a film series made by film-makers (though we do not really know who), and not by politicians. This means that contradictions sometimes emerge in the films, as the film-makers go 'offline' from time to time, under the influence of their own art and craft-based inclinations. In a film such as *A New Look at Housing* (1967), for example, an aesthetic treatment of the image occurs which makes the housing on show appear somewhat dehumanised; while, in a film such as *Maintaining Cleanliness* (1965), which seeks to claim that the rubbish problem in Singapore is being dealt with, the imagery shows, precisely, rubbish – probably because such images of debris were relatively filmic. However, the fact that the films of *Berita Singapura* do not show such contradictions and anomalies to the extent that other official films of the period were able to is testament to the degree of control exercised over them by Tom Hodge, Cathay Film Services and the paternalist Singapore state.

ACKNOWLEDGEMENTS

HKBU FRG1 13–14/44: A study of the 1960s Singaporean film series *Berita Singapura*.
HKBU GRF 240213: A study of the 1960s Singaporean film series *Berita Singapura*.

NOTES

1. SNA, Ministry of Culture, Hodge to Permanent Secretary, 12 February 1963.
2. Ibid.
3. NAS MC. 244/62, Minister for Culture to film Sub-committee, 1 December 1962.
4. NAS MC 244/61, Lawrence G. Mani to Permanent Secretary, 8 November 1962.
5. NAS MC 244/61, Hodge, Letter to the Prime Minister, 24 June 1963.
6. Noni Wright, no relation to Grierson's colleague Basil Wright, worked briefly within the documentary film movement prior to the war. During the war she worked for the BBC. She joined the Malayan Film Unit in 1953, shortly after Tom Hodge joined it, and left the MFU shortly after him, in 1958, to continue working under him at Cathay Film Services.
7. No information on him is available.
8. Hokkien, a Southern Chinese dialect initially brought into Singapore in the nineteenth century from Fujan province. It was largely replaced by Mandarin in Singapore in the early twentieth century.
9. See the Introduction to this anthology.
10. NAS MC, 244/62, Hodge to Ministry of Culture, 30 October 1962.
11. SNA MC, 244/62/, Minister for Culture to Film Sub-Committee, 1 December 1962.
12. NAS MC, 244/62, Hodge to Ministry of Culture, 30 October 1962.
13. SNA, MC, Lee Kong Chong to A. Kajapathy, 14 February 1963.
14. Ibid.
15. Ibid.
16. Ibid.
17. NAS MC, 244/61, Chong to W. S. Woon, Permanent Secretary Ministry of Culture, 24 June 1963.
18. NAS MC, 244/61, Chong to W. S. Woon, Permanent Secretary Ministry of Culture, 24 June 1963.
19. NAS MC 244/61, Hodge, Letter to Permanent Secretary, Ministry of Culture, 18 October 1963.
20. Accessed on 30 April 2016 at www.nas.gov.sg.
21. These category titles are the author's, and are not formal titles associated with the series. They were generated during the research process of viewing the films. The categories are also not mutually exclusive, and there is a degree of overlap between films in the various categories in some cases.

REFERENCES

Aitken, Ian (2012), 'The development of official film-making in Hong Kong', *Historical Journal of Film, Radio and Television*, 32: 4, 531–55.
Aitken, Ian (2015), 'British governmental institutions, the Regional Information Office in Singapore, and the use of the official film in Malaya and Singapore, 1958–1961', *Historical Journal of Film, Radio and Television*, 35: 1, 27–52.
Barr, Michael, D. (2014), *The Ruling Elite of Singapore: Networks of Power and Influence*, London/New York: I. B. Tauris.

Bernays, Edward, L. (1955), *The Engineering of Consent*, Norman: University of Oklahoma Press.
Habermas, Jürgen (1993), *The Structural Transformation of the Public Sphere: An Inquiry into a Category of Bourgeois Society*, Cambridge, MA: MIT Press.
Lingle, Christopher (1996), *Singapore's Authoritarian Capitalism: Asian Values, Free Market Illusions and Political Dependency*, Barcelona: Editions Sirocco, S.L.
Margolin, Jean-Louis (2010), 'The People's Action Party blueprint for Singapore 1959–65', in Jean-Louis Margolin and Karl Hack (eds), *Singapore: From Temasek to the 21st Century: Reinventing the Global City*, pp. 292–322.
Mauzy, Diane, K. and Milne, R. S. (2002), *Singapore Politics under the People's Action Party*, London: Routledge.
Tan Tai Yong (2008), *Creating 'Greater Malaysia': Decolonization and the Politics of Merger*, Singapore: Institute of Southeast Asian Studies Publishing.
Turnbull, C. M. (1989), *A History of Singapore 1819–1988*, Oxford/New York: Oxford University Press.

CHAPTER 2

Merdeka for Malaya: Imagining Independence across the British Empire

Tom Rice

'And now an era comes near to its close', announces the British commentator, 'as the last few minutes of 170 years of British protection over Malaya tick away'. A shot from below of the clock striking midnight is interspersed with the image of the Union Flag, now lowered from its pole. The sound of the chiming clock competes with that of the British national anthem, before both are replaced by the noise of cheering crowds. The camera pans down to reveal a neon sign, stating 'Merdeka' (Freedom). The shot fades to black.

This short sequence within the Malayan Film Unit's (MFU) official record of Malayan Independence, *Merdeka for Malaya* (director unknown, 1957), visualises the country's move from colonial to independent state. This complex, contested and often violent process is contained and imagined throughout this thirty-minute film within succinct visual displays, through public celebrations, airport departures and official ceremonies. The film offers a record of the ceremonial events of independence, illustrating the ways in which states are symbolically imagined through such pageantry. While there has been much excellent recent scholarship on independence ceremonies, I want to think more closely in this chapter about the film record. In doing this, we might usefully examine the spectacle of colonial handover as a distinctly 'filmic' moment, one that is organised visually and constructed on film. In short, how is changing statehood visualised through film? Furthermore, what role do government film units play within this process? A closer examination of the production history of *Merdeka for Malaya* provides a further way to explore the move from 'colonial' to 'post-colonial' within film. Much literature on film continues to present independence as a point of rupture, a starting point for national cinema histories, but in looking at the personnel, the unit and indeed equipment involved in *Merdeka for Malaya*, we might better understand the continuities, as well as the ruptures, that mark the very moment of the post-colonial.

In many respects, the films of independence and the events that they depict follow a prescribed path, although given the plethora of states that would achieve independence in the decade following Malaya (Malaysia) in 1957, the spectacle of new nationhood is partially worked through and made visible in this example. In his examination of Merdeka Day, A. J. Stockwell illustrates the level of planning involved in the ceremonial handover of power – from the selection of dignitaries to the drafting of goodwill messages – but also notes that the pattern for independence ceremonies would follow 'a more of less standard form of flag ceremonies, military tattoos, firework spectacles and state banquets' (Stockwell 2010: 117). Richard Rathbone, in his study of Ghanaian independence, which took place earlier in the year in March, characterises these moments with a dash more cynicism as sharing 'similar quotients of military display, fireworks, pious sentimentality at midnight and the profoundly implausible pledges of eternal friendship between long-term antagonists' (Rathbone, 2010: 57). All are present in *Merdeka for Malaya*, but what is particularly striking is the way in which the MFU seeks to articulate this message of 'eternal friendship' through these displays, at once mourning the loss of the British empire while simultaneously projecting a continued colonial influence within the new nation.

The filmed pageantry in *Merdeka for Malaya* serves both to celebrate British influence and validate the transition to independent statehood. A lengthy sequence in the recently built Merdeka stadium depicts crowds 'representative of every race and every walk of life' watching as the British national anthem is played 'for the final time'. The first King of Malaya is introduced, seated alongside the heads of state, while the Prime Minister and the new cabinet arrive in 'their newly designed uniforms'. British royalty and the emerging Malayan leadership are used to mediate this handover to both domestic and international audiences. The Duke of Gloucester stands to deliver a speech, in which he notes the 'close cooperation' involved in the formation of the constitution, before the Prime Minister states that the new nation 'will always remember with gratitude the assistance that we have received from Great Britain down our long path to nationhood'. In the next sequence, it is the 'people's turn' as the film depicts public street celebrations. While relatively brief compared with the focus on official ceremonies, the film again celebrates the continued European influences here, through shots of colonial architecture and sports events. The film shows Europeans supporting a local swimming meeting, local Malays watching cricket, a cycling race and finally a bullfight, a coming together of the varied cultures, customs and sounds that now make up Malaya.

Merdeka for Malaya comprises a series of performances that were, or would become, common to films of independence ceremonies. The ceremonial handover is represented by the passing of the constitutional instrument from Duke to Prime Minister, a 'simple gesture' that, the commentator explains, now makes 'Malaya responsible for her own destiny'. The Prime Minister raises his right hand and repeats the call 'Merdeka', the Federation Flag is raised – 'and with it the hopes and aspirations of a people, the symbol of nationhood' – and the new national anthem plays. 'The guns boom, the flags flutter, a pledge is honored and a nation is born', surmises the British commentator. Later, the film records the elaborate investiture ceremony of the King, an event described by historian T. N. Harper as 'a medieval sacerdotal ceremony in a month-old throne room; an invention of tradition that projected a pre-colonial sovereignty for the new nation state' (Harper 1998: 356). The review of troops ('the pageantry associated with nationhood') emphasises the different races, states and genders paying respects to the new King, before the monarch opens the new parliament. The structures here – in the events depicted, the government formation and indeed in the film form – closely follow established British models.

In this way, the film does more than merely record the major ceremonial events, carefully constructing a narrative that negotiates loss and celebration, the old and the new. Significantly, the MFU articulates its vision for the new nation to both a domestic and global audience. On the domestic front, the MFU's films played to an estimated non-theatrical audience of ten million in 1954, while also providing 6,910 screenings in Malaya's commercial cinemas (*Film News* 1955). Shortly after independence, the MFU claimed that its films regularly played in 378 cinemas in Malaya, through 134 mobile film units and, what is more, in sixty-eight different countries (Department of Information 1959: 3). Given the mass decolonisation that would follow across the empire over the next decade, *Merdeka for Malaya* represents a significant example of the ways in which film was used to explain and manage this British 'loss', while simultaneously circulating images of independence around the world. These films of independence addressed, and circulated, a subject that was often avoided in official British film. As one example of many, the 1950 Central Office of Information (COI) documentary, *Spotlight on the Colonies* (Diana Pine, 1950), which offers a 'survey' of the empire, makes no mention of India, which had achieved independence less than three years earlier. The film largely eschews any reference to the potential dissolution of the empire, though by 1957 this issue starts to be worked out and played through these official films on independence.

THE MALAYAN FILM UNIT AND THE END OF EMPIRE

The independence ceremonies and celebrations in Malaya on 31 August 1957 would represent the largest production undertaken by the MFU in its eleven-year history. Seven cameramen worked 'flat out for 14 days' providing newsreel footage within twenty-four hours of the celebrations. Intended for 'all countries in the free world', the footage was followed a few weeks later by the more extensive documentary, *Merdeka for Malaya*. The images of independence would now play in other territories seeking and witnessing the processes of independence from British rule. *The Straits Times* noted barely three weeks later that 'millions of people throughout the world next week will be able to see how Malaya celebrated the advent of independence' (*Straits Times* 1957b). The paper further explained that the MFU was turning out 120 prints of *Merdeka for Malaya*, which would go initially to America, Australia, England, India and Jakarta where the unit had its own agencies (*Straits Times* 1957a). The MFU produced commentaries in Malay, Mandarin and Tamil, while there were at least two different versions of the film in English. For example in Singapore, the film played in Tamil and in Malay at the Diamond cinema, in Malay at the Taj cinema and in English at the Rex. In addition, the MFU made copies of the film available at a cost of $250 to 'any member of the public', suggesting a further use for this film, as a historical keepsake to be shown at private parties (*Straits Times* 1957c).

As *Merdeka for Malaya* attests, the MFU recorded the major historical incidents leading up to independence but it also claimed a more active role in prefiguring the formation of a modern, self-governing Malaya. The official company catalogue noted in 1953 the Unit's part in assisting Malaya's 'progress towards self-government' (Department of Information 1953: 13), while Tom Hodge, the Director of the Malayan Government Films Division, which oversaw the work of the MFU, wrote on his departure from Malaya in 1957 of this broader political role. 'Recording every stage in Malaya's march towards independence', wrote Hodge, helped establish 'that unity and harmony among Malaya's many races which alone make independence a workable aim' (Hodge 1957: 539).

The film works within a longer colonial tradition by presenting 'racial' unity as the foundation for 'national' unity, and this emphasis on racial harmony was a common feature of British documentary in Malaya. Alexander Shaw's 1938 film, *Five Faces* (Alexander Shaw, 1938) presented five cultures, clearly delineated, but all 'living in harmony', with each culture shown in turn and defined by a different way of life or product. This formal structure, which endorsed a British policy that sought to maintain ethnic boundaries within Malaya, was evident a decade later in *Voices of Malaya* (Ralph Elton, 1948), which now examined the five voices within post-war Malaya. *Voices of Malaya* was a seminal film in the history of the MFU, a first foray into production and a training ground for many leading local figures, including Ow Kheng Law, who was head of the MFU in 1957 when *Merdeka for Malaya* was produced.

The origins of the MFU owe much to British documentarians such as Ralph Elton and Denny Densham, who arrived on Penang at the point of Japanese surrender in 1945 and proceeded to record, over the next year, the rapidly changing situation within Malaya. This initial Crown Film Unit expedition would provide the personnel, ideologies and equipment for the emerging MFU, which was set up in 1946. By the time of Crown's departure in October 1946, the trainee Malay and Chinese film-makers who had travelled with the Crown Film Unit, including Ow Kheng Law, had all been absorbed into the MFU. By 1953, Ow Kheng Law was one of thirty Chinese working for the MFU alongside seventy Malays, twenty-two Indians, nine Eurasians and four Europeans (see Rice 2013; Department of Information 1953: 13).

Such a narrative serves in part to present the developments within the MFU as indicative of the nation as a whole, a manifestation of the broader political moves to self-government in post-war Malaya as these two histories – of imperialism and film history – are inextricably enmeshed. It also highlights the movement of British documentary film-makers and their ideologies and practices into the colonies after the war, as the so-called Griersonian tradition – with its purported humanist, liberal, paedagogical agenda – found a fresh outlet within the post-war colonies as part of the 'nation-building' process. Yet this narrative becomes more complicated during the 1950s, both with the intensification of the Malayan Emergency, a decade-long war (in all but name) in the jungles of Malaya between the colonial forces and the 'communist terrorists', and also with shifts in personnel, most notably the arrival of Tom Hodge, who was seconded from the Foreign Office to become Director of Films Division in the summer of 1952.

The Emergency would dominate the work of the MFU during this period, as the Unit became an integral part of the government's Emergency propaganda campaign. The MFU initially held broader ambitions – 'it is important that the idea of the three races living in harmony should be preserved and fostered' – but after the British government declared a State of Emergency in June 1948, the MFU focused on bringing government propaganda to those communities, such as the rural Chinese, that were involved with the insurrection (*Colonial Cinema* 1947: 15). The MFU grew up alongside these tumultuous events and was framed by this history. In his lengthy report on the function of the MFU in 1950, the Producer in Chief for the Australian National Film Board, Stanley Hawes, determined that the MFU should 'concentrate mainly' on 'films designed to assist the Government in the emergency by showing the positive side of democratic government and the strength of the British Commonwealth' (Hawes 1953). Having produced nineteen films in its first three years, the MFU delivered fifty-two films for distribution in 1950 and 111 in 1951 (Ramakrishna, 2002: 110–11). As the MFU became more fully integrated into the Emergency Information Services (EIS) in 1952, it increasingly produced films that directly endorsed Emergency propaganda campaigns, such as *The Knife* (Ow Kheng Law, 1952), and expanded and centralised its mobile cinema network. By 1954, there were ninety-two mobile units (giving a total of 17,092 shows during the year); this was extended to 123 by 1957 and 134 by 1959 (*Kinematograph Weekly* 1955; Hodge 1957: 538; Department of Information 1959: 3). The units played not only in Malay villages but also in Chinese resettlement areas, as the government used film within a political campaign, which was at once both imperialist and part of the Cold War.

Yet while the Emergency dominated Malayan political life and was at the forefront of the MFU's work, it is almost entirely absent from *Merdeka for Malaya*. Aside from one brief mention when showing the parading troops – 'to all of whom Malaya owes gratitude in helping her rid the country of communist terrorism' – which suggested that the problem was now fully resolved, this defining and all-pervading aspect of post-war Malayan history is ignored. The MFU was ultimately a product of the Emergency, shaped and expanded through its ties with the EIS after 1950, yet this ongoing tale of dissension and anti-colonial struggle is pushed beyond the frame, obfuscated in a narrative of racial harmony and nation building. As with so much of colonial film, these films are most interesting for what they do not show or, put another way, they reveal through what they conceal.

The presence of Tom Hodge would also help to reshape the MFU. He was to offer, in his own words and using patriarchal language common to colonial literature, 'strict parental guidance to this brilliant and exuberant youngster [the MFU]' (*Straits Times* 1952). While he oversaw the continued expansion of the Unit, his focus on quantity and on short instructional films represented something of a break from the Griersonian 'prestige' model previously favoured. Ian Aitken has recently argued that Hodge was 'openly critical' of the early Griersonian elements he found at the MFU (Aitken 2015: 34). The MFU's 1953 catalogue of films had listed quotations from John Grierson on the inside page, celebrating film's ability to 'bring the outside world alive to the growing citizen' and to 'bring to the stubborn fact a measure of imagination and inspiration'. It further quoted Grierson as stating that 'Any medium which can help government to give an account of its stewardship, elucidate its legislation or otherwise help to provide a background of civic understanding is very precious'. In this way, Grierson's words were used to endorse, justify and define the MFU's work, but the influence of Grierson, evident in the government's pre-war and immediate post-war film work, would become ever more marginal with the arrival of Hodge (Department of Information 1953). A later production such as *Merdeka for Malaya* deviates significantly from the more 'poetic' work seen in productions like *Voices of Malaya*. While Ow Kheng Law described *Merdeka for Malaya* as a 'documentary', he further labelled it an 'objective record of the merdeka celebrations' (*Straits Times* 1957e). While such claims to objectivity may appear spurious, the language hints at the ways in the MFU imagined and positioned the film. Indeed *Merdeka for Malaya* more closely follows a form seen in other MFU 'special news films', such as the 1953 film *Malaya Celebrates* (director unknown, 1953), which depicts the response in Malaya to the coronation of Queen Elizabeth II. It is to this film that I turn briefly now.

CELEBRATIONS ON SCREEN: FROM THE CORONATION TO GHANAIAN INDEPENDENCE

The MFU dispatched seven mobile camera teams to film the coronation celebrations throughout Malaya in 1953. In sending the footage to newsreel companies overseas, Hodge predicted that it would 'reach a world audience exceeding 100 million people' (*Straits Times* 1953). At the time this was the largest project undertaken by the MFU and the completed film, *Malaya Celebrates*, would share many characteristics with *Merdeka for Malaya*. *Malaya Celebrates* opens with fireworks and contains celebratory crowd scenes, official ceremonies – featuring the British national anthem and the raising of the Union Flag – and inspections carried out by Sir Donald MacGillivray. There are scenes of British welfare work (visiting hospitals), the arrival by aeroplane of dignitaries (in this case General Templar, the British High Commissioner in Malaya) and ceremonial handovers (the insignia of 'Honorary Knight Commander of the British Empire' to Malay politician, Dato Onn).

As Tom Hodge indicated in planning the production, *Malaya Celebrates* also illustrates the different religious ceremonies held freely within the country, as the film promotes an image of a multiracial community united through its support for the British Empire. Integral to this is the image of the Queen, foregrounded as a unifying symbol of the Empire (both the banners and commentary refer repeatedly to 'our' Queen). In this later period, as focus shifts towards the Commonwealth, the royal family serves as a means of legitimising imperial control and authority overseas. 'Never has there been such widespread enjoyment', the commentator states, 'and never have the people's feelings been expressed so spontaneously and so generously'.

While the emphasis is on celebration and national unity, the film does make one mention of the political situation within Malaya, acknowledging, albeit briefly, the anti-imperial struggle dominating and decimating Malaya at the time. As security forces make their way through the jungle, they stop, lay out a commemorative rug emblazoned with the Queen's face, pull out some drinks and toast the new Queen. The scene neatly encapsulates an imperial ideal, showing a multiracial country (represented by British, Malay, Chinese and Indian forces) united through the image of the Queen, while also illustrating the 'civilised' nature of the security forces as they pay due respect and drink together. *Malaya Celebrates* manages here to offer a fervent, uncritical, endorsement of the British Empire during a period of sustained anti-imperial unrest. There is a clear trajectory from these celebratory scenes of the coronation (or royal visits), which are common to most colonial units, to the subsequent films of independence celebrations. These events, of celebrations and parties, traditional pageants and displays, are visually striking and can be largely isolated or removed from the politics of the time. They stand alone, tied up in symbols and rituals, and serve to represent, construct and encapsulate a national history.

A comparison with another government film of colonial handover, produced by the Ghana Film Unit a few months earlier, reveals another model for such nation-building and further indicates what was at stake in these widely circulating representations. On first glance *Freedom for Ghana* (Sean Graham, 1957) appears to adopt a similar format to the subsequent MFU film, *Merdeka for Malaya*. The opening minutes comprise a map, fluttering flags, dignitaries arriving at the airport, a royal procession and religious ceremonies within a stadium. Later there are formal state banquets, royal visits and the unveiling of the Independence Monument. Yet, what is perhaps most striking here is the commentary, which offers a much more critical perspective on the colonial influences within Ghana. The film celebrates those that have lost their lives fighting for freedom, and when the British flag is removed, the British commentator is replaced by a local voice stating 'too long up there making us other people's property'. Despite this more critical approach, which appears to reflect more clearly the tensions marking the end of empire, the film still qualifies what the flag represents and seeks to negotiate a peaceful handover. 'But behind that flag, fine, sincere people devoted to this country's good', the commentator adds, 'there is a friendship and affection between us'.

Freedom for Ghana is notably more 'poetic' – both sonically and visually – and more closely aligned to the earlier Griersonian *Voices of Malaya* than *Merdeka for Malaya*. Indeed the Ghana Film Unit (formerly Gold Coast Film Unit or GCFU), which produced *Freedom for Ghana*, held closer ties with the 'prestige' work of the British Documentary Movement than the instructional work adopted by other colonial units in Africa. This is, in some ways, surprising. The Colonial Film Unit (CFU) was at its most active in West Africa during the 1940s and set up its first training school in Accra in 1948, which provided the founding personnel for the GCFU. Yet, the head of the GCFU, Sean Graham, was a self-proclaimed 'disciple of Grierson', who vehemently rejected suggestions that the GCFU was a colonial unit; 'colonial was a dirty word' (Sandon et al. 2013: 530). Martin Stollery recalls GCFU filmmaker Chris Hesse's recent description of Graham as a 'rebel' within the Gold Coast Information Services, marked out by his integration within Ghanaian culture and his more liberal, humanist politics (Stollery, 2014: 193). There is a notable shift within both units during the 1950s. While in Malaya, a more instructional cinema associated with William Sellers and the CFU replaces the 'Griersonian' influences, in the Gold Coast, the reverse is true as the 'Griersonian' influences come to the fore. The GCFU is also able, surprisingly, to invite more critical and radical voices to work on its films. Indeed the credited writer on *Freedom for Ghana* was Basil Davidson, a radical journalist, noted African historian and champion of liberation movements.

The latter sequences of *Freedom for Ghana* also deviate from the more 'prosaic' form of *Merdeka for Malaya*. After the raising of the Ghanaian flag at midnight, the film conveys the energy and excitement of Ghana through travelling shots, which follow Prime Minister Kwame Nkrumah's car, and the multiple cuts, which capture the urgency of the crowds. The commentators celebrate Nkrumah's rise and struggle ('the government put him in prison. They tried to forget him. They failed'), but also, once more, attempt to locate Britain's place within this process. As the procession moves through the streets, a British voice-over states, 'I suppose we could have hung on of course, we could have gritted our teeth and called in the troops and somehow muddled through, shot our way through'. The commentator concludes that such an approach is 'out of date, greedy, stupid'. An Indian voice-over then responds by recalling how the Indians felt about the British 'before they decided to leave India'. 'We used to dislike the British, we don't now', he concludes. At the departure of the Duchess of Kent, the commentator outlines the 'warmth of friendship that will continue to unite Ghana with Great Britain'. As with *Merdeka for Malaya*, the film celebrates the confluence of influences and styles, although in this instance it is marked by an infiltration of African culture on colonial structures more than the colonial influences on local life. For example, the film presents the formal dance at the Hotel Ambassador as a sign of progressive racial integration and gleefully champions the African influences now creeping into the European club, 'that dear old department of the stiff upper lip'.

Freedom for Ghana continued to circulate well beyond independence and was presented as a positive call to arms for other nations. The Ghana Film Unit's catalogue recognised that the film 'attempted more than the conventional record of a happy royal tour', setting a 'pattern for the wider picture' and presenting Ghana 'as a symbol for the whole of Africa' (Ghana Film Industry Corporation 1974). The film's conclusion, which features Nkrumah's moonlit speech, represents a much more provocative and politicised moment than we see at any point in *Merdeka for Malaya*. Nkrumah introduces the new national anthem over a shot of the Ghanaian flag, before proclaiming 'freedom' once more with his right hand raised. While this is not dissimilar from sequences in the MFU's film, the British commentator also speaks here, noting that Africa has 'woken up' and that other countries will follow Ghana. 'Courage, freedom, these are Ghana's words for you wherever you are, whoever you are . . . humanity is indivisible. Indivisible.'

FLAGS, ANTHEMS AND THE CONTESTED SYMBOLS OF A NEW NATION

Freedom for Ghana concludes with a shot of the national flag fluttering in the night sky. The flag, as a manufactured symbol of the new nation, features in much the same way as a framing device in *Merdeka for Malaya*. The flag was, however, a somewhat contested symbol in Malaya. It was initially chosen through a public contest overseen by a committee chaired by Sir Alec Newboult, the colonial Chief Secretary. The committee discussed at length their hopes for the design, with Dato Onn suggesting that the flag should 'denote the birth of a new nation and should indicate the unity of the nine States and the two Settlements and partnership with the United Kingdom'. After a public call brought forward 373 designs, a shortlist of three was presented for public vote in the *Malay Mail*. The chosen flag was not without controversy as the favoured five-pointed star too closely resembled communist symbols. Further points were thus added to the star to represent each of the eleven states before it was approved by King George VI in 1950 and first raised by Sir Henry Gurney, the British High Commissioner in Malaya, in the Sultan Selangor's palace. Gurney referred once more to the flag as a 'symbol of unity' (see Nasruddin and bin Zulkhurnain 2012).

The public was also initially invited to select the national anthem, listening to the final seven entries on the radio in 1956. Historian Cheong Soon Gan argues that the national anthem would ultimately become a more prominent and significant symbol of the new nation, but the debates over its selection – concerning whether the anthems represented the traditions, customs and cultures of Malaya – and, moreover, over the public responses to the selected anthem, attest to the broader, imagined function of the anthem within the new nation. Indeed the government ultimately rejected those tunes put forward for public vote and curiously commissioned one of the most prominent British composers, Benjamin Britten, to write its anthem in June 1957. Britten's composition was also rejected in favour of 'Negaraku', an established tune and the existing anthem for the state of Perak (Gan 2015: 61–78; Marshall 2015).

The selection of the anthem illustrated the tensions between existing colonial authority and emerging local voices. Furthermore, Gan shows how the chosen anthem became imbricated in anxieties around local resistance. In particular, he notes the escalating discourse around its performance after film shows, when audience members would leave before it was played (Gan 2015). The British national anthem had formed a pivotal part of the colonial film show and had cemented the anthem as a daily feature of the nation-building process. The earliest mobile film tours in Africa in the 1930s had ended with a picture of the King and a performance of the national anthem. The performance was imagined here as an integral part of the colonising process, a means of creating British citizens. There are numerous reports of audience reactions at MFU film shows that challenged this stated ideological aim. For example some cinemagoers reportedly cheered the appearance of communist leader Chin Peng at a screening of the MFU's film *1955: The Year in Malaya* (director unknown, 1955), which resulted in the government removing the film from screens. At film shows across the empire, any failure to observe protocol during the anthem was invariably construed as a political act of protest (*Straits Times* 1956a).

The emphasis on the flag and anthem within the film, as carefully constructed symbols of the new nation, echoes much colonial cinema, symbolically representing a changing of the guard by using the form and conventions of its colonial predecessors. Through film, radio and photography, these symbols are used to mark, celebrate and circulate news of the new nation, but film also attempts to overlook the disagreements and political tensions that are stitched onto these symbols, stabilising this fluid and contingent history. These films of independence are part of a myth-making process, fantasies that are integral to the narrative of 'amicable' handovers and new nation building. However, when we look beyond the frame at the film's reception, these tensions often come to the fore as the sounds, images and symbols were critical sites not only for the imagination, but also the contestation, of national and global identities. For example, the United Malay National Organisation (UMNO) complained that *Merdeka for Malaya* placed too much emphasis on the role played by non-Malays in the Merdeka celebrations, in particular by omitting shots of thanksgiving ceremonies at mosques (*Straits Times* 1957d). As noted earlier, the film attempted to show the different cultures 'of this multi racial country rolled into one', the 'rich and varied cultures' working together in harmony. Ow Kheng Law defended the film from the UMNO criticisms. 'In the film we have shots of the mosques, faces of the Malayans and children celebrating merdeka and the Nobat (royal drums) at the installation of the Paramount Ruler', he wrote. 'Surely these are Malayan scenes and background' (*Straits Times* 1957e). The validity of the UMNO criticisms is of less relevance than the fact that they were made. These criticisms endorse widely held British fears of communal division and dissension, as these disparate groups sought to promote their own image within an emerging national identity. Evidently the stakes are high here for the many invested parties; the film represented, as a government document projected around the world, a microcosm of the new nation, a way to work through a new national identity.

Merdeka for Malaya also seeks to preserve British prestige at this moment of loss, perpetuating the idea that Britain had controlled and carefully planned the handover of power. This historical reworking is most neatly articulated through the movement of personnel. Just as much early colonial cinema highlighted arrivals and departures – the movement on trains and boats across the empire – *Merdeka for Malaya* visualised this shift in power through the technological advances that the colonial powers have brought. In one sequence, we witness the departure by plane of Sir Donald MacGillivray, the last high commissioner. Once more, the departure is marked by military pageants as MacGillivray says 'farewell to personal friends of all communities'. The commentator emphasises the amicable nature of the handover – 'the citizens of Malaya salute you' – and almost mourns the loss of empire here, explaining that 'there are some ties that are painful to break'. The commentator's words endorse a particular revisionist account of this pathway to independence. Suggesting that MacGillivray served Malaya well 'in the crucial years when independence became possible', the film reinforces the notion that independence was long imagined and willingly offered by the British. It was, of course, a much more rapid and unforeseen development, with the move towards independence in Malaya gaining sustained momentum after the Federal elections of July 1955. The Alliance Party, headed by Tunku Abdul Rahman, had somewhat surprisingly won fifty-one of the fifty-two elected seats and, on assuming power, the Tunku had immediately pushed for independence, arguing that 'the only real alternative to Communism is nationalism' (*The Times* 1955). The British remained suspicious of the political coalition, and had repeatedly stated that independence would only be considered once the state of emergency had ended. However, by October 1955, British ministers retreated from this position, in part to ensure that the Tunku avoided striking a deal with Chin Peng. In January 1956, the Tunku led a delegation to Britain, and on 8 February signed an agreement (the Independence Treaty), which granted Malaya independence on 31 August 1957 'if possible'. Piers Brendon argued that 'the British were stampeded into granting *Merdeka*', while T. N. Harper noted that once a date had been agreed, 'an unstoppable momentum built up towards it' (Brendon 2007: 459; Harper 1998: 348).

This subtext is carefully omitted from this official presentation of independence. Tom Hodge's account in 1957 presents a similar picture of a supportive MFU, preparing and enacting the moves to self-governance: 'It has helped to train the people in the methods and standards of elections and census taking and to encourage a sense of responsible citizenship' (Hodge 1957: 539). In endorsing a post-war rhetoric of welfare and development, the films served as 'visual education', outlining, for example, the benefits of literacy (*The Letter*, director unknown, 1953), the welfare of the blind (*Touch and Go*, director unknown, MFU, 1953), the government's pension scheme (*Worry Free*, director unknown, 1954) and rehabilitation through the prison services (*A Better Man*, director unknown, 1953). In promoting self-sufficiency, modern welfare services and a Western model of citizenship, the Unit sought to play an active role in the modern nation state-building process. Hassan Muthalib has more recently illustrated the ways in which the MFU awakened 'a sense of nationalism' during the 1950s, while also presenting Tunku Abdul Rahman, the Chief Minister, as a viable, 'heroic' leader: a process completed with *Merdeka for Malaya* (Muthalib 2011: 191).

In these ways, the films of independence are essential historical records, not simply through their depiction of the people and events, but for the myths and fantasies they create or perpetuate. In a period of intense, tumultuous change, these recorded ceremonies seek to preserve a moment of reconciliation and celebration. The rigid structure and recurring patterns may attest to a continuing colonial influence and to an attempt to control and manage this loss, but as Rathbone and others have shown, they also serve to conceal the tensions and struggles that led to independence and that marked the very process of arranging these celebrations. Government records illustrate that the ceremonial plans were invariably contested (who stands where, who is invited, where and when this should take place). Power is visual, and the positioning and organisation of personnel (through editing, buildings and events) is one of the ways in which power is transformed into spectacle. Ultimately the on-screen fantasy, comprising fireworks, parades and flag waving, encourages viewers to surrender to a form of amnesia. These ceremonies, hypnotic in their repetition and order, are an integral part of a process that invites British viewers not to remember and to mourn, but rather to forget and move on. This process still continues today. For example, British education continues to focus on world wars, rather than the empire, on narratives of victory or good versus evil, while surprisingly little fiction film confronts Britain's loss of empire and the more complicated process and repercussions of decolonisation.

CONCLUSIONS: BEYOND INDEPENDENCE

In July 1957, on the eve of Malayan Independence, Tom Hodge left the MFU. In discussing his departure, and the position of Ow Kheng Law at the head of the unit, Hodge suggested that the MFU 'now lives proudly up to the first word of its title, reflecting the nation in its composition as in the films which leave its laboratories' (Hodge 1957: 539). Shortly after completing work on *Freedom for Ghana*, Sean Graham would leave his role in charge of the Ghana Film Unit and return to Britain. The moves to independence also led to the promise of new equipment and studios. Ow Kheng Law announced plans to rehouse the MFU in the 'biggest and most up to date studio' in South-East Asia in 1956. The MFU's existing studio was a reminder of Japanese occupation – a former Japanese paper mill – and was described by the Kuala Lumpur fire authorities as the 'biggest fire hazard in the country' (*Straits Times* 1956b). In Ghana, Nkrumah soon announced plans to modernise film production and instal a modern recording and film processing plant in Accra. He reportedly paraded the African film crews as a model for modern Ghana, suggesting that the film units were not only responsible for creating the new nation in the popular imagination but were also positively enacting this process, exemplars of the shift from colonial to post-colonial state.

These narratives of change, however attractive to politicians of the time and historians today, oversimplify and conceal a more nuanced transition in both countries after 1957. Many of the personnel retained close ties to, and were developed through, the colonial era. Ow Kheng Law, for example, had travelled and trained with the Crown Film Unit in 1945–6 and was a founding member of the MFU, while Mohammed Zain Hussain, who would later become Director General of the MFU, was a cameraman on the very earliest MFU productions like *The Kinta Story* (director unknown, 1949). Sam Aryeetey, who would later serve as the Managing Director of the Ghana Film Industry Corporation – a further successor to the GCFU – was one of six film-makers who attended the inaugural training school organised by the Colonial Office's CFU in Accra in 1948, and was a founding member of the GCFU. While Aryeetey is often credited as the director of the first Ghanaian feature film, *No Tears for Ananse* (Sam Aryeetey, 1968) this film would not appear until 1968, a full decade after independence. Indeed, during the early 1960s, films were still sent to London for processing, while the senior staff consisted of five expatriate officers and six Ghanaians. Graham even claimed that Nkrumah asked him to stay on after independence and, despite the government's stated desire to 'make the film productions completely

Ghanaian in character', the unit continued to bring in European directors (Ministry of Information and Broadcasting 1961). Likewise, much of the equipment and structures remained in place – development work on the MFU's new studio was postponed and it only finally opened in 1965 – while films produced within the colonial era continued to circulate. A film catalogue from the Ghana Central Film Library in 1971-2 (Public Relations Department 1972) is dominated by Gold Coast Film Unit productions (and productions from other colonial-era units, including the MFU), which still played on the mobile film circuit.

The government films of independence ceremonies, like *Merdeka for Malaya*, are hugely significant parts of the nation-building process, celebrating the new nation, while in their homogenous form and conciliatory narratives of partnership, still retaining strong ties to the colonial powers. The symbols of change – the raised flag, the handover, the departing dignitary or the new anthem – are powerful visual (and sonic) signifiers of this change, yet in capturing a few moments, the films become fantasies, seemingly removed from the politics and tensions that led to independence and that would invariably continue after the plane took to the skies and the cameras switched off. In a similar vein, the units that captured these moments are often celebrated and presented as microcosms of the nation at large. In many respects they are, but not always in the ways imagined. Instead they reveal, like the films they produce, a moment of uncertainty and transition, one that often retains a close tie to the colonial influences that shaped its cinema cultures, but often fails to confront and address the tensions, frustrations, failings and successes of the colonial era. In preserving a moment, these films too often seek to forget what has gone before and what will likely come after. The legacy of this process continues to this day.

ACKNOWLEDGEMENTS

I would like to thank Kay Gladstone and the Imperial War Museum, and James Kearney and the AP Archive, for their help in accessing the films.

REFERENCES

Aitken, Ian (2015), 'British governmental institutions, the Regional Information Office in Singapore and the use of the official film in Malaya and Singapore, 1948–1961', *Historical Journal of Film, Radio and Television*, 35: 1, 27–52.
Brendon, Piers (2007), *The Decline and Fall of the British Empire, 1781–1997*, London: Jonathan Cape.
Colonial Cinema (1947), 'Films in Malaya', March, 13–15.

Department of Information, Federation of Malaya (1953), *Catalogue of Films Made by the Malayan Film Unit*, Kuala Lumpur: Department of Information.
Department of Information, Federation of Malaya (1959), *Catalogue of Documentary Films in the Federal Film Library*, Kuala Lumpur: Department of Information.
Film News (1955), 'Presenting – the Malayan Film Unit', 15: 3, Fall, p. 13.
Ghana Film Industry Corporation (1974), *Films We Have Produced*, Accra.
Harper, T. N. (1998), *The End of Empire and the Making of Malaya*, New York: Cambridge University Press.
Hawes, Stanley (1953), the 'Hawes Report', *Malayan Film Unit: Proposed Investigation and Reorganisation* (1949–1950), FO 953/757, National Archives (UK). Accessed on 1 July 2015 at http://digital.lib.hkbu.edu.hk/documentary-film/index.php.
Hodge, Tom (1957), 'Eleven years of the Malayan Film Unit: a record of solid achievement', *Educational Screen and Audio-Visual Guide*, November, 538–9.
Kinematograph Weekly (1955), 'Vintage year for Malayan Film Unit', 10 March.
Marshall, Alex (2015), 'Benjamin Britten's "lost" Malaysian anthem', accessed on 12 October 2015 at http://www.bbc.co.uk/news/magazine-34417765.
Ministry of Information and Broadcasting, Ghana (1961), *Ghana: An Official Handbook*, Accra.
Muthalib, Hassan Abdul (2011), 'The End of Empire: the films of the Malayan Film Unit in 1950s British Malaya', in L. Grieveson and C. MacCabe (eds), *Film and the End of Empire*, New York: Palgrave Macmillan, pp. 177–96.
Nasruddin, Muhamad Razif and Zarul Nazli bin Zulkhurnain (2012), 'The history and design chronology of Jailur Gemilang', accessed on 1 July 2015 at http://www.malaysiadesignarchive.org/jalurgemilang.
Public Relations Department (1972), *Catalogue of Films*, Ghana Central Film Library Accra, 1971–2.
Ramakrishna, Kumar (2002), *Emergency Propaganda: The Winning of Malayan Hearts and Minds 1948–1958*, Richmond: Curzon Press.
Rathbone, Richard (2010), 'Casting "the Kingdome into Another Mold": Ghana's troubled transition to independence', in R. Holland, S. Williams and T. Barringer (eds), *The Iconography of Independence: Freedoms at Midnight*, London: Routledge, pp. 57–70.
Rice, Tom (2013), 'Distant voices of Malaya, still colonial lives', *Journal of British Cinema and Television*, 10: 3, 430–51.
Sandon, Emma, Tom Rice and Peter Bloom (2013), 'Changing the world: Sean Graham', *Journal of British Cinema and Television*, 10: 3, 524–36.
Stockwell, A. J. (2010), 'Merdeka! Looking back at Independence Day in Malaya, 31 August 1957', in R. Holland, S. Williams and T. Barringer (eds), *The Iconography of Independence: Freedoms at Midnight*, London: Routledge, pp. 113–30.
Stollery, Martin (2014), 'White fathers hear dark voices?: John Grierson and British Colonial Africa at the end of Empire', in Zoë Druick and Deane Williams (eds), *The Grierson Effect: Tracing Documentary's International Movement*, London/New York: BFI Palgrave Macmillan, pp. 187–208.
Straits Times (1952), 'Child prodigy gets an expert', 6 October, p. 9.
Straits Times (1953), 'Surprise from the MFU', 21 June, p. 13.
Straits Times (1956a), 'Chin Peng cheered as KL audiences see peace talks newsreel', 6 January, p. 4.
Straits Times (1956b), 'New film unit studios will be S-E Asia's best', 7 April, p. 4.
Straits Times (1957a), 'Free Merdeka films for free world', 20 July, p. 7.

Straits Times (1957b), '"Merdeka" film for foreign lands', 19 September, p. 7.
Straits Times (1957c), '$250 for film memento of Merdeka Day', 21 September, p. 7.
Straits Times (1957d), 'Art in uniform', 24 September, p. 6.
Straits Times (1957e), 'Film Unit Head: we did our best', 25 September, p. 9.
The Times (1955), 'Malayan plea for speedy self-government', 1 September, p. 7.

CHAPTER 3

The Language of Counterinsurgency in Malaya: Dialectical Soundscapes of Salvage and Warfare

Peter J. Bloom

Counterinsurgency remains a source of refrain that came to rely upon the deployment of film and radio as indexical formulations of national ideology during the post-Second World War era. This chapter examines the media-specific language of counterinsurgency within the context of the Malayan Emergency (1948–60) and draws on 'the long tail' of British documentary film and BBC radio as its most significant source.[1] The rich and varied scholarship about the deployment of film and radio in Britain during the Second World War has emphasised a transformation of the conceptual address to the 'people', and the correlative 'we' as an increasingly inclusive register. The expansive repositioning of regional and accented speech associated with musical and localised ambient soundscapes specified distinct British voices that came to describe and circumscribe the narrative envelope for 'emergency'.

This contribution explores how transformations associated with the voice references sound effects as integral to the audio-visual staging of the Malayan Emergency. It is within the realm of such effects in their immediacy and quality of authentication that the communist insurgency in Malaya became named. Through a discussion of a jungle imaginary that relied on the relationship between native Malay, aboriginal Orang Asli, and ethnic Chinese populations, this chapter describes how the mobilisation of sound effects – including sounds of the jungle and the mechanisation of warfare – became a critical site in authenticating the legitimacy of the British-led counterinsurgency campaign. Within an articulation of the radio-cinema voice, evoked by Adorno's perceptive address to its radio physiognomy, the chapter suggests that an extended conception of the voice may refer, echo and become re-imagined within the reverberating 'symphony space' of the auditory.[2] The projection of the voice as the strategic deployment of a vocabulary of conflict also served as a foundation for political objectives during the counterinsurgency campaign itself. The 'communist terrorist' eventually came to serve as concept and agent of an insurgency paradigm that contributed to a Cold War realignment during the post-war era. It also remains the underlying historical and political footing for current evocations of 'counterterrorism'.

During the Second World War, the British propaganda film campaign organised by the Ministry of Information (MoI) took as its point of departure three primary themes: what Britain is fighting for, how Britain fights and the need for sacrifice if the fight was to be won (Chapman 1999: 44; Taylor 1981: 59–65). These themes served as points of reference in the development of war propaganda during and after the war. While the immediate effectiveness of MoI-produced documentary films as war propaganda has been cast into doubt (Pronay 1983: 72), the emergence and stabilisation of nationally distinct voices in newsreels, public service announcements and especially feature films served to amalgamate a new mode of address allied with the enlargement and intimacy of radio broadcasting. These films resorted to the vocabulary of the popular as the assemblage of voices that came to reinvigorate British sound cinema and widen the BBC broadcasting ethos during this unprecedented period of expansion. In particular, the scope and context for BBC operations grew from a staff of 4,233 with twenty-three transmitters in 1939 to 11,417 and 138 respectively by 1945. Foreign-language broadcasts also dramatically expanded from eight languages in 1939 to forty-seven in 1945, reaching an extended empire of listeners (Richards 2010: 44).

The so-called 'wartime wedding' between documentary and fiction film became a means by which the winning of the Second World War was to become a popularly held conviction (Chapman 1999: 44; Higson 1995). Its address to the home front relied on Winston Churchill's well-known rhetorical phrasings that emphasised historic and linguistic community within a heroic narrative that nominated the working class as 'champions' of national progress in the name of 'blood, toil, tears and sweat'.[3] Repositioning the media context at home was a means of addressing the widening context for participation in the war effort. This was accomplished through the expansion of documentary and feature film productions, but also crucially with the initiation of the BBC Forces Programme Broadcast station on 7 January 1940. Featuring light background entertainment among other programmes for casual listening, BBC Forces Programme radio was conceived to address the tastes of the troops (Nicholas 1999: 71).[4] It also expanded the BBC middle-brow broadcasting ethos of the 1930s beyond that of 'elevated classlessness' as founded on vestiges of 'cultural elitism' and 'self-improvement', to more representative popular-accented voices such as Wilfred Pickles's broad Yorkshire accent as Billy Welcome in the eponymous radio serial (Richards 2010: 44).[5]

Though the war effort itself may be said to have facilitated a shift in national cultural parameters, the BBC Listening Research Department, established in 1936 as a variation of Mass Observation, had already begun analysing and measuring listener tastes leading to a continued pattern of experiments with the variety-show format. It was in fact this spirit of ongoing experimentation that contributed to the eventual formation of an inclusionary national culture that was mirrored in the culture of documentary film, such that John Reith, founding director of the BBC (1923–38), may be said to have closely resembled John Grierson, the leading figure in the British documentary film movement.

The expanding popular appeal of BBC radio programming was also mirrored in the cinema. In documentary films such as *Spare Time* (1939), directed by Humphrey Jennings, and those by Harry Watt among others, as well as feature films such as *In Which We Serve* (Noel Coward and David Lean, 1942), *Millions Like Us* (Sidney Gilliat and Frank Launder, 1943) and *The Way Ahead* (Carol Reed, 1944), an emphatic populism came to emerge. The use of the 'we' and the 'us' in wartime propaganda posters and documentary was embodied, as John Ellis suggests, by an image of Churchill in hat and overcoat against a background of Spitfire aircraft with the caption, 'Let us go forward together' (Ellis 1981: 59). The ideological shift at work here from this rarely used invocation of the 'we' of the interwar years to a legible collective identity relied on the effect of the wartime emergency as a call to mobilisation. The legibility and stereotyping of radio-cinema voices resulted in a normalisation of accent within a hierarchy on the basis of clarity rather than authenticity. Nonetheless, accent still functioned as an index or, as Jo Fox explains, a significant 'device in the formation of both the collective experience and individual identities' (Fox 2006: 820).

STAGING THE MALAYAN EMERGENCY IN THE LANGUAGE OF COUNTERINSURGENCY

An extensive literature has examined the extent to which the modulation of accent and a more broadly conceived notion of the radio-cinema voice became integral to the emerging construct of propaganda on the home front during the Second World War.[6] It is my contention here, however, that adaptations of wartime propaganda also served as foundational sources for staging the Malayan Emergency, which has been described as the defining post-war counterinsurgency paradigm (Hack 2009). More specifically, the expanding narrative and technological sophistication of recorded sound media during the Second World War, as relayed through sound film and on radio, became the basis for developing a language and register for counterinsurgency. In fact, Richard H. S. Crossman, a principal figure in developing the psychological warfare campaign against Germany during the war, explained that there was not only an extensive staff that coalesced at Supreme Headquarters under Dwight Eisenhower's command by the end of the war, but that during his six-year involvement with psychological operations many techniques were tried and 'they made almost every mistake possible'. Instead, he explained, it was rather the careful coordination of diplomatic and military activity with the deployment of media that became the essential feature of wartime propaganda (Crossman 1952: 320). Hugh Carelton Greene, a close associate of Crossman during the war who was attached to the Political Warfare Executive German Section, was later appointed as Head Staff Officer of Emergency Operations during the early strategic phases of the Malayan Emergency from 1950 to 1952.[7] There were significant continuities in personnel from one theatre of conflict to another. The technological development of audio recording technologies also followed. Large hearse-like recording vans were followed by the cumbersome but portable Midget disc recorder. As a result, the rhetorical context for counterinsurgency as a cinematic spectacle and broadcasting event became a means by which to reassert colonial administrative prerogative, while also accepting the principle of eventual independence for Malaya.

The lexicography of conflict in Malaya, as John Deery has explained, was carefully considered and then scripted into the authoritative diction, vocabulary and phrasings of newsreaders, commentators and invisible narrators in film and radio. A particular logomachy of the conflict was developed and refined by the Information Research Department (IRD) based in Singapore as a 'top secret semi-autonomous unit' created under the aegis of the British Foreign Office in 1948 (Deery 2003: 233).[8] The crafting of terminology was also mindful of legal implications in the actual deployment of an 'emergency', rather than colonial war. This allowed the Malayan rubber estates and tin-mining companies to claim losses of stock and equipment from London insurance companies under the terms of 'riot and civil commotion' without further aggravating the dollar gap crisis that had plagued the Attlee Administration of the period (for example Derry 2003: 237; White 1998: 170). In addition to the nomenclature of 'Emergency', it was the ubiquitous use of the term 'bandit', and 'anti-banditry' campaigns that were most often broadcast on Radio Malaya, and referred to by the incrementally active and remarkably accomplished productions of the Malayan Film Unit (MFU). The MFU came into being partly thanks to the availability of a full range of 35mm film equipment being sold by the departing United States Army Film Unit, and on the urging of Ralph Elton, then head of the Crown Film Unit. The first post-war Director of Public Relations in Malaya, Mervyn Sheppard (aka Abdul Mubin Sheppard), negotiated its purchase in May 1946 (Sheppard 1956).[9]

Elton, who was accompanied by cameraman Denny Densham, arrived in the region to film the British invasion of Singapore, code-named Operation Zipper, and compile a series of newsreels. As Tom Rice has explained, from 1945–6, Elton, with four Englishmen and six Malayans shot 250,000 feet of film, which became the basis for the film *Voices of Malaya* (Ralph Elton, 1948), which was also the initial film made in association with the newly founded MFU (Rice 2013: 431). Elton's involvement in the creation of the film unit was of limited duration, and the task of training the Malayan staff and making films fell more to Harry Govan, an army film-maker who became the first director of the MFU, and his assistant R. E. D. 'Gillie' Potter (Muthalib 2011: 179). This initial phase of the unit lasted until 1952 under Govan initially, who left in 1950 and was succeeded by Ben H. Hipkins. The unit was completely reorganised however as a professional organisation for propaganda, starting in October 1952, under Alec D. C. Peterson. Peterson has been described as Gerard Templer's very own propaganda 'supremo', an oblique term frequently evoked to describe Churchill's mandate for Templer himself in Malaya, who was granted extraordinary military decision-making power (Aitken 2014: 94–7; Ramakrishna 2002: 49, 64).

Much of this transformation in the organisation of the MFU was also facilitated by the Hawes Report, which made recommendations for revitalising the staff and organisation of the MFU.[10] The MFU documentary films and shorts that followed addressed specific themes allied with particular strategic objectives related to the Emergency, and were frequently made with voice-over narrations in multiple languages (including English, Malay, Mandarin and Tamil) for distribution in mobile caravans, theatres and schools throughout Malaya (Chan 2016). The themes of these short films would address questions of resettlement, as with *Proudly Presenting Yong Peng* (1953), the modernity of radio as in *Malaya Speaks* (1955), farming and irrigation techniques in *Tanjong Karang* (1953), fishing collectives in *United We Stand* (1959), the loyalty of the common people against the newly dubbed Communist Terrorists in *The Knife* (1952), as well as the modernity of military operations in *Jungle Fort* (1953). The style of the documentary shorts was derivative in format and narrative address of British documentary sound cinema and public service announcements during the war years. They incorporated the use of local voices of Malay characters and protagonists (as in *United We Stand*), supplemented by neutral voice-over narration, albeit British accented within the general parameters of Received Pronunciation. RP, as it is widely known, is the standard educated accent of southern England, carrying with it a certain quality of cultural prestige within England and especially abroad, particularly during this mid-century era. Within a continuing cycle of themes derived from popular wartime features in Britain, the theme of banditry was cast in relation to home defence squads on the rubber plantations in Malaya. The imperturbability and endurance of the British character synonymous with war films such as *In Which We Serve* continued in the imagined realm of a Malayan rubber plantation. *The Planter's Wife* (Ken Annakin, 1952), starring Claudette Colbert and Jack Hawkins, evokes these very same themes through the lens of a family defending their rubber plantation against communist insurgents from the jungle.

The notable shift from the vocabulary of 'bandits' to 'communist terrorists' by May 1952 was specifically mandated by the Colonial Office as a strategic move related to the emerging register of American Cold War public opinion. As John Deery has suggested, the change in nomenclature was enacted to better dissolve international perceptions of colonial struggle. Those referred to as bandits and later communists were in fact highly trained, disciplined and skilful soldiers. They were veteran fighters who actively resisted the Japanese occupation from 1942–5 as part of the Malayan People's Anti-Japanese Army (MPAJA). Many were initially trained by and liaised with Force 136, a branch of the British Special Operations Executive, later becoming the backbone of the communist insurgency led by Chin Peng, a former member of the

MPAJA, who was decorated by the British for his heroism against the Japanese occupation (Stockwell 1999: 479).[11]

VOICES AND GEOGRAPHIES OF THE EMERGENCY

While a detailed history of the Emergency has been examined elsewhere (Hack 2001; Harper 1999; Milner 1995), the narrative register of film and radio auditory has received less attention. Significant innovations in mobile sound recording and propaganda techniques more generally were derived from experience on the home front during the Second World War. This allowed for an increasingly scripted narrative that framed oppositions between nature and culture, while also modelling a multiracial context for civil society that privileged the Malays in a discourse of paternalistic underdevelopment. It was precisely within the terms of neutrality and equanimity in relation to citizenship rights that *Voices of Malaya* claimed that the return of the British administration was fortuitous. The voice-over narration served as a sound bridge across distinctively accented first-person narrators; it also functioned as the arbiter of opinion within a multiracial context in the name of hygienic and educational reform. Thus, the increasingly active deployment of film and radio inferred an emerging temporal and spatial dynamic of technological modernity that became a central feature of the counterinsurgency paradigm.

A clearly articulated mode of argumentation was prevalent in documentary film voice-over narration. The tactics of the correlative 'us' and 'we' took the form of accented English among Tamil, Chinese, Malay and British speakers who narrated their own perspective in *Voices of Malaya*. Episodic uses of first-person narration referred to a particular figure within the diegetic space of the film. It was then woven together by an omniscient voice-over narration that appeared in many MFU documentary film productions. The neutral British voice-over narrator would often function as foil for the equanimity of British administrative authority but was set in opposition to the locality of voices pictured as individuals on location in Malaya. In many of the MFU productions, the ethnic Malay majority was also portrayed as the dominant, though underdeveloped, national identity matrix through the use of subtle contrasts with Chinese-Malays. The less numerous but significant population of Tamils, among others from India, who arrived en masse to serve British labour needs on the rubber estates after the turn of the twentieth century, are portrayed as part of the supporting cast of British modernising interests. In addition to the device of ethnically accented voices aligned through an omniscient voice-over in English-language versions of the MFU films, there is also the question of how these voices were contextualised as part of a local soundscape, and it is here that locality was lodged by reference to sounds of the Malayan jungle and the aboriginal people of Malaya, known as the Orang Asli, who were neither Malay, Chinese, nor Tamil. Representing the originary people of Malaya, the early recordings of the Temiar people in particular, among the Orang Asli, came to serve as a vanishing point for the sounds that technologies of audition could detect, protect and adjudicate.

Although technologies of audition were incorporated into the extensive array of films produced during the Emergency which reached a wide audience in theatres, schools and through caravans among other public venues, radio became a primary source of listening throughout Malaya and it was within this context that Radio Malaya expanded rapidly once the Japanese occupation ended in 1945. Initially established in 1936 at studios located on Caldecott Hill in Singapore, it came to be known as the Malayan Broadcasting Corporation in 1940 and operated from the Cathay Building in Singapore before being abandoned in 1942 as a result of the Japanese invasion. Nonetheless, the evacuated staff continued to broadcast from Java, and later Jakarta, on the same wavelength during the occupation until Broadcasting House for Radio Malaya was established in Singapore as the initial hub that quickly expanded through the establishment of relay stations in Kuala Lumpur, Malacca and Penang making it the most extensive radio network in South-East Asia of the era.[12] By 1953, three networks had already been established and 153,305 licences for shortwave radio sets had been registered.[13] Malay and English were broadcast on the Blue network, Chinese and Tamil on the Red medium wave network, and the Green network produced programming exclusively in the seven major Chinese dialects from Singapore.[14] While there is much fascinating detail regarding the nature and organisation of this broadcasting arrangement, my particular interest here is the development and function of sound effects that served as part of a circulating archive to punctuate all types of programmes including school broadcasts, news and radio dramas.

SOUND EFFECTS AND THE CIRCULATION OF JUNGLE EFFECT

The recording and sourcing of jungle sounds came to inform a vanishing point for broadcasting and screening the Emergency itself as a space to be protected and appropriately administered. It was the remarkable intermingling of sounds of the jungle and implements of war through which the Malayan Emergency came to resonate as a new theatre of conflict. In effect, it recast visual metaphors of geographic mapping and human physiognomy to a more internalised and individuated quality by which to influence judgement in the international circulation and fluency of mid-century sounds of geographic and historical difference. As Hugh Clifford, the late nineteenth-century colonial resident, asserted, the vast stretches of forest in Malaya remained 'one of the few remaining blanks on the map . . . [which included] . . . untouched aboriginal blocks of Malayan territory' (Clifford as quoted by Roseman 1998: 106). As Maureen Sioh (1998) has explained, a search for the 'noble savage' in unmapped territory came to be successively anchored by the transposition of 'forest', as a protective and inventive space of nature, to 'jungle'. This emphasis on depicting otherness contrasts with the emerging emphasis on the correlative 'we' and 'us' as a claim for national unity in Britain. It was from the perspective of forest being remade in the imagination of Kipling's jungle that Herbert Deane 'Pat' Noone's ethnographic fieldwork began, with the mapping of 8,000 square miles that extended the colonial cartographic record in the northern states of Perak and Kelantan leading to his encounter with the Temiar among the Orang Asli aboriginal people (Roseman 1998: 108).

While Roseman's remarkable ethnographic work details the wonders of musical genre and invention among the Temiar, Noone's early research served as a foundation for the evolving sonic signature of the jungle in Malaya. It was a signature that inferred a particular kind of exotic reference to esoteric knowledge associated with the culture of aboriginal dreamwork among the Orang Asli within a larger archive of sound effects. The Temiar, as a people who were the purveyors of the jungle, served as the subject of the important and well-regarded MFU documentary, *Timeless Temiar* (Mohammed Zain Hussain, 1956). This film refers to folkloric conceptions of their life including references to the cosmology of their spirit world. Its ethnographic quality harkens back to Noone's work, particularly the act of bringing a group of Temiars to Singapore in 1936, when he supposedly recorded some of their songs and spoken language for broadcast during the first year of Radio Malaya (*Singapore Free Press* 1937). Noone later returned to Malaya prior to the fall of Singapore in 1942 as a member of a British paramilitary unit called 'Frontier Patrol', which operated along the Thai/Malay border.[15]

During this time, he also made a series of local recordings of Temiar songs with Eric D. Robertson in 1941, which was later published by Ethnic Folkways records.[16] These recordings also became integrated into an archive that constituted a distinctive array of Malayan sound effects circulated by Radio Malaya to the BBC and other Commonwealth radio stations.

The subsequent sound recordings in the years to follow were on a continuum with the early recordings of the Orang Asli as aboriginal exotic subjects, who served as a significant basis for asserting a culture of British protectionism. Initiated within the register of physiognomy and the mapping of territory, these sounds served to reinforce the developmental imagination. It was a construct that expanded a search for otherness as the very reconciliation of internal differences in speech and culture within Britain itself. The descriptive anthropology of Pat Noone, who was the first field ethnographer of the Perak State Museum, was followed by that of his brother Dick Noone, after Pat mysteriously disappeared and then was reportedly killed during the Japanese occupation. Their work became an important basis for arguing in favour of protecting the Orang Asli. It was within this context that the British administrators were able to situate themselves as adept purveyors and preservationists upon their return in 1945. While Noone proposed a sixteen-point aboriginal policy in 1936, it was only after the war that an expanded version was embraced, such that the idea of a 'controlled reservation' including a reserve of land could eventually be adopted along with Malayan citizenship rights (Noone 1936: 62).

Following Pat Noone's early work, which included descriptions and recordings of the dream-songs of the Temiar, an extensive array of field-sound recordings was further created by Tony Beamish and Stewart Brook Wavell. Along with Edward Ward, they were among the best known broadcasters for Radio Malaya during the Emergency, and their radio documentaries were featured on BBC radio and broadcast on BBC External Broadcasting Services.[17] Their close ties with British intelligence have also been variously mentioned, leading us to see that sound recording was not merely about esoteric knowledge, but involved establishing links with the Orang Asli as a means of eventually fighting against the communist insurgency, and became linked to the eventual establishment of the Senoi Praaq paramilitary unit established in 1956, which was partially facilitated by Dick Noone's efforts (see Jumper 2001).

By 1953, there were more than 5,000 recorded sound effects available for insertion by producers in their programing at Radio Malaya. In addition to on-the-spot sound effects created in the studio, there was also a sound effects library of a different nature that was being developed gradually, and that drew on 'wild' sound recordings by Beamish and Wavell. As the 1953 Radio Malaya annual report recounts, the idea to create a sound archive was born in 'the heart of the natural park', when they heard the cry of 'the racquet-tailed Drongho'. With this recording, a number of other wild sounds were recorded of 'the bellow of a charging saladang, the cry of a giant leather-back turtle, the morning song of the ungka and so on'.[18] Some of the locally recorded sound effects were integrated into the wide ranging Historical BBC Sound Effects Archive, which was widely circulated to Commonwealth radio stations on vinyl discs, and incorporated a wide range of exotic sounds from Malaya and other parts of South-East Asia, Africa and beyond, in the museumification and circulation of colonial affect.

Pat Noone was among the first to describe and record the dreamsongs of the Temiar and his uncompleted work directly influenced Tony Beamish and Stewart Wavell. In fact, Wavell explains that he was one of the founders of the sound library at Radio Malaya in 1953, which began with his own sound recordings of healing ceremonies that he attended in the jungle near Perak, among another Orang Asli ethnic group known as the Semai Senoi, in addition to other recorded sounds. While the coding and analysis of songs among the Orang Asli has served more generally as a source for an ongoing thread of ethnographic study that became aligned with storytelling and songs associated with dreamwork, this theme of research has reinforced a native quality of otherness that contrasted with the sounds of modernity. While the sophisticated work of Roseman among others describes the adeptness and adaptation of the Temiar and Semai to historical circumstances, the emphasis on preindustrial otherness as communicated through song, as well as sounds of the jungle, bear the markings of the 'salvage paradigm' (see Clifford and Marcus 1986). In this sense, 'salvage' asserts a critical intervention against a form of anthropological positivism that continues to project an idealised conception of timelessness and authenticity into the study of indigenous cultures. The evocation of otherness as sound may be said to enable a structural space that allows for cohabitation with and a means by which to code an enemy presence. It is here that the declination of forest to jungle as a negative space nominates a dialectical relationship that helps define the political invention of the Emergency itself.

CONCLUSIONS: DIALECTICAL SOUND SIGNATURES OF COUNTERINSURGENCY

The partial rendering of the Malayan Emergency that I have briefly sketched in this chapter refers more broadly to a chain of associations that refers to the well-known opposition between savage and civilised as allied with a sound signature of counterinsurgency that was first established within the context of documentary film and Second World War-era British cinema. In the specific situation of mid-century Malaya, the alignments and differential codings asserted the purported underdevelopment of Malays, which was contrasted with the pre-industrial proclivities of the Orang Asli. Additionally, this alignment was cast in opposition to stereotypes of Chinese entrepreneurialism. By extension, there was a significant melding of sounds and songs of the Orang Asli that was contrasted with the wildlife in the forest. Crucially, this forest soundscape was then set in opposition to weapons of war, particularly the sound of aircraft, artillery and the very troops charged with fighting against the communist insurgency. As Eric Robertson had explained in his introduction to the early songs recorded by Pat Noone of the Temiar, they were both commissioned to record interviews with British, Indian and Australian troops in December 1941 on the first expedition of a mobile recording unit commissioned by Radio Malaya.¹⁹

In conclusion, there is a fundamental dialectical relationship at work, which I have tried to examine in this chapter, that positions a metropolitan fascination with pre-industrial songs in relation to industrial sounds of warfare. These sound categories are crucial extensions of the words and language of counterinsurgency. It was these overcoded sounds that become part of a larger archive of circulating sound effects that were used to punctuate radio programming. These sounds and words, supplemented by human voices, became integrated as an amalgamated language that functioned as a significant political register of the BBC Empire and latter-day Commonwealth orbit of broadcasting and film productions. It is within the overcoding of sounds in relation to words, and voices in relation to the moving image, that shifters, *pace* Jakobson (1996), mobilised a vocabulary that provided a foundational coding in the language of counterinsurgency used to wage the Malayan Emergency.

NOTES

1. As Patrick Russell and James Piers Taylor write, 'If this was but the tail end of the British documentary [i.e. in the post-war era], then it was in a fashionable twenty-first century phrase, a *long tail*. In fact, the true fall of the British documentary film tradition came not in the late 1940s but over the course of the 1970s, as British industry, under recessionary financial pressures, began reducing investment in film, and tightening its criteria for it' (Russell and Taylor 2010: 5).
2. See Adorno's 'Radio physiognomics' for further discussion of this point in Hullot-Kenter (2009: 41–132).
3. 'Blood, toil, tears and sweat' refers to Winston Churchill's first speech as Prime Minister to the House of Commons on 13 May 1940. For the text, see http://www.winstonchurchill.org/resources/speeches/1940-the-finest-hour/blood-toil-tears-and-sweat, accessed on 17 February 2015. Churchill served as Prime Minister from 1940 to 1945, then from 1951 to 1955.

4. BBC Forces Programme was broadcast between 7 January 1940 and 26 February 1944; it was later relaunched after Victory Europe Day (8 May) in 1945 as the BBC Light Entertainment Programme until 1967, when it was rebranded as BBC Radio 2.
5. For further discussion, see also Briggs (1995), Nicholas (1996), Scannell and Cardiff (1991).
6. See in particular the extensive commentary around the theme of the 'people's war' in Aldgate and Richards (1986), Burton et al. (2000), Eley (2001), Ellis (1981), Fox (2006), Hayes and Hill (1999), McKibbin (1998), Nicholas (1996), Richards (2010) and Short (1983).
7. Greene's credentials were enmeshed in the politics of the British Special Branch and the MI6 (predecessor to the MI5). His work in Malaya was closely coordinated with the newly established International Research Department run by Maurice Oldfield of the MI6 and based in Singapore (Deery 2003: 235). Greene was quickly becoming a trusted figure within the BBC establishment, especially by Ian Jacob, and was later appointed as Director General of the BBC from 1960 to 1969 (Tracey 1983: 73–9, 127–32).
8. The IRD predated by one year its American counterpart, the United States Information Agency (USIA), which funded the 'Voice of America'. At its peak in the early 1970s, the IRD was a massive operation, employing 400 staff based at Riverwalk House on the South Bank in London and with an annual budget in excess of £1 million. See Brian Crozier (1993: 104): Crozier worked for the IRD throughout the 1960s and early 1970s.
9. The equipment included a Mitchell camera, a number of Eyemos lenses and a Wall camera, an animation unit and a laboratory processing plant: Anon (June 1950), *Colonial Cinema*, 8: 2, 834–6.
10. 'Federation of Malaya Annual Report 1950: Film Unit', National Archive of Malaysia (ANM), Kuala Lumpur (Archive # 1957/575902, file # 12948/1950 XXVI). See also the Hawes Report: 'Malayan Film Unit: Proposed investigation and reorganisation (1949–50)', FO 537/657, National Archives (UK), accessed on 1 July 2015 at http://digital.lib.hkbu.edu.hk/documentary-film/index.php. See also Muthalib (2011). Stanley Hawes, producer-in-chief of the Australian National Film Board, was appointed by the British Secretary of State for the Colonies to lead the commission.
11. Resistance to the return of the British in the post-war era was organised through the Malayan National Liberation Army [aka the Malayan Races' Liberation Army], which was aligned with the Malayan Communist Party (MCP). However, the MCP was not initially considered to be a threat. Instead, the British post-war recognition of the MCP was to serve as a reward for their service during the war.
12. *Report of the Department of Broadcasting for the years 1946–52*, Singapore: Acting Government Printer, 1953: 1. Central Library, National University of Singapore Library.
13. *Report of the Department of Broadcasting, 1953*. Singapore: Government Printing Office, 1954: 20. Central Library, National University of Singapore Library.
14. Ibid., 8. The seven major Chinese dialects included Mandarin (for the younger generation), Cantonese, Amoy and Teochew (for commercial and industrial communities), Hakka (for mineworkers and farmers), as well as Foochow and Hylam (for clients in coffee houses and eating houses).

15. 'Letter to Tony Beamish of 13 March 1983', Senio Collection, Robertson_Senoi_Doc_30, University of Cambridge Depository, D Space. Accessed on 16 February 2015 at www.repository.cam.ac.uk/handle/1810/230148.
16. *Temiar Dream Music of Malaye* (1955), Ethnic Folkways Library Album no. P 460, Recorded under the direction of H. D. Noone by the Malaya Broadcasting System, New York: Folkways Records and Service Corp.
17. Tony Beamish and Stewart Wavell's radio programmes about the Malayan Emergency were a significant feature of broadcasting during the Emergency. Beamish was selected to serve the Malaya Command for intelligence duties from February to April 1941, and was then transferred on 10 April 1941 to the Malaya Broadcasting Corporation to serve as head of talks, planning and production (see 'Letter to Tony Beamish of 13 March 1983'). Wavell also started his own show called 'Comment is Free' in Malaya which he claims was the first call-in radio show (Wavell 1969: 61). Several programmes remain of great interest: see 'Ambush feature' (presented by Stewart Wavell, aired on 20 March 1953 , 'Ambush at Windy Corner' (presented by Stewart Wavell, aired on 2 April 1953) and Tony Beamish's thumbnail radio sketch of Gerald Templer (presented by Tony Beamish, aired on 16 January 1952). Research on these programmes was conducted in the P. Ramlee radio archive collection at Radio Television Malaysia (RTM), Angkasapuri, Kuala Lumpur, Malaysia, where Sheela Gangadharan assisted me with my research, and RTM Director General Dato' Norhyati Ismail approved my access to the research collection. It should also be noted that an important BBC radio feature included 'Fighting the bandits in Malaya' (presented by Edward Ward, 8 March 1952) and, more recently, the radio documentary from 1984, which is a compilation of a wide range of audio sources of the era. Please consult 'Last tales from the South China Seas: bandits: the anti-terrorist war in the Malaysian jungle, 1948–1956' (presented by Charles Allen, aired on 31 January 1984). These final items are available courtesy of the British Library Sound Archive Listening Room, London.
18. *Report of the Department of Broadcasting*, 1953, p. 28.
19. Eric D. Robertson, 'Foreword' (Programme notes), *Temiar Dream Music of Malaya*, Ethnic Folkways Library Album no. P460, 1955. It was thanks to permission granted by Eric Davis, then chairman of Radio Malaya, that Noone and Robertson made these early recordings of the Temiar.

REFERENCES

Aitken, Ian (2014), 'The Griersonian influence and its challenges: Malaya, Singapore, Hong Kong (1939–73)', in Zoë Druick and Deane Williams (eds), *The Grierson Effect: Tracing Documentary's International Movement*, London/New York: BFI/Palgrave Macmillan, pp. 93–104.

Aldgate, Anthony, and Jeffrey Richards (1986), *Britain Can Take It: The British Cinema in the Second World War*, Oxford: Oxford University Press.

Briggs, Asa (1995), *The History of Broadcasting in the United Kingdom*. vol. III: 'The war of words', Oxford: Oxford University Press.

Burton, Alan, O'Sullivan, Tim and Wells, Paul (eds) (2000), *The Family Way: The Boulting Brothers and Postwar British Film Culture*, London: Trowbridge.

Chan, Nadine (2016, forthcoming), 'Making Ahmad "problem conscious": educational cinema and the rural lecture caravan in 1930s British Malaya', *Cinema Journal*, 56: 4.

Chapman, James (1999), 'British cinema and the people's war', in N. Hayes and J. Hill (eds), *'Millions Like Us'? British Culture in the Second World War*, Liverpool: Liverpool University Press, pp. 33–61.
Clifford, James and Marcus, George (1986), *Writing Culture: The Poetics and Politics of Ethnography*, Berkeley: University of California Press.
Crossman, Richard H. S. (1952), 'Psychological warfare', *Journal of the Royal United Service Institution*, 97: 587, 319–32.
Crozier, Brian (1993), *Free Hand: The Unseen War 1941–1991*, New York: Harper Collins.
Deery, John (2003), 'The terminology of terrorism: Malaya, 1948–52', *Journal of Southeast Asian Studies*, 34: 2, 231–47.
Eley, Geoff (2001), 'Finding the People's War: film, British collective memory, and World War II', *American Historical Review*, 106: 3, 818–38.
Ellis, John (1981), 'Victory of the voice?' *Screen*, 22: 2, 69–72.
Fox, Jo (2006), 'Millions like us? Accented language and the "ordinary" in British films of the Second World War', *Journal of British Studies*, 45: 4, 819–45.
Hack, Karl (2001), *Defence and Decolonisation in Southeast Asia: Britain, Malaya and Singapore, 1941–1968*, Richmond: Curzon Routledge.
Hack, Karl (2009), 'The Malayan Emergency as counter-insurgency paradigm', *Journal of Strategic Studies*, 32: 3, 383–414.
Harper, T. N. (1999), *The End of Empire and the Making of Malaya*, Cambridge: Cambridge University Press.
Hayes, Nick, and Hill, Jeff (eds) (1999), *'Millions Like Us'? British Culture in the Second World War*, Liverpool: Liverpool University Press.
Higson, Andrew (1995), *Waving the Flag: Constructing National Cinema in Britain*, Oxford: Oxford University Press.
Hullot-Kenter, Robert (ed.) (2009), *Current of Music: Elements of a Radio Theory*, Malden, MA/Cambridge: Polity Press.
Jakobson, Roman (1996), 'Shifters and verbal categories', in P. Cobley (ed.), *The Communication Theory Reader*, London: Routledge, pp. 292–8.
Jumper, Roy Davis Linville (2001), *Death Waits in the 'Dark': The Senoi Praaq, Malaysia's Killer Elite*, Westport, CT: Greenwood Press.
McKibbin, Ross (1998) *Classes and Cultures: England 1918–1951*, Oxford: Oxford University Press.
Milner, Anthony (1995), *The Invention of Politics in Colonial Malaya*, Cambridge: Cambridge University Press.
Muthalib, Hassan Abdul (2011), 'The end of empire: the films of the Malayan Film Unit in 1950s British Malaya', in L. Grieveson and C. MacCabe (eds), *Film and the End of Empire*, London/New York: BFI Palgrave Macmillian, pp. 177–98.
Nicholas, Sîan (1996), *The Echo of War: Home Front Propaganda and the Wartime BBC, 1939–45*, Manchester: Manchester University Press.
Nicholas, Sîan (1999), 'The people's radio: The BBC and its audience, 1939–1945', in N. Hayes and J. Hill (eds), *'Millions Like Us'? British Culture in the Second World War*, Liverpool: Liverpool University Press, pp. 62–92.
Noone, H. D. (1936), 'Report on the settlements and welfare of the Ple-Temiar Senoi of the Perak–Kelatan Watershed', *Journal of the Federated Malay States Museums*, 19, part 1, December, 1–85.
Pronay, Nicholas (1983), 'The land of promise: the projection of peace aims in Britain', in K. R. M. Short (ed.), *Film and Radio Propaganda in World War II*, London/Canberra: Croom Helm, pp. 51–77.

Ramakrishna, Kumar (2002), '"Telling the simple people the truth": the role of strategic propaganda in the Malayan Emergency', *Journal of the Malaysian Branch of the Royal Asiatic Society*, 75: 1, 49–68.
Rice, Tom (2013), 'Distant voices of Malaya, still colonial lives', *Journal of British Cinema and Television*, 10: 3, 430–51.
Richards, Jeffrey (2010), *Cinema and Radio in Britain and America, 1920–60*, Manchester: Manchester University Press.
Roseman, Marina (1998), 'Singers of the landscape: song, history, and property rights in the Malaysian rain forest', *American Anthropologist*, New Series, 100:1 (March), 106–21.
Russell, Patrick and Taylor, James Piers (eds) (2010), *Shadows of Progress: Documentary Film in Post-War Britain*, London/New York: BFI Palgrave Macmillan.
Scannell, Paddy and Cardiff, David (1991), *A Social History of British Broadcasting: 1922–1939, Serving the Nation*, vol. 1, Cambridge, MA: Wiley-Blackwell.
Sheppard, Mervyn C. F. (1956), 'The birth of the Malayan Film Unit', *Tenth Anniversary Malayan Film Unit 1956* (programme guide), National Archive of Malaysia (ANM), Kuala Lumpur (Archive #2007/0023079).
Short, K. R. M. (ed.) (1983), *Film and Radio Propaganda in World War II*, London: Croom Helm.
Singapore Free Press and Mercantile Advertiser (1937), 'Temiar Sakais come to Singapore: bewildered by their first contact with the big city', *Singapore Free Press and Mercantile Advertiser*, 13 January, p. 3. Accessed on 9 March 2015 at http://newspapers.nl.sg/Digitised/Article/singfreepressb19370113-1.2.30.aspx.
Sioh, Maureen (1998), 'Authorizing the Malaysian Rainforest: configuring space, contesting claims and conquering imaginaries', *Ecumene*, 5: 2, 144–66.
Stockwell, A. J. (1999), 'Imperialism and nationalism in South-East Asia', in J. Brown and W. R. Louis (eds), *The Twentieth Century*, vol. 4, Oxford: Oxford University Press, pp. 465–89.
Taylor, Philip M. (1981), 'Documents: techniques of persuasion: basic ground rules of British propaganda during the Second World War', *Historical Journal of Film, Radio and Television*, 1: 1, 57–66. [Reprint of National Archives (Kew) Document: INF 1/724: Memorandum by the International Broadcasting and Propaganda Inquiry, 21 June 1939.]
Tracey, Michael (1983), *A Variety of Lives: A Biography of Sir Hugh Greene*, London: Bodley Head.
Wavell, Stewart (1969) *The Art of Radio: A Ceylon Broadcasting Corporation Training Manual*, Colombo, Ceylon: Ceylon Broadcasting Corporation.
White, Nicholas J. (1998), 'Capitalism and Counter-insurgency? Business and Government in the Malayan Emergency, 1948–57', *Modern Asian Studies*, 32: 1, 149–77.

CHAPTER 4

Figures of Empire: American Documentaries in the Philippines

José B. Capino

In *Barbarian Virtues*, historian Matthew Frye Jacobson writes of a modern American nationalism that, strange as it may sound, had its 'coming of age in the Philippines' (Jacobson 2001: 261). Then as now, 'dominant notions of national destiny and of proper Americanism draw upon charged encounters with disparaged peoples whose presence is as reviled in the political sphere as it is inevitable in the economic' (Jacobson 2001: 9). Americanness, as we know it, 'took shape within an international crucible of immigration and empire-building' (Jacobson 2001: 4). That process of overseas empire building began and was then developed in the Philippines, the US's first colony, from 1899 to 1946 and, since then, an important site of the US informal empire. The maturation of the US Empire in the Philippines also coincided with signal moments in the development of documentary cinema. Throughout America's colonial occupation of the Philippines, numerous types of non-fiction films were utilised in programmes of screenings established by the colonial state to serve various ends. Private individuals and organisations also made documentaries to educate, entertain and promote their concerns. While very diverse in their forms and aims, these films collectively established a transnational imaginary of American presence overseas and chronicled the Filipino experience of living under empire.

This chapter explores the parallel development of documentary cinema and US imperialism in the Philippines during and shortly after colonial occupation. The chapter aims to show how non-fiction cinema shaped the ways in which American imperialism was realised in the archipelago. At the same time, the chapter will sketch out an account of how American imperialism utilised and reconfigured the form and style of documentary cinema. The chapter will also argue that, more often than not, the documentary's affordances functioned to reconcile the contradictory goals of empire, namely, to assert American influence while hiding its imperial face; to invoke history while actually trafficking in myth; and to aggrandise empire's benevolence while promoting conditions of inequality for the native population. These sharp contradictions were mitigated by recourse to the representational mode of realism, the rhetoric of facticity, the prestige of scientific discourse and the power of sentiment – elements that developed variably as the documentary became more deeply implicated in the project of imperialism. While this argument is based on an examination of America's Philippine documentaries, this chapter also recognises its broader significance for an understanding of the colonial documentary film. The films to be discussed here represent a small fraction of extant films at the National Archives and Records Administration (NARA), the Library of Congress, the Smithsonian Institution and the Philippine Information Agency. At the risk of imposing a false coherence on a disparate archive, films have been selected that span the relevant historical period and will allow an illustration of the dynamic relation between the form of documentary film and the rhetoric of the US Empire to emerge. The familiar term 'documentary' will also be used here instead of the more precise 'non-fiction cinema', though reservedly. The latter more accurately represents this essay's main objects of study, namely a diverse array of films at or outside the margins of what we call documentary. Such films include movies shown in vaudeville presentations, narrative films and newsreels. That said, the prefix 'non-fiction' tends to obscure the fact that colonial films and cultural productions are as much works of social and geopolitical fantasies as they are representations of fact. Moreover, the term 'documentary' is more versatile than non-fiction. Although often equated with films, 'documentary' also refers to other cultural forms (such as photographs, picture books, writing, video and audio recordings, performance) that represent actuality, often through a combination of words and images. Many of the films described here were not seen in isolation but rather experienced in combination with those other types of documentary.

THE COLONIAL ENCOUNTER

In 1898, in the middle of the Spanish–American War, the United States ventured to the Philippines to battle the Spanish colonists who had occupied the archipelago since 1521. While waiting for reinforcements and supplies, the Americans invited the Filipinos to resume their failed bid to expel the Spanish just two years earlier. Running separate campaigns, the Filipinos and the Americans built an effective de facto alliance. But the relationship failed when the US secretly negotiated with the Spanish for the latter's surrender and for the sale of their interests in the Philippines for twenty million dollars. The Philippine–American War began on February 1899 when a handful of Filipino soldiers entered the contested limits of an American-occupied suburb outside Manila. The bloody campaign of 'pacification' was represented in contemporaneous forms of early cinema to exploit the American public's patriotic sentiment and their curiosity about the war. Film companies such as the Edison Manufacturing Company hastily staged re-enactments of American battles against the 'dusky' natives (Kramer 2006: 190). The films were shot in New Jersey with African-Americans playing Filipinos. In *Advance of Kansas Volunteers at Caloocan* (Edison, 1899), the native soldiers charge and fire directly at the camera, engaging viewers in playhouses and salons across the US. The dark enemy advances, hindered only by the cloud of smoke from their weapons. Suddenly, the frightful attack is countered by a band of American soldiers. They jump out of the foreground, coming out as it were from the spectators' location. A big American flag is carried to the centre of the fight, clearing the smoke. More soldiers emerge from right and left, swiftly charging towards the enemy. A big hit at movie parlours, films such as *Advance* built popular support for the war. They also fanned the flames of jingoism and prettified the violence of hundreds of thousands of Filipino deaths (Kramer 2006: 170).

Other film producers, such as the American Mutoscope and Biograph Company, filmed short actualities – or 'foreign views' – that demonstrated the more banal processes of colonial occupation and pacification. One of these films, *Unloading Lighters, Manila* (C. Fred Ackerman?, 1903),[1] records the early years of colonialism and represents the incursion of colonial power upon the native landscape and bodies. It shows a parade of water buffalos (also known as *carabaos*) – the Filipino beast of burden – dragging cargo along a city street. Factory buildings with imposing chimneys loom in the background, functioning as emblems of colonial modernity. A portly Caucasian orders the natives around, pointing them forward. He even grabs a *carabao* by its horn to correct its path. In this early incarnation of the colonial travel film, the imbalanced relationship of power between natives (persons and beasts) and colonisers testifies to a strengthened assumption of the legitimacy of colonial rule. Historians of the American film have suggested that the success of these early 'colonial' films gave the movies a new lease on life, bringing in money just as they were losing their novelty and cultural relevance in the US (Musser 1994: 225, 261). They also furnished US cinema with the *mise-en-scène* of an imperialist nationalism, one defined by a naturalised and affectively charged image of American presence in foreign spaces and near racialised bodies.

ILLUSTRATED LECTURES AND COLONIAL POLITICS

During its colonial occupation of the Philippines, the United States variously portrayed itself as a reluctant imperialist, an entitled colonialist and a benevolent civilising force, and nowhere are contradictions within these portrayals more manifest than in the highly popular illustrated lectures – combinations of films, lantern slides and live talks – given by entertainers and political figures. The most famous of these lectures were given by Elias Burton Holmes. A leading figure in the history of travel literature, travel photography, and travel cinema, Holmes popularised the term 'travelogue' and ran various multimedia enterprises. From the late nineteenth century to the 1960s, he helped Americans learn 'about the world and their place in it in a pleasurable but also educational manner' (Roan 2010: 32). Holmes took his first trip to the Philippines in the summer of 1899, spending two months there as the 'war of conquest' raged on. He took numerous still photographs and also shot motion pictures, the latter becoming a novel addition to his illustrated lectures. The subjects of the films include street scenes, a cockfight, water buffalos, a firehouse, and the staged burning of a straw hut that ostensibly belonged to a Filipino insurgent (Holmes 1920: 319).[2] The movies, many of them hand-tinted, were shown 'at the end of Mr Holmes's lecture proper, as a fifteen-or-twenty-minute added attraction' (Depue 1983: 60). Images from the movies and anecdotes about the filming were included in book versions of Holmes's travelogues (Holmes 1920: 260, 268, 284, 287, 320). A few years before Holmes returned in 1913 the status of America's far eastern colony once again became the subject of public debate. In 1910, the Philippine Assembly – the native legislature in training – filed a resolution calling for independence. Nothing came of it. The situation began to change when Woodrow Wilson was elected in 1912, the first president from the Democratic Party to occupy the White House in the twentieth century (Golay 1998: 163). Wilson ran on an anti-imperialist platform, and so did other democrats who retained control of Congress in the same elections. In March 1912, the first version of the Jones Bill – the proposal to terminate American political rule – was filed in the US Congress. The so-called 'Philippine Question' was brought up by the press whenever Holmes lectured about the archipelago, but he refused to talk politics. Holmes's films studiously avoided denigrating the natives and overpraising the colonial regime. But many of his chosen topics – reformed headhunters, tropical landscapes, mixed-race women, colonials among natives – drew from Orientalist stereotypes and were implicated in the politics of empire.

Holmes's approach to colonial film-making is signalled by the title of his film *In Old and New Manila with Burton Holmes* (Elias Burton Holmes, 1916), one of several Paramount-Burton Holmes Travel Pictures based on his 1913–14 lectures. During his first visit, Holmes wrote that 'it was something to have been witness to the transformation of Manila, to have seen the sleepy haunt of Spanish inactivity suddenly become the busy centre of American enterprise in the Far East' (Holmes 1905: 336). This trope was his once and future strategy for representing the Philippines. Colonial modernity – especially its ability to engender fascinating transformations – is his central motif. The film begins with a trans-Pacific journey from San Francisco to Manila. In the capital city, the camera is mounted on a vehicle and tours structures erected during American times (a hotel, the unfinished monument to national hero José Rizal, the Army and Navy Club). Via trolley, the camera enters Intramuros, the walled city of Manila. From then on the film's main interest turns to showing the stark contrasts between, on the one hand, American colonial modernity and, on the other, the medieval-style structures and tropical lifestyle of the former Spanish colony. In one section, the camera moves past the luxe modern awning of Clark's soda fountain (emblazoned with the Coca-Cola logo) and, moments later, ends up near the old 'Binondo Café', housed in a run-down wooden structure (Figure 4.1).

Holmes and his film-making partner Oscar Depue use the specificities of film language to dramatise the idea of colonial transformation. A series of travelling shots, often joined seamlessly through the uniform direction and apparent continuity of their movement, eases the audience into the journey from old to new and back again. In one example, a series of pans shot from a moving vehicle takes the viewer from short ramshackle barges called *cascos* (a mode of transportation representing the native past) to the enormous American steamships berthed just on the opposite side of the canal. At times, the moving shots reveal contrasts by framing shots in a way that enhances the appearance of depth

Figure 4.1: In the travelogue *In Old and New Manila with Burton Holmes*, the contrast between the legacy of the Spanish Empire and the promise of American colonial modernity is dramatised through the juxtaposition of a horse carriage in the foreground and a soda fountain in the background. Courtesy of the Library of Congress, Ref: 46929.

and capturing the moment when a strikingly modern object emerges from the layers of medieval-looking space on-screen. In one instance, the camera (mounted on a trolley) frames a native carriage before encountering a zig-zagging automobile that seems to come out of nowhere. Similarly, the film's inter-titles mimic the schema of contrasts in the images. One title card reads: 'The busiest corner of the "Escolta" where the new traffic clashes with the old. Trolleys and motor trucks, calesas and carabao carts.' At times, Holmes and Depue practise restraint, adopting the stillness of older travel films or 'views'. In one section, the camera remains stationary or reframes just slightly as it beholds – in a series of brief shots – a hulking motorised grass mower spinning in the lawns outside the medieval ramparts (Figure 4.2).

The combination of stasis and motion in the filmed image reinforces the contrast between modern technology and centuries-old structures. In his reminiscences, Depue recalls jazzing up his films by taking 'single-frame exposures at intervals to speed up the action',

Figure 4.2: In the travelogue *In Old and New Manila with Burton Holmes*, the hoariness of Spain's 400-year-old empire in the Philippines and the youthfulness of American colonial modernity is dramatised through the juxtaposition of a motorised lawnmower in the foreground with the medieval-style ramparts in the background. Courtesy of the Library of Congress, Ref: 46929.

what he termed 'crazy pictures' (Depue 1983: 61–2). It appears that he used this technique – along with ramping up the speed of filming – at various times, as if to convey the frenzy of moving people and vehicles, and the pace of colonial modernity. In the penultimate shot, the Filipino soldiers and their American superior rush past the portal of the medieval city, charging towards the camera. The intertitle links the pattern of contrasts to the discourse of colonial justification: 'Out through the old gate of the crumbling Spanish city comes the new blood of a race that has found freedom under the Stars and Stripes.' The preceding title also betrays Holmes's attachment to colonial power: 'The Constabulary has done splendid work for Uncle Sam, putting down small revolts, rounding up "ladrones" [bandits], policing lawless districts.'

If Holmes was the most famous of the lecturers on the Philippines, then Dean Worcester was the most prolific at taking pictures of the colony. Originally a zoologist and botanist from the University of Michigan,

Worcester gathered specimens of Philippine flora and fauna and published a book on the archipelago before it became an American colony (Worcester 1899). He was Secretary of the Interior from 1901 to 1913, a tenure marked by draconian policies, including the burning of a district in Manila to rid it of cholera. He famously quarrelled with Filipino politicians (including Manuel L. Quezon), many of whom he would later characterise as belonging to a 'mestizo class' with a secret racist antipathy for 'the great dark mass of the [Filipino] people' (Worcester 1914: 939). Worcester used his official inspection trips throughout the archipelago to take thousands of still images and 12,000 feet (about two-and-a-half hours) in aggregate of edited motion pictures. He took the images with the help of a government photographer named Charles Martin. Rodney J. Sullivan notes that Worcester used 'his annual reports and articles published in the *National Geographic* to circulate photographs intended to manipulate public opinion in favour of the indefinite retention of the colony' (Sullivan 1992: 156). He escalated this campaign upon leaving public office, preparing a lecture series incorporating his slides and films, along with a two-volume book. He also took the position of Vice-President of the American–Philippine Company (APC), a '$5,000,000 corporation organised to develop the Philippines with American money'.[3] Since the company's mission to exploit the colony would directly benefit from Worcester's campaign against Philippine independence, the APC put Worcester and his films in wide circulation. The epitome of an unabashed imperialist, Worcester took pride in being called 'the great white father' or 'the White Father' to the 'non-Christian tribes' (Brooklyn Institute of Arts and Science 1914; Rice 2014: 143). He preferred the tribes over educated Filipinos because they did not argue with him and illustrated his position that the colonised were not ready for independence. Not surprisingly, therefore, much of Worcester's images featured tribal people. The two film programmes accompanying the lectures were called *The Headhunters* and *From Savages to Civilization*, and they were presented in an omnibus as *Native Life in the Philippines* (Dean C. Worcester, 1914).

Benefiting from his skill in popularising ethnological representation, Worcester's lectures and films blended actuality and fiction in a manner similar to *documentaires romancés*, the 'scripted fictionalised travelogues' (Rony 1996: 85) being developed elsewhere by colonial filmmakers in the 1910s. This novel type of documentary was characterised by an idealised, Western-influenced depiction of the life and rituals of the primitive man, typically representing tribal people as noble savages who live in an eternal past. Worcester's shooting plans illustrate this approach:

> Start with a young baby cared for by its mother. Get a youngster just able to walk, dressed in a Gee-string and decked with Ifugao [a northern Philippine tribe] ornaments. Show for his mother and father a typical Ifugao pair about their house. Show a small boy putting the chickens in baskets under the house toward dusk.[4]

By placing his subjects within a nuclear family and observing them in their daily routines, Worcester gives his exoticised subjects a measure of common humanity recognisable to the modern spectator. To enliven his programme and depict the Filipinos as primitives, Worcester staged an elaborate headhunting sequence using a papier-mâché head (Rice 2014: 132). Worcester introduces it thus: 'The headhunting scenes which follow were taken in connection with the last head hunt which ever occurred in Bontoc . . . By the rarest chance the government photographer of the Philippines was on the ground'.[5]

Worcester adds to the fakery by stating that the decapitation was prompted by a man's rejection 'by his sweetheart because he has never taken a head'.[6] More controversially, Worcester and Martin filmed an actual scene of animal sacrifice as part of a tribal ceremony. Due to horrified reactions from audiences, the distributors excised footage of animal killings while retaining the headhunting scenes.[7] Worcester and the APC's imperialistic designs did not go unnoticed by either Americans or Filipinos. A fiery editorial entitled 'A scandalous anomaly' appeared in the Spanish-language Filipino newspaper *La Democracia*.[8] The article bases its criticism upon a February 1914 advertisement in *The Moving Picture World*. The author protests the 'half-nude' photographs that were taken 'for the manifest purpose of ridiculing the non-Christian tribes'. The editorial criticises Worcester and Martin for imprudently using government resources in producing their films. US newspapers, however, ignored Filipino protest against misrepresentation and focused instead on the conflict of interest involved in Worcester's move to the private sector so soon after leaving his government job.

THE FUNCTIONS OF EMPIRE FROM THE 1920S TO THE 1940S

Public health was a significant arena of colonial relations, determining how the bodies of natives and colonials were to be nurtured and regulated. A film entitled *Leprosy* (Roger Hilsman, Sr, 1929) shows the peculiar mix of colonial humanitarianism and social control that characterised the American Empire's biopolitics, its management of human life. The film-maker was a retired US Army colonel and then commandant of cadets at the Ateneo de Manila University, the Jesuit university of Manila. The silent film depicts the residents of Culion, a leper colony founded by the American colonists in 1906 to isolate leprosy patients from the rest of the population, including family members. The images show the progression of leprosy in various patients, from the innocuous looking first lesions (just 'depigmented spots' and 'anesthetic patches of skin', say the inter-titles) to the 'burnt out stage' marked by the 'destruction of digits and ears, deformity of the nose, and paralysis of the muscles of the mouth'. Taking advantage of cinematic motion, an off-screen person apparently coaches one of the patients to shut his gaping mouth close with his 'burnt out' fingers, as if to prove that the muscles in his mouth were indeed paralysed. The film catalogues the varieties of leprosy by asking the patients to strike awkward poses and keep still – as in photographs – in order to showcase body parts ravaged by the disease. In many instances, the patients pose with upraised arms, like creatures in a photographic bestiary (see Figure 4.3).

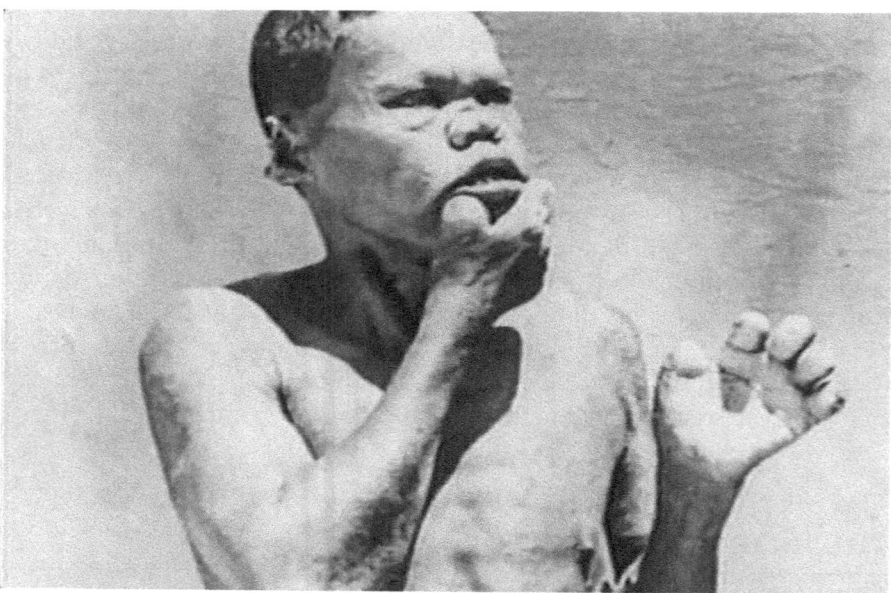

Figure 4.3: A leprosy patient uses his hand to close his mouth, apparently with instructions from someone off-screen, in *Leprosy*. Courtesy of the Human Studies Film Archive, Smithsonian Institution, Ref: HSFA 81.2:2.

While the native bodies are exposed in their most vulnerable and unflattering states, the figure of the coloniser appears only as hands and arms that gently reposition the patients or point sticks at their affected areas. In one instance, the colonial medic appears by proxy, as a native man in white uniform who vigorously and repeatedly injects a hypodermic needle into a native woman's cheek. The procedure demonstrates the use of chaulmoogra oil in the treatment of the disease. Playing to the camera and his foreign superiors, the man pounces on the patient's face with such frequency that one wonders if the woman's already swollen cheeks would burst before the needle bends in half. Meanwhile, the virtual absence of colonial figures only serves to exaggerate their power. That power is reinforced by the use of inter-titles touting the superior knowledge possessed by those colonial figures and their charge of the helpless natives. Archivists at the Smithsonian Institution believe that Hilsman's documentary was 'commissioned by the Philippine government' and toured 'around the islands in an effort to encourage victims of leprosy to seek treatment' (Wintle and Homiak 1995: 31). In his study of colonial health in the Philippines, Warwick Anderson recalls that 'doctors from the Bureau of Health gave lectures on leprosy and showed photographs and films of the colony' as part of its efforts to relocate lepers to Culion (Anderson 2006: 166). He goes on to say that the humanitarianism at Culion had a dark underside. While the patients received good medical care, their banishment from their families and society took its toll. As Anderson notes, 'Americans insisted on calling Culion the Island of Hope, Filipinos knew it as "la Isla del Dolor" [the island of sorrow]' (Anderson 2006: 173). To be sure, living the rest of one's life in isolation is a cruel requisite for obtaining medical care.

Empire's dubious benevolence is also glimpsed in a Depression-era newsreel segment identified as *Filipino Repatriation Act (free transportation home for Filipinos) Passed by Congress* (director unknown, 1936). The title refers to a 1935 law that sought to voluntarily deport Filipino residents in the US in exchange for one-way passage. According to Rick Baldoz, the law was prompted by such factors as stiff competition for agricultural jobs, fear of miscegenation and a desire to suppress the growing 'militancy of Filipino labour' (Baldoz 2011: 184). The newsreel segment opens with silent images of Filipinos toiling in lettuce fields. The scenes have a pastoral quality but the romance of the beautiful environs is tempered by the absence of lush vegetation (harvest is over), the appearance of the farmhands and their back-breaking work. The portrait of labourers is followed by a prepared statement given directly to the camera by California Congressman Richard Welch, the sponsor of the Repatriation Act and unsuccessful Filipino exclusion bills. He is surrounded by more than a dozen Filipino adults and children. Although the Repatriation Act was intended to help indigent Filipinos, Welch's dusky guests are all impeccably dressed in fine three-piece suits, tailored dresses and stylish trench coats. Not surprisingly, they assume a stiff posture, betraying the ventriloquist nature of their interactions with the Americans. Welch begins his statement with a lie, saying that the law is 'the result of an appeal of thousands of Filipinos to President Roosevelt to help them return to the homeland'. Welch is followed by Edward Cahill, San Francisco's Commissioner of Immigration and, according to Baldoz, one of the leads in the day-to-day logistics of repatriation in the West Coast. Cahill asks a man named Jack Santos why he 'desire[s] to return to the Philippine Islands?' Santos replies:

> I want to take advantage of the recent act of Congress . . . And I believe I've been away from home for too long. And whatever experience I have learned in this country might help make me a better citizen in the Philippine Islands when I get back there.

The interview with Santos is followed by two speeches, 'giving Filipino viewpoint[s]'. The first speaker portrays himself as tough on fellow Filipinos, saying he 'would rather see them go back with their own money', and that 'they [should] leave with a feeling of gratitude for the American people'. The next person calls Welch's bill 'the best economic legislation ever enacted by Congress for the benefit of the Filipino'. Because of their apparently sincere obsequiousness and self-abnegation the testimonies of these last two speakers are especially difficult to watch. The segment ends with an image of a door labelled 'US Department of Labor Immigration Service'. The silhouettes of what appear to be Filipino men are shown passing through the door before it closes. In another shot, one sees the figure of a man sporting an officer's visor hat walking behind the same door's mottled glass window. Both shots use dramatic staging conventions taken from fiction cinema, demonstrating the influence of narrative feature films that were shown together with newsreels in the cinemas.

The newsreel segment is dated 2 March 1936 and appears to have been part of a campaign to boost the dismally low rate of applications for repatriation. Baldoz notes that:

The Department of Labor chartered a special train that departed from New York City in April 1936 to pick up Filipinos at designated stops across the country and to transport them to San Francisco, where they would board the President Coolidge ocean liner bound for the Philippines. (Baldoz 2011: 211)

Records of the holding archive indicate that the film was never released (UCLA Film and Television Archive 1998: 25). The lack of musical scoring and the presence of alternate takes in the surviving film elements suggest that the film was not even completed. As for Welch's voluntary deportation programme, Filipinos recognised its opportunism. The law also failed because it barred deportees from re-entering the US in the future and did not provide transportation for their white spouses. In fact, the programme's success would have been inconsequential. A decolonisation law passed a year earlier than Welch's bill was already set to reduce the number of Filipino immigrants in a far more substantial and permanent fashion.

PROJECTING DECOLONISATION

In 1934, the US legislature voted to grant independence to the Philippines. The decision was ultimately determined neither by the natives' three-decade campaign for national selfhood nor by colonial altruism, but by American self-interest. During the Great Depression, American farmers put pressure on their government to end the colonial affair, citing the adverse effects of competition from Filipino immigrant labour and US trade preferences for Philippine agricultural exports. Congress provided for a twelve-year transition period, significantly culminating on American Independence Day (4 July) of 1946. With the independence law in place, the rhetoric of colonial justification drastically ebbed and, at least temporarily, so did much of the production of government-sponsored documentaries about the Philippines. When film-making efforts resumed with the outbreak of the Second World War, the hierarchies previously essential to colonial rule collapsed instantly, if not in real life then at least in films. One example is *This is the Philippines* (US Army Signal Corps, 1945), an orientation film from the War Department, assembled largely from extant footage (including captured newsreels from the Japanese). The film's unseen narrator, whose folksy tone is reminiscent of the narration in Frank Capra's *Why We Fight* documentaries, implores his GI viewers to 'Take a good look at this town. This is Manila before the Japs took it . . . This is the Philippines in 1940, a modern, civilised country. A piece of America.' The screen teems with images of buildings in the neo-classical style, American cars, soda fountains and English signage. Prior to the war, the Philippines had been characterised as a mere 'possession' and was not even accorded the recognition of being the colony that it was. The distinction was based on an early nineteenth-century US court opinion, which held that a 'colony' is 'settled by the citizens of the sovereign, or mother state', while a possession is not (Malcolm 1916: 380). In fact, the US did settle the Philippines and ran it as a colony but simply refused to apply the correct label. 'So, during its half century in the archipelago', Stanley Karnow writes, the United States refused to be labelled a colonial power and even expunged the word colonial from its official vocabulary' (Karnow 1990: 197). In *This is the Philippines*, the status of the islands is upgraded, catapulting the archipelago into a geographic and mental equivalent of America. Near the ending, a stirring segment of voice-over narration declares: 'Just one more word: it's a word that covers a lot of ground. It covers 48 states, it covers 7,000 islands. The word is America. The Filipinos are Americans; treat 'em like Americans.' While US imperialists had long used the term 'little brown brother' to describe Filipinos in a condescending manner, it is in wartime films such as this that we find – arguably for the first time – effusive representations of Filipinos. The rhetoric of equality serves a mercenary purpose but its significance should not be overlooked. Apart from upending colonial hierarchies with their message of equality, they render in audio-visual terms a regime of social control aimed not at the natives but squarely at the colonisers.

When the Second World War ended in the Philippines on 3 September 1945 the archipelago was left in ruins. Four-fifths of the capital was destroyed. As Nick Cullather notes, more than half of the Philippine livestock was lost and the necessities for planting staples were in great shortage (Cullather 1994: 34). Facing tremendous commitments to rebuild other allies and enemies, the US was relieved to forgo its colonial burden at the predetermined date. This did not mean, however, that it could afford to sever its military, political and economic ties with its only former colony. The Americans offered Filipinos preferential trade benefits and $620 million in rehabilitation funds. In exchange, they demanded parity rights (i.e. 'the same rights as to property, residence and occupation as the citizens of the Philippines') (Cullather 1994: 37). In 1947, the US and the Philippines also reached a new military bases agreement that allowed the former to retain control of twenty-three military installations in the Philippines for a period of ninety-nine years (Cullather 1994: 59). An accompanying military assistance agreement promised equipment and training. American efforts to shape the decolonisation process – and how it was to be projected to Filipinos and Americans – are captured in several newsreels and informational films from the late 1940s. While nostalgically announcing the end of formal colonialism, these movies engage in the still-imperialistic cultural work of rewriting the history of colonial intervention, consolidating the legacy of the colonial enterprise and projecting an American-inspired image of the liberated Filipino nation.

In the documentary film *The Philippine Republic* (Time, 1946), the beginning and end of empire are marked by dramatic images of the void. At one end, there is the inchoate vacuum of pre-colonial times: 'A land inhabited by 43 different racial groups with no common culture or tradition', says the narrator. At the other end is the apocalypse of the Second World War:

> Of all the countries invaded by the axis powers in WWII, few were more completely ravaged and devastated than the Philippines. As peace came to their ruined cities and farms, the Filipinos, with the independence the US had promised them only a year away, found they had little left with which to begin life as a nation.

The aporias at both ends of the American colonial project echo the rhetoric of sudden, impossibly drastic transformation, represented in this instance by the capacity to erase and alter the history of imperialism. At one point, the narrator conveniently discounts the impact of the previous coloniser: 'Entirely dominated by their Spanish rulers, the Filipino people, in three centuries, made little economic or political progress.' In a reversal of imperialist discourse, the narrator also recognises the validity of Filipino nationalism, saying that: 'The Filipinos had looked forward to their Independence Day – July 4, 1946 – as the achievement of a goal never lost sight of through more than three hundred years under American and Spanish rule.' The film enumerates the colonial regime's achievements, emphasising their relation to the natives' development into nationhood. The denouement of this narrative is the presentation of the 'finished product': the well-educated, freedom-loving citizen of a new nation, the image of the internally colonised but sovereign native. The story does not end there, however, and is linked into a narrative of post-coloniality. According to the film, the benefits granted by the colonial master – security, progress, democracy – are only as durable as the natives' resolve to preserve them. Consider, for instance, this foreboding piece of narration about the precariousness of the national defence situation after empire:

> Until Philippine independence would finally take effect, defence of the islands rested upon US fleet units based at Cavite and Manila Bay and upon the US air forces assembled and maintained in the Philippines. But Filipinos knew that from the day their freedom became an accomplished fact, the responsibility for national defence might well be theirs.

The seeds of these future problems (attributed to the natives' weaknesses) are then identified by the narrator, as in the following passages that intimate future economic troubles:

> The Philippines under US rule had achieved a degree of progress and prosperity unmatched among any of the dependent people of the Far East. But this prosperity was not widely distributed and the living standard of the masses of Filipinos was high only in comparison with the rest of the Orient . . . And the economy of the Islands, based almost entirely upon trade with the US, depended chiefly upon tariff concessions which gave Philippine products a favoured position in American markets.

The politically sensitive issues of rehabilitation and veterans' benefits are conveniently omitted in the discussion of the former colony's economic and security woes. The film culminates in a spectacular celebration of the coloniser and an anticipation of the new nation's birth. At a parade in what appears to be a provincial town or a Manila suburb, a sign reads: 'Welcome, Victory Festival'. Several floats slowly wend their way through jubilant natives. One of the floats includes a Filipino dressed as an American soldier, carrying an American flag and standing by a much shorter Filipino boy (Figure 4.4).

The infantilisation of the native – even the post-colonial one – is a throwback to colonial rhetoric, a condescending representation of his prolonged tutelage in Western civilisation. A Filipina woman, in native dress, stands beside them. The shot of the floats is succeeded by images of Filipinos hoisting placards that say: 'Thanks Uncle Sam', 'Long Live Philippines' and 'Mabuhay [long live], President Truman'. This vision of a post-colonial 4 July rehearses the tale of imperial benevolence

AMERICAN DOCUMENTARIES IN THE PHILIPPINES 95

Figure 4.4: The legacy of American rule is highlighted in this float for a parade celebrating the liberation of the Philippines in the Second World War. Courtesy of the National Archives and Records Administration, Ref: 111-EF-261.

once more as America bestows its cherished legacy – independence and democracy – upon the nation that it ostensibly fashioned out of the void. The cultural work of the film is not only to rehabilitate empire but to turn its history into myth.

DOCU-DRAMA AND THE RED SCARE

Beginning in the 1950s, US worries about the spread of communism drove the feverish production of films aimed at Asian nations and other countries that were thought to be vulnerable to the influence of the Soviet Union and Red China. The US government, mainly through the United States Information Agency (USIA) and its predecessors, developed multi-media campaigns aimed at projecting the American way of life as a model society, reporting on American charity and development projects abroad, touting the benefits of US-style democracy and helping the US in protecting the 'free world'. The English-speaking and American-friendly Philippines served as a central hub of content production and distribution in Asia, especially for print and motion picture materials. Some of these tools of Cold War propaganda – alternately referred to as public diplomacy – were designed for Philippine consumption. In the early 1950s, the Philippines was reeling from the Huk rebellion, a peasant-based armed resistance movement tenuously allied with the Philippine Communist Party but only shallowly penetrated by communist ideology (Kerkvliet 1979: 263–6). The rebellion was effectively quelled with the American-aided fortification of the Philippine Armed Forces, the capture of the entire communist politburo in Manila and the amnesty programme initiated by the charismatic, American-supported Filipino President Ramon Magsaysay (Shalom 1986: 111–23). The State Department put the county on the second tier ('the danger zone') of its list of countries deemed most vulnerable to communist influence.[9] For an agency flush with government funds (Cull 2008: 103), even this second-rank designation meant that plenty of films would be created for the Philippine audience and, when necessary, dubbed in other languages for use abroad.

Many of the films fit the mould of what the film scholar Bill Nichols has called docu-dramas, ostensibly based on factual content but almost wholly staged in dramatic form (Nichols 1991: 160). They were made in collaboration with the finest directors in the Philippine commercial film industry, directors such as Ramon Estella, Manuel Conde and Lamberto Avellana. In an attempt to remove the stigma of propaganda, the docu-dramas were packaged as Filipino creations, their sponsorship by the US government concealed through the use of Filipino talent and fictitious production companies such as Freedom Films. Government personnel referred to these works alternately as 'unattributed' materials[10] and 'grey propaganda' (Belmonte 2008: 38). A small number of these productions, such as *Huk sa Bagong Pamumuhay/The 'Huk' in a New Life* (Lamberto Avellana, 1952), were packaged by major film studios as big-budget narrative feature-length films with excellent production values, star actors and an accomplished director in Avellana. As with *The Huk*, some of these features were distributed abroad. The majority of the films, however, were shorter docu-dramas. One of the most representative of these is *This Is My Home* (director unknown, c. 1953). The twelve-minute film dramatises the effects of a communist takeover on the life of a Filipino farmer. The film uses a before-and-after scenario, in which an idyllic rural existence in the present gives way to a nightmarish future under communist rule. The film's Filipino narrator speaks in English and calls himself Mang Tasio (Mr Tasio). As he introduces other members of his family and describes their frugal but blissful life, the visuals depict a succession of picturesque scenes. There is no hint of agrarian unrest in his idyll of the countryside. As Tasio declares, he is satisfied with his 'own small cut of land' which 'under our democratic system, all are free to win more [of] by hard toil'. The menace of communism is introduced in the second half of the film. Instead of accurately depicting the insurgency problem that was still being felt in the Philippine countryside, the film offers a scenario inspired by Hollywood melodrama and even science fiction films about human-looking aliens taking over the earth. Although likely voiced by the same person, the narrator adopts a 'harsh tone . . . with foreign accent' to simulate the locution of a communist official.[11] The communist characters in the film alternately behave like robots (such as stiff posture, blank facial expression, mechanical speech) or Hollywood villains (including lots of sneering and broad gesticulations). Furthermore, the communist version of Tasio's life is rendered in histrionic fashion: in one scene after another, the simulated destruction of Tasio's life is staged with overblown rhetoric, spectacle and music.

In line with propaganda goals in the Far East, the film realises 'the exposition of the threat of communism to family and religion' (see Figure 4.5).[12] Tasio's son is 'taken to a communist centre', possibly for brainwashing. His teenage daughter is assigned to waitress at a soldiers' mess hall, where the diners (wearing Nazi-style armbands) freely harass her. Tasio himself is forced to labour in a 'faraway collective farm'. As with the majority of docu-dramas created for predominantly Catholic Filipinos, *This Is My Home* shows Tasio's family and community deprived of their religion. Tasio's wife is shown praying in front of an empty spot where a picture of the Holy Family of Jesus used to hang before it was confiscated by the authorities. The laughable gesture is repeated by the community when they pray at vespers while looking at a belfry that had lost its bell to the communist state. The bell had been melted down for its metal. Following the presentation of the communist scenario, the narrator poses a rhetorical question to Tasio and, by extension, to the film's viewers: 'All the communist regulations dictated by our Soviet leaders will improve the Filipino way of life. Don't you agree, Comrade Tasio?' Tasio's voice, suddenly recovering the role of narrator, emphatically objects: 'No, I,

98　JOSÉ B. CAPINO

Figure 4.5: A montage of shots depicts the perils of a communist takeover in the Philippines in *This Is My Home*. Courtesy of the National Archives and Records Administration, Ref: 306.3:805.

Mang Tasio, do not agree! There are still two ways of life open to us. It is for us Filipinos to choose.' The narration and the triumphant closing music affirm Tasio's commitment to the 'Filipino way':

> I chose the right to work under a free democracy for the great happiness of my wife and children. Whatever its faults, that is the better way, the Filipino way of life. For only under a democracy can this truly remain our home!

To avoid dealing with the real plight of sharecroppers in the 1950s, the film makes several convenient substitutions to reality. In the film, a small-land-owning farmer replaces his real-life equivalent: the desolate sharecropper. The film's foreign-sounding communist supplants the greedy landlord as the face of evil in rural society. Finally, a Hollywood version of communism replaces an anachronistic feudalism as the bane of the sharecroppers' existence. To sell this fabricated version of reality, the film commits itself to an aesthetic of melodrama bearing little resemblance to the dominant forms of non-fiction cinema. Here we see how the fantasies and half-truths of the Cold War substantially altered the practice of making documentaries. Films like *This Is My Home* significantly exceed the penchant for aesthetic expressiveness[13] seen in landmark British documentaries such as *Housing Problems* (Arthur Elton and E. H. Antsy, 1935) and the tendency to bend the truth in the American *March of Time* newsreels (1935–42). A continuity script for *This Is My Home* notes that the film was dubbed in multiple languages, including Spanish, Bengali and Malay. This suggests that the film was distributed well beyond the Philippines despite its marked cultural specificity. The film anticipates the famous non-fiction short *The Red Nightmare* (George Waggner, 1962). Featuring a small American town beset by robot-like communists, the film was produced by the government and Warner Bros' production head Jack Warner. It featured movie actors Jack Webb and Jeanne Cooper.

In view of anti-imperialist movements in many parts of the world, the government-sponsored films of the 1960s and 1970s mainly trafficked a dissimulated version of US interventionism and anti-communist propaganda through programmes of 'mutual understanding between the people of the United States and other countries' (Belmonte 2008: 27). *Skilled Tradesmen in Peace Corps* (Kennedy/Lee, 1970), a film aimed at recruiting American workers to provide technical training in rural places abroad, features a brief segment on a volunteer in the Philippines. The film depicts a white American named Steve Leahy teaching a class on elementary farm engineering at a dilapidated rural school ('hit by a typhoon and there's no money for repairs'). The documentary pegs the value of Peace Corps assistance in wholly altruistic terms, as 'helping others to help themselves', 'bringing about change for the better' or 'doing good things' in the world. The film leaves out the political implications of Peace Corps volunteerism, namely the use of its community development projects as a deterrent to communist insurgency movements, its surveillance of rural communities and its role in Cold War public diplomacy.

The drastic bracketing of politics can also be observed in the educational films disseminated abroad by the USIA through its film lending libraries. *From Mindanao to Milly Martin* (director and production company unknown, 1969) is framed by a narrative about a father who is refurbishing his daughter's room. The inquisitive child, who sees the lumber delivery truck pull away from the house, asks her father where the plywood came from. Her father, exceptionally well-informed about geography and the technology of lumber processing, gives her an almost five-minute lecture about plywood from the Philippines. Actuality footage shot in the Philippines and the US illustrate his lesson. The choice of Mindanao as the source of the wood and the inclusion of the southernmost Philippine island's name in the film's title is not insignificant. Mindanao is a place known for strife between the country's largest Muslim community and the predominantly Christian population. The late 1960s – when the film was made – saw the revival of Muslim civil rights and separatist movements in Mindanao, triggered by massive Christian migration to the island and anti-government sentiments (Wurfel 1988: 155–6). Not surprisingly, Milly's father makes no mention of Mindanao's political situation, its sociocultural background or the environmental impact of the trade in precious wood. After tracing the lumber's path to the American plywood store, he simply dismisses his child, telling her, 'Yes, honey, this is going to be your room if you ever let me finish!' At the end of the film, we see a montage of the fabrication and transportation of the plywood superimposed over Milly's face. The film depicts her thinking process but is silent on what she (and the film's viewers) is supposed to make of her father's lesson about the third world or the ex-colony and its relation to America. It appears that for the film's sponsors, merely conveying the idea of a connection between Mindanao and America was already a sufficient form of everyday Cold War politics. The documentary's superficial treatment of Filipino–American relations is typical of the films of the USIA and its predecessor institutions. Superficiality and vagueness are necessary to dissimulate the real nature and extent of American involvement in Philippine affairs, past and present.

To be sure, the US during this time made documentaries whose martial themes carried a greater risk than usual of exposing American neo-imperialist doings. The participation of Filipino troops in the wars in Korea and Vietnam were memorialised in films such as *Philippine Troops in Korea* (USIA, year of release unknown) and *The Battle for Peace* (USIA, 1967) The films' titles indicate the contrasting nature and representation of the Filipino role in these 'American' wars. Whereas the Filipino engagement in combat activities in Korea was something the US wanted to tout as exemplary free-world citizenship, the anti-imperialist protests against the Vietnam War necessitated the opposite approach. *The Battle for Peace* shows the community-oriented work of the Philippine Civic Action Group (aka PHILCAG), a force of 3,000 engineers. Marcos deployed PHILCAG at the insistence of American of officials but, in a concession to Philippine sovereignty and anti-imperialist protesters, made it an entirely non-combat force. These films contributed to America's Cold War effort to legitimise American intervention in Asian countries by deeply involving allies from the region in overseas wars against communism. The documentaries studiously omit the role of the US in brokering and funding the Philippine missions to these countries. The effacement within the documentaries of American involvement in the cooperative war efforts seems to be at odds with the USIA's advertised sponsorship of the films. As with other films discussed here, such contradictions are inherent in the American documentary's twin post-Second World War projects of projecting US global engagement after decolonisation and trafficking in dissimulated propaganda.

CONCLUSIONS: EMPIRE'S PERSISTENT VISIONS

The Philippines changed from a colonial state to a client state of the United States after independence, and the documentary films discussed here belie the claims of historians such as Lewis Gleeck, Jr and Nick Cullather who minimise America's post-colonial influence on the Philippines (Gleeck 1998: vii, Cullather 1994: 97). Since colonial times, the US has seen the need to engage with the Philippines as a place of strategic importance and as a close ally in the Pacific. Following decolonisation, America's role in Philippine affairs has fallen under the banner of what William Appleman Williams calls an 'informal empire' (Williams 1988: 47). Williams holds that:

> When an advanced industrial nation plays, or tries to play, a controlling and one-sided role in the development of a weaker economy, then the policy of the more powerful country can with accuracy and candour only be described as imperial. (Williams 1988: 55)

He uses the term 'informal' to convey 'the sense that the weaker country is not ruled on a day-to-day basis by resident administrators, or increasingly populated by emigrants from the advanced country, but it is nevertheless an empire' (Williams 1988: 55). While it is important to recognise the agency of the Filipinos in thwarting American designs, it would be inaccurate – as these documentaries suggest – to ignore three decades of efforts to represent the Philippines and influence its history since decolonisation. In the Philippines, US imperialism changed faces, at times with the aid of documentary cinema. By examining films closely as well as placing them within a broad historical context, this chapter has attempted to show how particular documentary forms have been shaped by the history of empire and how certain figures of imperialism were constituted through the technology of non-fiction film.

ACKNOWLEDGEMENTS

This research was funded by Conrad Humanities and Helen Corley Petit scholarships from the College of Liberal Arts and Sciences, University of Illinois. Thanks to the film division staff at NARA (Audrey Amidon, Steve Graybill, Dan Rooney, Nicholas Schwartz, Carol Swain, Rob Thompson), the Library of Congress (Mike Mashon, Madeline Matz, Rosemary Hanes, George Willeman), the Philippine Information Agency (Bel Caipul, May Padilla), and the Smithsonian Human Studies Film Archives (Pam Wintle, Daisy Njoku, Mark White). Much gratitude to Gerry Nepomuceno and Jim Erickson for hosting me in DC through the years.

NOTES

1. Nick Deocampa (Deocampa 2011: 104) has identified Ackerman as the cinematographer of the film but, as in most works of early cinema and institutional films, his name appears nowhere in the credits or publicity materials. Alternately, I use the phrase 'director unknown' numerous times in this chapter.
2. 'Lectures by two authors: William Dean Howells will speak on "Novels and Novel Writing" and Burton Holmes on "Manila"', *Chicago Daily Tribune*, 22 October 1899, p. 38.
3. 'Worcester replies to newspaper critic', [Philadelphia] *Public Ledger*, 23 January 1914, Dean C. Worcester Papers, Box 2: Newspaper Interviews, 1899–1915, Bentley Historical Library, University of Michigan.
4. D. C. Worcester, 'Scheme for moving picture film showing inspection trip of Secretary of the Interior through Nueva Vizcaya and the Mountain Province', undated, Worcester Papers, Box 1: Concerning the Production of a Film on the Philippines, 1911–13, p. 4.
5. D. C. Worcester, 'Lecture to accompany film and slides illustrating "Native life in the Philippines" Series I', undated, Worcester Papers, Box 2: Lectures and Speeches, 1908–13, p. 10.
6. Ibid., p. 7.
7. 'See Filipinos at best and worst', *Baltimore Star*, 17 April 1914, Worcester Papers, Box 3: Newspaper Clippings.
8. 'A Scandalous anomaly', *La Democracia*, 3 April 1914, as translated by the Philippine Constabulary, 'P' File for Dean C. Worcester, RG 350: Records of the Bureau of Insular Affairs, Box 21, National Archives and Records Administration II, College Park, MD.

9. T. L. Barnard, memorandum to media divisions about country priorities in 1952 (p. 26), September 1951, RG 306: Records of the USIA, Murray Lawson Card File, Box 49.
10. W. Schwinn, letter to Mr. Sargeant regarding distribution of anti-Soviet materials, 9 December 1949, Lawson Card File, Box 52.
11. Shooting script of *This is My Home* and foreign version script of *This is My Home*, undated, RG 306: Records of the USIA, Movie Scripts: 1942–65, Box 57.
12. W. B. Connors, Letter to John Hamilton regarding Berrigan letter, 27 April 1951, Lawson Card File, Box 51.
13. See the earlier paragraph on communist characterisation, staged rhetoric and spectacle.

REFERENCES

Anderson, W. (2006), *Colonial Pathologies: American Tropical Medicine, Race, and Hygiene in the Philippines*, Durham, NC: Duke University Press.

Baldoz, R. (2011), *The Third Asiatic Invasion: Migration and Empire in Filipino America, 1898–1946*, New York: New York University Press.

Belmonte, L. A. (2008), *Selling the American Way: U.S. Propaganda and the Cold War*, Philadelphia: University of Pennsylvania Press.

Brooklyn Institute of Arts and Science (1914), *Bulletin of the Brooklyn Institute of Arts and Sciences*, 10 January, 12: 1, 7.

Cull, N. J. (2008), *The Cold War and the United States Information Agency: American Propaganda and Public Diplomacy, 1945–1989*, New York: Cambridge University Press.

Cullather, N. (1994), *Illusions of Influence: The Political Economy of United States–Philippines Relations, 1942–1960*, Stanford: Stanford University Press.

Deocampo, N. (2011), *Film: American Influences on Philippine Cinema*, Mandaluyong City: Anvil.

Depue, O. (1983), 'My first fifty years in motion pictures', in R. Fielding (ed.), *A Technological History of Motion Pictures and Television*, Berkeley: University of California Press, pp. 60–4.

Gleeck, L. E. (1998), *The American Half-Century, 1898–1946*, Quezon City, Philippines: New Day Publishers.

Golay, F. H. (1998), *Face of Empire: United States–Philippine Relations, 1898–1946*, Madison, WI: University of Wisconsin-Madison, Center for Southeast Asian Studies.

Holmes, B. (1905), *The Burton Holmes Lectures*, vol. 5, 'Hawaiian Islands, Edge of China', Manila/New York: McClure, Phillips.

Holmes, B. (1920), *Burton Holmes Travelogues*, vol. 11, Chicago: Travelogue Bureau.

Jacobson, M. F. (2001), *Barbarian Virtues: The United States Encounters Foreign Peoples at Home and Abroad, 1876–1917*, New York: Hill and Wang.

Karnow, S. (1990), *In Our Image: America's Empire in the Philippines*, New York: Ballantine Books.

Kerkvliet, B. J. (1979), *The Huk Rebellion: A Study of Peasant Revolt in the Philippines*, Quezon City: New Day.

Kramer, P. A. (2006), *The Blood of Government: Race, Empire, the United States & the Philippines*, Chapel Hill: University of North Carolina Press.

Malcolm, G. A. (1916), *The Government of the Philippine Islands: Its Development and Fundamentals*, Rochester, NY: Lawyers Cooperative Publishing.
Musser, C. (1994), *The Emergence of Cinema: The American Screen to 1907*, Berkeley: University of California Press.
Nichols, B. (1991), *Representing Reality: Issues and Concepts in Documentary*, Bloomington: Indiana University Press.
Rice, M. (2014), *Dean Worcester's Fantasy Islands: Photography, Film, and the Colonial Philippines*, Ann Arbor: University of Michigan Press.
Roan, J. (2010), *Envisioning Asia: On Location, Travel, and the Cinematic Geography of U.S. Orientalism*, Ann Arbor: University of Michigan Press.
Rony, F. T. (1996), *The Third Eye: Race, Cinema, and Ethnographic Spectacle*, Durham, NC: Duke University Press.
Shalom, S. R. (1986), *The United States and the Philippines: A Study of Neocolonialism*, Quezon City: New Day Publishers.
Sullivan, R. J. (1992), *Exemplar of Americanism: The Philippine Career of Dean C. Worcester*, Quezon City: New Day Publishers.
UCLA Film and Television Archive (1998), *The 1930s: Prelude to War*, Los Angeles: UCLA Film and Television Archive.
Williams, W. A. (1988), *The Tragedy of American Diplomacy*, New York: W. W. Norton.
Wintle, P. and Homiak, J. P. (1995), *Guide to the Collections of the Human Studies Film Archives*, Washington, DC: National Museum of Natural History, Smithsonian Institution.
Worcester, D. C. (1899), *The Philippine Islands and Their People*, New York: Macmillan.
Worcester, D. C. (1914), *The Philippines Past and Present*, London: Mills & Boon.
Wurfel, D. (1988), *Filipino Politics: Development and Decay*, Ithaca: Cornell University Press.

PART II

Missionary Films and Christian Evangelism

CHAPTER 5

Two Films and a Coronation: The Containment of Islam in Flores in the 1920s

Sandeep Ray

In January 1931, the evening edition of *De Tijd*, a Dutch newspaper covering religious and political stories, carried a report about a coronation ceremony in Ruteng, Flores Island, Eastern Indonesia (*De Tijd* 1 May 1931). It was organised for the first Catholic king of Flores, the young Alexander Baroek. The article described the solemnity of the historic event and its accompanying pomp and rituals. Among these were the very unexpected projections of films by a Dutch pastor named Simon Buis. The reporter recorded the astonished reactions of the local population. In 1930, Flores was far from urban centres of the Netherlands East Indies and distanced from the many advancements of modernity and technology, including movie theatres. This essay explores the pioneering cinematic work of Simon Buis, a Dutch Catholic priest-turned-film-maker, and the political underpinnings of his innovative evangelical efforts. The films Buis produced are significant because they provide us with unique visual coverage of a greatly under-studied region of the former East Indies during an era of Dutch colonial re-expansion.

JOURNEY TO FLORES

The Societas Verbi Divini (SVD), the denomination that Simon Buis belonged to, was a Catholic group founded in 1875 in Steyl, in the south of the Netherlands, by Arnold Janssen during the Kulturkampf – a rising wave of secularism that greatly reduced the power of the Roman Catholic Church in Prussia. In exile but still influential, it comprised many German and Dutch priests and had a penchant for the close study of diverse cultures. During the early 1920s, Brother Berchmans, an SVD priest from the Netherlands, was impressed with the evangelical films his mission had commissioned in the Congo and in Uganda. Supported by his diocese, Berchmans approached German film-maker Willy Rach to create non-fictional works in China. When that enterprise proved to be politically risky, Rach lobbied instead for permission to film in the East Indies, and Arnold Verstraelen, the bishop in charge of the mission in Flores, gave his consent. In 1924, Rach went to Flores and filmed 15,000 feet covering his journey and encounters with native life on the island. Back at the seminary in Steyl, another SVD priest, Simon Buis, a former Superintendent of Schools in Flores, became fascinated with the material Rach had brought back and took on the responsibility to develop the project further. He envisioned a new strategy for promoting the evangelical cause in Flores.

Buis transformed what he considered slow visual ethnography, into a faster-paced film with clearer plotline (Willemsen 2012: 62–3). He organised the footage into a narrative about Catholic priests leaving the Netherlands on an epic, arduous journey through Flores while observing its 'primitive' culture. Though Buis himself would not return to Flores for another five years he edited this footage in the Netherlands to produce a two-hour long film. He also filmed several scenes on a ship docked in the port in Amsterdam to signal the long journey to the east. The creation of a narrative plot in an ethnographic film, with re-enacted scenes blended into non-fiction footage, was a new trend in international documentary cinema. His new collaborator, Father Piet Beltjens, admiringly observed that, 'His rich imagination flourished as he found new methods and his sentimental romanticism could express itself' (Appels 1997: 13–14: Beltjens 1992: 2). Buis was a consummate film promoter and evangelist; he made Flores a recognisable name in the Catholic churches of the Netherlands. But before describing the ethnography embedded in this footage and Buis's remarkable efforts at outreach, it is important to establish the power struggle that emerged in Flores during the early twentieth century, as this constitutes the geopolitical backdrop to these films.

THE WAR OF PACIFICATION

At the turn of the twentieth century, the Dutch colonial government scoured the outer islands of the East Indies for areas that could provide them with new tax bases. Although Flores had not been considered particularly lucrative in this respect, it now came under scrutiny. Central and western Flores remained predominantly Muslim along the coasts with many autochthonous groups residing in the highlands. The powerful Islamic Sultan of Bima, just across the waters to the west, controlled the western region of Manggarai (Steenbrink 2007: 89). But there was a Catholic presence in the east of the island, a remnant of the long Portuguese rule from 1613 to approximately the mid-1800s. In 1907, emboldened by the mandate of expansion given by the new Dutch Controleur A. Couvreur, Captain Hans Christoffel carried out what noted historian Karel Steenbrink describes as a 'blitzkrieg' in the central and western parts of Flores. The mass murder, characteristically dubbed as *Perang Pasifikasi*/War of Pacification, was notably barbaric. In one incident, fifty-two men, women and children who had sought refuge in a cave were killed as Christoffel had evidently promised his soldiers the equivalent of 2.5 guilders for each head. Couvreur began writing letters in secrecy to the Catholic mission in Larantuka. He beseeched them to populate the area with their missions as a matter of urgency:

> If we do not act fast, Islam will occupy the interior and we will have lost this cause forever . . . If we act fast, Flores, with the exception of a few coastal places, can be secured for the Catholic Church . . . If we succeed in inducing them to say *saya orang serani* (I am a Christian), we still have thousands of years to make them true *serani*.[1]

While there was a clear tussle for political influence over the native non-Islamic community, the colonial administration, in principle, was not permitted to favour faith. The extent to which Jesuits could be involved locally was by bringing in teachers. As they were not allowed any direct form of evangelism, a gradual indoctrination through the education system was attempted. The island soon began to fill with young native recruits hired to start schools and spread Catholicism. In addition, European priests, leaving colonies in Africa after the conclusion of the First World War began arriving in the 1920s. It was around this time that Simon Buis came to Flores and became Superintendent of Schools. The dynamic Buis bore the dual evangelical and colonial cudgel quite fervently. His writings in *De Katholieke Missien*, a religious magazine in the Netherlands, reveal a priest dedicated to denouncing Islam and championing a greater influence for Catholicism. In a section titled 'Pas Op Voor De Schloen/Beware of the Schools', he writes that one must be very suspicious of Islamic 'fanatical opposition to Christianity' (Buis 1925: 21). He bemoans that because schooling was not compulsory in Flores, the Muslim opposition could not be countered properly. In a subsequent section called 'Beleedigende Taal/Insulting Language', he states dramatically that 'one of the heaviest crosses' that a missionary has to bear are the daily insults from Muslims who typically saw Catholics as intruders and referred to them as 'dogs and boars' and 'enemies of Muhammad' (Buis 1925–6: 35).

Urgently wanting schools and missionaries to encourage conversions across Flores, Buis was eager to engage in alternative forms of propaganda in addition to his writing. Making films, he imagined, could serve this purpose of depicting unenlightened or uncivilised behaviour and help his proselytising cause. The attempt produced the very records that provide us with a unique ethnographic history of the region today. Missionaries like Buis and his colleagues were thoroughly trained in ethnology and linguistics in their home countries. In their foreign missions, their spiritual philosophy compelled them to 'discover evidence of the supposedly primordial and monotheism among those to be proselytized' (Schroeter 2010 145). The belief was that the primitive, animist systems of the local autochthonous were essentially not in contradiction with Christianity, the natives were just not aware of the similarities. But while the SVD took a paternal approach to highlanders in Flores, they demonstrated intolerance towards the coastal Muslims. The vitriol that Buis demonstrated towards Islam is not surprising. In the years to come the SVD would join with the colonial government to foist a stratagem of ridding Flores as much as possible from the religious and political influences of Islam.

FILM AS EVANGELICAL PUBLICITY

In 1926, after working with the material for almost a year, Buis released *Flores Film* (Simon Buis, 1926) in the Netherlands. It was lauded for its ethnographic and evangelistic content. *De Tijd* gave it a glowing review:

> The simple viewer admires the *Flores Film* for its beautiful pictures and the pleasant variety of performances. The scholar, the connoisseur of the Indies, sees even more: he sees the beautiful presentation of tropical opulence ... the grace of our Indian brothers and sisters. This the botanist, ethnologist, the geologist, psychologist and especially the sociologist, enjoys. It is a singular fact that the film captivates everyone, but each according to his own knowledge of the East. This is the greatest merit of the *Flores Film*. (*De Tijd* 15 December 1926)

Buis would capitalise tremendously on the popularity of the ensuing screenings, beseeching audiences to support the religious cause:

> All together there are nearly twenty thousand children who have been to see the film been in Utrecht, Amsterdam, Den Hague and

> Tilburg . . . What fun we had . . . Do you think that the Mission no longer needs your help? Well, as long as a thousand million pagans are not converted (and that will take a while), we have hard work to continue for the Mission. And so we must keep the fire in it. (Willemsen 2012: 62–3)

The SVD's aim was to show people in the Netherlands that Flores needed priests, mass conversions and induction into the church. And to that end they displayed natives, mostly from the remote highlands, emphasising their primitiveness and their othering heathenness. In the process, however, they captured that very important moment of the colonial contact and established a visual essay of how exactly evangelism, buttressed with colonial military and administrative apparatus, entered a remote, non-Christian area and took over the local faith. Considering that there were very few early visual records of life in Flores, this aspect of Buis's (and Rach's) propagandistic work, makes the footage both rich and unique.

Buis, as mentioned, neither filmed *Flores Film* nor was present during filming. It was Rach who travelled extensively to capture the footage. While we do not have a clear record of how Rach's footage was initially assembled, it is evident that the SVD credits Buis as the creative force behind the project. Perhaps defensive, Buis was vocal about his perseverance in regard to editing Rach's footage to perfection. For example, in *De Tijd* in 1926:

> Interviewer: To get the movie to flow so well, do you need to cut a lot?
> Buis: Of course! I spent seven months to perfect its observations. There circulates at the moment 13 copies. They run in Austria, Poland, Germany, North and South America. In Rotterdam I had to stop, unfortunately. I would happily have stayed another 14 days. The hall was packed to the last evening.

Surprisingly, after many screenings and the critical discussion of the film in the newspapers, the idea of its potential as a historical document did not surface much. Simon Buis was not identified academically as a pioneering ethnographer until 1997 when Eddy Appels, a Dutch visual anthropologist, resurrected his role as ethnographic film-maker in a graduate dissertation at the University of Amsterdam (Appels 1996). To contribute to the record, this chapter will elaborate on this initial effort by Appels and identify key points that establish *Flores Film* among the first ethnographic documentaries in the East Indies.

EARLY ETHNOGRAPHY: *FLORES FILM*

In his 1997 essay 'Mission to Flores', Appels attested that the genre of the mission film, after some initial opposition on account of its low 'entertainment' content, had found a niche in the world of evangelical fund raising and advertising in 1920s Netherlands:

> In 1925 Father Simon Buis of the SVD assembled film material shot in 1923 by the German film-maker Willy Rach on Flores in the Dutch East Indies. *Flores Film* was thus the pioneer of the Dutch mission movie. The Dutch mission films focused on the ordinary church people, especially the farmers in the Catholic Brabant and Limburg. From those circles finally emerged the missionaries, and to a lesser extent the money for the missions. For many people found the screening an excellent opportunity to know about foreign nations and see exotic regions (it was also the only option for boys to see half-naked women). For the generally poor peasantry, the screenings in the parish house were often the only contact with the medium of film. (Appels 1997: 11)

Flores Film had done very well. In 1928, the Limburger Koerier, a daily serving the province of Limburg in the south of Holland, ran an advertisement for the movie *Ben-Hur* (Fred Niblo, 1925).[2] The most expensive film of the silent era, *Ben-Hur* was an international hit. Just above the advertisement for the blockbuster was the announcement for *Flores Film*. 'Where is Flores Film?' the advertisement asked readers, listing as many as eight screenings for the week of 16–23 November (Appels 2004) (Figure 5.1).

Marketed as 'The *Ben-Hur* of reality', it sold 2,000 tickets a week in Utrecht, with three screenings per day. The reason for this may have been the exciting narrative that Buis had crafted; the film created a vicarious sense of adventure for those imagining themselves as missionaries going to an uncharted, faraway land. The first twenty minutes of the *Flores Film* show various scenes of student life at a seminary in Steyl. The mission cross is then handed to a group who board a ship stopping at several destinations on its way to the East Indies. We fleetingly visit Italy, Gibraltar, Cairo and Colombo before the missionaries arrive in Batavia. As we now know, some of this footage was filmed long after Rach had handed over the material to the SVD. Buis appears a couple of times, inserting himself into the reconstructed narrative (Figure 5.2).

After arriving in the colony, there are cursory halts at the large Roman Catholic Cathedral in Batavia and the Buddhist temple of

Waar is de FLORES-FILM?

Na haar tocht door Zeeuwsch-Vlaanderen (September) en Westelijk Noord-Brabant (October) kwam de Flores-film in November naar de dorpen van noordelijk Limburg en zal in December vertoond worden, volgens haar

PROGRAMMA:

16 Zondag Houthem-St. Gerlach, „Witte Paard"
17 Maandag Beek, Zaal Patronaat.
18 Dinsdag Beek, Zaal Patronaat.
19 Woensdag Elsloo, Zaal Patronaat.
20 Donderdag Elsloo, Zaal Patronaat.
21 Vrijdag Roermond (Vertooningen van
22 Zaterdag Roermond de Flores- en de
23 Zondag Roermond Bali- Floti- film.)

Astoria Theaters

BRUNSSUM EN RUMPEN—

Zaterdag 15, Zondag 16 en Maandag 17 Dec
Vanaf 5 uur. Vanaf 3 uur. Vanaf 5 uur

De geweldigste film der wereld

BEN-HUR

12 Acten.　　　　ENORM.　　　　12 Acten.
ENZ.　　　　　　　　　　　　　　ENZ.
Aanvang Zondag te BRUNSSUM 4 UUR.
7620

Figure 5.1: Advertisements for *Flores Film* and *Ben-Hur*, *Limburger Koerier*, 1928.

Figure 5.2: Father Simon Buis in staged contemplation in *Flores Film*, 1926.

Borobodur. A celebratory reception in Flores occurs only fifty minutes into the film, when the local parish in Ndona receives the travellers with a brass band. The missionaries continue on their long, arduous journey on horseback, travelling along the river valley to the north of Ende. They are seen drinking from streams (Figure 5.3), asking for directions and, on one occasion, falling clumsily into the water (Figure 5.4). The scenes appear staged but are effective.

The first long significant sequence in the film is the tracking and killing of a Komodo dragon (see Figure 5.5). This appears to be the first time the large, prehistoric creature is captured on film, even before the well-known footage shot by Douglas Burden in 1926 as described by Timothy Barnard in his chapter in this collection. The footage of several dozen men chasing the enormous reptile indirectly references a complex political situation. In an attempt to restrict the hunting of the exotic lizard, that had become a zoological fascination in several countries in the early twentieth century, the Dutch colonial government issued a series of bureaucratic measures in the 1910s requiring permits to be procured for hunting. The Sultan of Bima, however, was in a position to control much of the hunting activity from adjacent

CONTAINMENT OF ISLAM IN FLORES IN THE 1920S 115

Figures 5.3 and 5.4: Missionaries braving the mountainous and riverine terrain of Flores in *Flores Film*, 1926.

Figure 5.5: Killing a Komodo dragon in *Flores Film*, 1926.

Sumba as many groups stopped there to gather coolies. In response, the Dutch authorities strategically placed the island of Komodo under the jurisdiction of Mangarrai in western Flores, effectively wresting authority away from the Sultan. The stubborn Sultan, however, continued to act autonomously, creating consternation within the colonial authority. Flores thereafter became a political battleground with both SVD and the local Muslims straining to win influence over the native, autochthonous dwellers.[3]

The next scenes are replete with close-ups of native inhabitants, flora and fauna, and several short sequences of dance and fairground-type festivities including gambling. Notably, a large local place of prayer is shown being built, preceded by an inter-title that reads 'Dieper in't heidendom/Deeper into paganism'. There does not however seem to be much judgement or comment on the activity depicted in these scenes. Historian Karel Steenbrink is of the opinion that there would have been professional explicateurs (lecturers) accompanying the screenings of *Flores Film* who may not have been guarded about their opinions on non-native 'heathens' in Flores.[~] Based on the inter-titles and the visuals, however, it cannot be said that the film either embellishes conditions in Flores or expresses anti-autochthonous sentiment.

The last section of *Flores Film* is dedicated to showing the efforts of the mission workers in more detail. Karel Steenbrink makes the observation that it depicts Catholic missions as a modernising movement rather than as a new and powerful religion. Indeed, the effort of the mission workers, despite their evangelical base, seems akin to the Dutch Ethical Policy, which operated sporadically in other parts of the archipelago and focused on infrastructure, education and agriculture rather than overhauling sociocultural systems.[5] The inter-title at the start of this end section reads, 'De Missionaries Brenger der beschaving' ('The Missionary: Bringer of Civilisation'). It covers events where the native population is trained or assisted: furniture making, livestock and poultry farming, planting seeds in large gardens. A section of tree planting that is supervised by a missionary is preceded by the title 'Om meer gebedel te voorkomen Plant de Broeder kokosboomen/To do away with begging, the Brother plants coconut trees.' A mission nurse is shown at an outdoor blackboard teaching what appears to be fairly complex algebra to a large class of teenaged girls. In other classrooms the language of instruction is Jawi (an Arabic script form) as Malay was still being taught in the Arabic script in the early 1920s. This conforms with Steenbrink's observation on the containment of Islam – that it was in the classrooms where the Dutch evangelists tried their best to secure and convert native non-Muslims to Christianity.[6]

Direct examples of proselytising are also shown in this film. A robed priest gives an elderly native man a photograph of himself, which is viewed with much conviviality. The inter-title then says 'Van vriend tot leeraar/From friend to teacher'. The ensuing scene resembles a large congregation of people at a Sunday outdoor church session. A priest narrates to them what appears to be a sermon from the Bible and then demonstrates how to make the sign of the cross (see Figure 5.6). We finally arrive at a very instrumental instance in this epic sojourn from the Netherlands, when non-Muslim natives are converted (see Figure 5.7). Right after this there is a title stating, 'Offervaardige en ijverige christenen/Sacrificial and zealous Christians', and we are shown hordes of locals; boys, men and even women carrying infants, bringing in rocks and beginning the construction of a church. In the penultimate sequence, a large congregation attends a marriage ceremony but the priest is soon pulled away to say the last words over a recently deceased man.

If the Catholic community in the Netherlands, and in several other parts of Europe, heard about Flores and saw its peoples, it was to Buis's credit. In order to train himself to become more adept at cinematography and directing, Buis went to the United States for a second time to enrol at the New York Institute of Photography. Father Piet Beltjens, a colleague

Figures 5.6 and 5.7: Stills from *Flores Film*, 1926: (upper) natives in Flores learn how to make a Christian prayer cross; (lower) Bishop Verstraelen blesses new converts.

from the SVD, accompanied him. In 1930, feeling more technically capable and artistically confident, they headed back to Flores to make films.

ETHNOGRAPHIC FICTION: *RIA RAGO*

The first fiction film Buis directed, *Ria Rago* had an uncomplicated theme (the poster is shown in Figure 5.8). He used locals to play the various roles, an innovative approach for that period. 'Good' people and 'bad' people are rarely more black and white. A Christian girl, Ria, is forced to marry Dapo, a Muslim boy who has grown tired of his first wife. A Muslim broker encourages and arranges the deal. Her greedy pagan father, Ragho Dago, accepts the money readily and welcomes his prospective son-in-law. Ria, however, refuses to give in and seeks help from local Catholic priests. They intervene and warn her family against the forced marriage. Realising she will eventually be married off to Dapo, she escapes to a nunnery. After being kidnapped by her family members and brought back, Ria is beaten and tied up. When Dapo tries to force himself on her, she outwits him and escapes again. This time, however, she falls ill. By the time her family finds her again she is at her last breath. She forgives her parents just before dying, clutching onto her cross.

While *Ria Rago* (Simon Buis, 1930) was fiction, it clearly strived to build a reputation on being based on actual, or at least plausible facts. Appels has speculated that Buis may have been influenced by the film *Nanook of the North* (Robert Flaherty, 1922) during his stay in the United States. Did he incorporate Robert Flaherty's style of blurring fact and fiction to provide an impression of authenticity in *Nanook of the North*? Appels writes:

> It seems plausible that Buis during his film studies in New York saw *Nanook of the North* by Robert Flaherty although nowhere does he mention this being his cinematic inspiration in his letters or diaries. Or maybe he saw *Nanook* on a mission exhibition, where it was played frequently. His method and approach to *Ria Rago* seem very much that of Flaherty. (Appels 1997: 14)

I hazard the speculation that Buis may also have been influenced by a scene that was shot by Rach. In *Bali-Floti* (Simon Buis, H. Limbrock, Johannes van Cleef, Willy Rach, 1926) a twin to *Flores Film*, there is a rather obvious re-enactment of a young woman from the highlands being forcibly sold to a Muslim family. We do know for sure that Buis had been obsessed with the theme of forced marriage since his days as School Superintendent in Flores. If one were to look at some of his writings in the Catholic newspapers, this becomes evident. In an article

Figure 5.8: Poster for *Ria Rago*, 'a film of actuality', screening at the Polytechnic Cinema Theatre in February 1931. Courtesy of University of Westminster Archives, Ref: RSP/6/6/17.

section titled 'Onvriendelijkheden/Unfriendly Gift', written in 1925–6, he highlights the incidents of coastal-area Muslims in Maumere who forcibly take away girls from the highlands. The backdrop is the ongoing tension between the Christians and the Muslims to gain control over the autochthonous groups in the mountains:

> Elizabeth, a young girl of marriageable age, was sold by her parents to a young Mohammedan. Although they are pagan she had led an exemplary virtuous life. The parents tried to force her and chastised her but Elizabeth suffered patiently and remained steadfast. The parents gave up and finally returned the money to the young man . . . Our new converts in the villages of the Islam have sometimes hardships to endure battles. Very often they come to the mission and show their bruises and tears in their clothes, when they have opposed the Moslems. (Buis 1925–6: 36)

Lisabona Rahman, an Indonesian film restoration expert, has recently written an important account of the making of *Ria Rago* in the new online film essay portal *FilmIndonesia* (Rahman 2013). Like Appels, she situates the film in the historical timeframe of early cinema. As there are no film anthologies that detail any of this work, these references are precious. Rahman says that Soverdi collaborated with the native population, a strategy that was not unique although this was amongst the first of such efforts. According to her:

> This joint strategy was not merely for cost-saving purposes as commonly done by commercial film producers of exotic fantasy films such as *Tabu* (Murnau & Flaherty, 1932), or *Goona-Goona: An Authentic Melodrama Of the Island of Bali/Kris the Sword of Death* (both by Armand Denis and Andre Roosevelt, 1932). In the case of Soverdi Films, the involvement of local actors was essential to create an authentic description of local people's lives. (Rahman 2013)

Indeed, there is something tangibly genuine about the locations, costumes and props in the film. Whether the story would have appealed to an audience much beyond a narrow, sympathetic and religious group is of course debatable; it is after all a rather straightforward, flat tale of unwavering allegiance to Jesus. If the storyline appears to be too simplistic, Rahman reminds us that this type of plot structure was actually rather common during that period. While the father and the villages represent the collective interests of the greedy indigenous, Ria represents an individual moral voice guided by the Christian mission. This form of Western-influenced individual conscience versus a native-based ideology conflict was typical of the Dutch-produced Indonesian Balai Pustaka/Bureau of Literature stories popular in the 1920s and 1930s. Published as novels, the stories typically featured intergenerational conflicts around arranged marriages and cultural values (Siregar 1964: 33–49). While *Ria Rago* is shot in natural locations, utilises local participants and is based on a plausible story, it contains little primary-source value for historians when compared to *Bali-Floti* or *Flores Film*. But in this way Buis was able to elaborately recreate some of the core issues that he was battling against in his evangelistic work. The film also provides us with detailed and vivid visuals of Flores. The costumes are authentic. Roy Hamilton, in his book *Gift of the Cotton Maiden*, devotes a page with inset photographs to the costumes of *Ria Rago*. He makes note of the fact that Ragho Dago, the father of the rebellious Ria, wears a sarong in the film in a style only seen in the remote island of Palue to the north of Flores (Hamilton 1994: 39). Daniel Dhakidae, an anthropologist from Flores, has remarked that some of the ceremonial aspects of the film, such as Ragho Dago's animist offerings and the Hadji's ceremonies, are authentic (Rahman 2013). Thus, while not quite ethnographically evidentiary because of its reworking and staging of society in Flores, *Ria Rago*, as corroborated by other sources, appears to be ethnographically illustrative, making it a relevant historical record of secondary source status.

The impact that *Ria Rago* had at the time of its screening is noteworthy. On 11 December 1930, the day after its first press screening for journalists in Holland, several newspapers published long reviews about the film. They were mostly favourable. Some were complimentary of its innovative on-location filming:

> In judging a film like this, that is not acted by professionals and recorded in a studio with plaster backgrounds, paper scenarios and lights, but under the scorching heat of the tropical sun, it is necessary to consider the almost insurmountable difficulties that filming in such warm regions entails. (*Algemeen Handelsblad* 11 December 1930)

Others remarked on its moral lessons:

> This new film work visualizes how Christian love triumphs over pagan cruelty. One sees a Christian girl in Flores oppose the pagan laws of marriage *adat*, which her ancestors and her immediate family still remained loyal to . . . After undergoing very heavy persecution and ill treatment she dies, true to her Christian ideal, with a word of forgiveness on the lips and in full surrender after having received the HH Sacraments of the Dying. ('Werkzaamheden op Flores', *De Tijd* 11 December 1930)

But a month before *Ria Rago* opened in the Netherlands, far away from all the recognition in the Netherlands, Simon Buis had already made cinema history by projecting the film in Flores.

CONCLUSIONS: REVISITING TWO FILMS AND A CORONATION

According to the *Katholieke Missiën*, Buis travelled to Flores on 13 November 1930 to attend the coronation ceremony of Alexander Baroek. This was a monumental event as the thirty-year-old would become the first Christian Raja of Manggarai, symbolically ending the long Islamic rule of the Sultan of Bima (Buis 1930). Baroek, who was the son of a chief and had been educated in a mission school, had, in an unanticipated sleight of hand by the Dutch Governor General, replaced the previous nominee, an illiterate non-Catholic chief (Steenbrink 2013: 117). On the eve of the coronation, Buis screened *Ria Rago* and *Flores Film* in the presence of 4,000 villagers and thirty-eight district heads. This was possibly among the largest film audience ever assembled in the Dutch East Indies. The newspapers would describe the screenings as quite extraordinary:

> It was lovely clear weather at 7 o'clock in the evening, and Father Buis showed the old, well-known film in the Netherlands, *Flores Film* and the new film *Ria Rago*. All were astonished. Ancient pagans murmured: '*Toeanhitoe kanang Mori Kraeng*!/The pastor must be our Lord himself!', They saw new and strange things! A train in motion, Amsterdam, big boats and big cities, Dutch ladies and gentlemen and children and so many other things. The first moving images on the silver screen elicited cries of surprise . . .

The report continued about the coronation the following day:

> The imposing figure of the resident of Timor and dependencies came forward and announced to the people the decision of the Dutch government: The appointment of Alexander Baroek as manager of Manggarai. In Malay, he exhorted the young king, to always remain true to Her Majesty Wilhelmina and serve faithfully the Dutch government in pristine honesty and dedication. (*De Tijd* 1 May 1931)

Buis was embedded as an integral part of the ceremony and the newspaper bore pictures of him and the new Rajah (see Figure 5.9). It must have been a seminal occasion for him. Twelve years ago he had arrived with the first wave of SVD priests and had set up schools all over Flores. He had returned to the Netherlands, trained himself in America, started a film company and had tirelessly advocated for the missionary cause in Flores through evangelical work, his writings and his cinema.

The tussle for Flores had begun with the ghastly 'blitzkrieg' by Captain Hans Christoffel about two decades earlier, ostensibly to rid the

Figure 5.9: Father Simon Buis and the newly appointed Raja Baroek, *De Katholieke Missiën*, 1931.

island of the oppressive, slave-owning Bima rulers of Sumbawa. It had gradually transformed into more benign assistance via education, medical help and community building through the work of missionaries. Now there was a new Catholic Rajah. Simon Buis, priest and filmmaker, stood by and watched him being sworn in. Even though Buis and Soverdi would go on to release two more films, *Amorira* (1930) and *Anak Woda* (1933) over the next few years, *Ria Rago* would prove to be the most successful mission film ever. An entire generation of Dutch schoolchildren, and many of their parents and church attendees, would see the film in the 1930s. Appels has reported that all three films were thought to be lost during the German occupation of the Second World War, until *Ria Rago* and *Amorira* were discovered by Father Hank de Beer in the SVD archives in 1990.

This chapter has attempted to persuade the reader that despite the obvious propagandistic slant to the SVD film footage, there is historical value in the material, both as primary and as secondary sources. Academics working on various aspects of culture in Flores, including handicrafts and religious and social anthropology, have not been privy to much of the film material screened at the coronation that was shot by Willy Rach, Simon Buis and their crew. Perhaps during their era of research these films were not easily available. Or, very possibly, the idea that film footage, especially overtly propaganda material, could serve as a historical source was one whose time had not yet come. I have teased out several scenes that not only corroborate and augment existing scholarship but also, on occasion, serve as sole surviving primary sources of events. Rach and Limbrock's arduous journey through much of unchartered Flores and the close observation of social rituals are unique documents that lead us to sites of memory that have long been vanquished by encroaching modernity and the inevitable march of time. I argue that this effort of locating overlooked visual sources cannot be at odds with the most fundamental tenets of studying the colonial era. These films from Flores are just a sliver of the hundreds of hours of footage filmed by Dutch propagandists all over the archipelago in the early twentieth century that are only now being rehabilitated. What is hopefully a burgeoning 'pictorial turn' in the study of Indonesia's colonial history clearly contains deep and rich resources still waiting to be researched. It is now relatively easy to at least get a sampling of the vast collection. The archives at the Eye Film Institute and at Beeld en Geluid, where this research was conducted, are welcoming to academics who wish to view the well-catalogued, comprehensive collection. The many terminals at these Dutch repositories or individual screens that we may access from our personal computers transport us, quite amazingly, into fragments of vision from almost a century ago. Currently an Indonesian film group called 'Indonesia Film Center', based in Jakarta, hosts a website that has uploaded dozens of films from the Dutch colonial propaganda collection with permission.[7] The ease with which this can be done and the scope of the material that we can access was not possible even a decade ago. The marriage of computer advancements and painstaking archival work can now assist in democratising the hundreds of hours of film that were seen only in the captivity of cinema halls in the 1910s and 1920s by a relatively small fraction of Dutch citizens. This is visual archival technology's shining moment. It would behoove historians to delve deeper into these sources.

NOTES

1. Letter of Couvreur to Jesuit priest Jos Hoeberechts dated 12 February 1908. See Steenbrink 2013, p. 108.
2. Advertisement, *Limburger Koerier*, 15 December 1928. Retrieved from Delpher on 18 September 2015. Accessed on 20 October 2015 at http://resolver.kb.nl/resolve?urn=ddd:010348448:mpeg21:10267.
3. For details on this power struggle and to read more on Dutch attempts to manage the environment and ecology of their colony, see Barnard 2011.
4. I sent a digital link of *Flores Film* to Karel Steenbrink for his insights. He published these comments in an online blog. Accessed on 18 June 2014 at http://relindonesia.blogspot.nl/2014/05/sandeep-ray-and-colonial-movies.html.
5. Although there was no singular document or charter that outlined its mission and modes of application, the turn of the 1900s is regarded as the start of the 'ethical policy'. See Kingston 1987.
6. Steenbrink (2013: 113–14) discusses how from 1909 Jesuits sent Malay-speaking teachers to the area and by 1925 they were already teaching in twenty-five schools. During these years, visiting priests would baptise children, who were prepared for the conversion by their teachers.
7. Indonesia Film Center. Accessed on 2 April 2013 at http://www.indonesianfilmcenter.com.

REFERENCES

Appels, Eddy (1996), 'Traveling images a push for a historical–anthropological study on CD-ROM of the Dutch mission movies', PhD dissertation, University of Amsterdam.
Appels, Eddy (1997), *Mission to Flores: Father Simon Buis Flores and his Films, 1925–1934*, Amsterdam: Film and Science Foundation, Audiovisual Archive.
Appels, Eddy (2004), 'Faraway places and exotic cultures in a movie mission', accessed on 8 May 2012 at http://www.cultuurwijzer.nl/cultuurwijzer.nl/cultuurwijzer.nl/i000741.html

Barnard, Timothy P. (2011), 'Protecting the dragon: Dutch attempts at limiting access to Komodo Lizards in the 1920s and 1930s', *Indonesia*, 92, 97–123.
Beltjens, Piet, SVD (1992), 'Herinneringen aan pater Simon Buis', Teteringen: Archivist of the Provincial Archive, unpublished manuscript.
Buis, Simon (1925), 'Pas Op Voor De Scholen', *Het Mahomedanisme Op Flores, Katholieke Missiën*, p. 1.
Buis, Simon (1925–6), 'Beleedigende Taal', *Het Mahomedanisme Op Flores, Katholieke Missiën*, 51: 1–3, 21–2, 33–6.
Buis, Simon (1930), 'De Kroning van Koning Baroek van Manggarai', *Katholieke Missiën*, 56: 104–9.
Hamilton, Roy, W. (1994), 'Behind the cloth', in Roy W. Hamilton (ed.), *Gift of the Cotton Maiden: Textiles of Flores and the Solor Islands*, Los Angeles: UCLA Fowler Museum of Cultural History, pp. 20–38.
Kingston, Jeffrey Burke (1987), 'The Manipulation of Tradition in Java's Shadow: Transmigration, Decentralization and the Ethical Policy in Colonial Lampung', PhD dissertation, Columbia University.
Kunst en Letteren (1930), 'De Flores-klarikfilm Rio Rago: Propaganda voor de missie', 11 December.
Rahman, Lisabona (2013), 'Lembah Ndona di Dunia Maya: Roman Adat-Religius ala Flores tahun 1930-an', *Film Indonesia*, October, accessed on 15 June 2014 at http://filmindonesia.or.id/article/lembah-ndona-di-dunia-maya-roman-adat-relijius-ala-flores-tahun-1930-an#.VvtwXMfQ-Qs.
Schroeter, Susanne (2010), 'The indigenization of catholicism in Flores', in Susanne Schroeter (ed.), *Christianity in Indonesia: Perspectives of Power*, Berlin: Lit Verlag, pp. 137–58.
Siregar, Bakri (1964), *Sejarah Sastera Indonesia Modern/History of Modern Indonesian Literature*, vol. 1, Jakarta: Akademi Sastera dan Bahasa Multatuli.
Steenbrink, Karel (2007), *Catholics in Indonesia, 1808–1942: A Documented History*, vol. 2, 'The spectacular growth of a self-confident minority, 1903–1942', Leiden: KITLV Press.
Steenbrink, Karel (2013), 'Dutch colonial containment of Islam in Manggarai, West Flores, in favor of catholicism, 1909–1942', *Bijdragen tot de Taal-, Land- en Volkenkunde*, 169, 104–28.
Willemsen, Marie-Antoinette (2012), 'De *fictive* kracht: De missiefilms van de missionarissen van Steyl (SVD)', in J. P. A. van Vugt and Marie-Antoinette Willemsen (eds), *Bewogen missie: het gebruik van het medium film door Nederlandse kloostergemeenschappen*, Hilversum: Stitching Echo and Uitgeverij Verloren, pp. 59–82.

CHAPTER 6

Paradoxical Legacies: Colonial Missionary Films, Corporate Philanthropy in South Asia and the Griersonian Documentary Tradition

Annamaria Motrescu-Mayes

Enduring racial stereotypes packaged as corporate advertising can spin orthodox post-colonial assumptions into a rapid topsy-turvy. Filmed ninety years apart, the short story of two fathers, two daughters and several crates of fresh lemons makes an unlikely pairing with that of white-clad Catholic Sisters cleaning the face of a leper-disfigured Indian patient. However, interpreted from the perspective of the social engagement praxis advocated by John Grierson, the founding father of the British Documentary Movement, productions such as Hong Kong Shangai Bank Corporation (HSBC)'s *Lemon Grove* TV commercial (2013) and amateur films made by the Saint Joseph's Missionary Society in India in the 1920s are methodologically matching while simultaneously operating outside their original social and cultural meaning. The theoretical framework employed in this chapter anchors the analysis of these two types of media productions in John Grierson's 'First principles of documentary', published in 1932. Relying on Grierson's theoretical agenda, this chapter examines the visual literacy that informs ongoing racial and economic hierarchies across two narratives of philanthropic work and will argue that it is possible to identify paradoxical legacies in terms of racial policy and global issues of social engagement. The core research material – a twenty-first century corporate banking advertisement and an early twentieth-century amateur colonial missionary film rife with imperial ideology – allows for a comparison of seemingly different understandings and representations of social, cultural and economic networks and of their interchangeable narratives. Most importantly, this comparative exercise suggests that the visual and thematic rhetoric unifying these two films qualifies them as unexpected examples of British Documentary Movement productions.

Most of the HSBC TV commercials are available to watch on YouTube – a free access distribution platform that complements the company's corporate agenda for buttressing global financial networks. Titles such as *Golf – It's Anyone's Game*,[1] *Expat – A Different Perspective: Expat Life*[2] or *Johnny Yates Says Thank You*,[3] are advertisements produced as bite-size entertaining feature films relying on stunning cinematography, effervescent humour and a highly emotional charge that primes the viewer with a sense of globally shared altruism and belonging. From loud laughter to social engagement and heart-breaking stories of heroic motherhood – topics of ubiquitous relevance – the HSBC's TV commercials are successful in enforcing their unique selling proposition: the network is the heart of life and as 'one of the world's largest banking and financial services organisations', HSBC is encouraging personal banking within networks of globalised success stories.[4] There is however one commercial that appears to have fallen between the cracks of HSBC's publicity rhetoric and of today's political correctness: *Lemon Grove* (2013).[5] This commercial is a spin-off of *Lemonade* (2012),[6] which has attracted strong disapproval for its soundtrack's alleged paedophiliac pitch originating in Maurice Chevalier's song 'Thank Heaven For Little Girls' (from *Gigi*, Vincente Minnelli, 1958).[7] While continuing to bank on the same soundtrack and the implicit controversy provoked by the invocation of Chevalier's song, *Lemon Grove* adds insult to injury by inadvertently steering away from HSBC's equalitarian and community-driven narrative. Within post-colonial critiques of gender and racial representations, this TV commercial raises issues of discrimination and international (un)fair trade. By employing John Grierson's core theories of documentary film-making, with a particular focus on his film productions for the Empire Marketing Board (EMB) (May 1926–September 1933), it is possible to resituate *Lemon Grove* within a more accurate discourse about corporate (prestige) advertising and its long tradition of and affiliation to imperial popular culture. This theoretical exercise also gains added legitimacy and new interpretative perspectives in the comparative framework, in which one of the Saint Joseph's Missionary Society's colonial amateur films, also analysed by testing it against Grierson's theories of documentary film-making, emerges as a counterpart visual source functioning outside its original film genre and message.

'STEWARDS' OF MEDIA PERSUASION

In 1875, with only five priests and a medical missionary, the Saint Joseph's Foreign Missionary Society – the first Roman Catholic society in England, founded by Cardinal Herbert Alfred Vaughan in 1866 at Mill Hill, London – established its first mission in Madras, South-West India. Four years later the Mill Hill Fathers set missions across the northwest of India (currently Pakistan and Kashmir). Driven by evangelical zeal and fighting constant financial shortage, the Mill Hill Fathers and Sisters resorted to an unrelenting campaign of self-promotion via various visual records, from glass plates and lantern slides in the late nineteenth century to photography and moving images in the twentieth and twenty-first centuries. The Society's film collection, covering over 750 hours of footage, includes a large number of films about its South Asian missions.[8] The Society's missions in South Asia became known for their two core work strands – medical and food relief programmes, and the care for and support of women's welfare and better rights within Indian society. The Saint Joseph's Missionary Society composite film accessioned 'BECM 2002/107/014 India',[9] recorded on 16mm and dated late 1920s to early 1930s, shows numerous scenes of local customs, crafts and social interactions between the Mill Hill Fathers, Sisters and Indian villagers, hospital in- and out-patients and festivities organised to celebrate the missions' work in Kashmir and Punjab. Like all the other visual records held by the Society's visual archives of South Asia this film was also made with the explicit purpose of illustrating and promoting the pivotal part played by the Mill Hill missionaries in improving the living conditions of colonised rural Indian communities. Ultimately, it was an advertisement targeting the Society's congregations in Britain and, in the context of interwar audiences, it contributed to wider imperial publicity campaigns by placing its 'product' – Catholic faith and philanthropy – alongside more mundane imperial raw materials and luxury goods. Importantly, the Society's fundraising schemes relied on lecture tours that extensively used glass plates, and later films, to illustrate its key role in disseminating the Catholic faith across the British Empire, and pictured the Mill Hill Fathers and Sisters as modern-day archangels enabling the Society's core agenda. This strategy echoed that of prestige advertising – promotional campaigns that promoted the company or the brand rather than a particular product (Aitken 2013: 153). This metonymical approach is also found in HSBC's TV commercial, in which the bank's international network is signified by the powerful efficacy of global networks of entrepreneurial cooperation. Enthusiastic and industrious (anonymous) Mill Hill Fathers posted around the world, from India to Borneo and across Africa, secured a similar type of international entrepreneurial network for the Saint Joseph's Missionary Society by recording the mission's first (promotional) amateur films. Apart from inter-titles rich in an unequivocal religious tone and message, these mid-1920s missionary films imitated the visual style (establishing and medium shots rudimentarily edited) and thematic strands common to early travelogue films.[10] Of note, the self-advertising elan and the common goal to promote the brand rather than specific 'by-products' such as medical aid or financial programmes, are two key features that bridge the thematic and time gap between . . ./o14 India and Lemon Grove.

John Grierson's alleged encouragement to avoid social meaning in cinematographic productions – he is known to have claimed that 'it is more important to make a myth than a film' (Russell 2007: 57), which some defined as 'Grierson's hamartia' (Winston 2014: 105), is one of the theoretical axes on which to develop several interpretations of the Saint Joseph's Missionary Society films, including . . ./o14 India. For instance, it could be argued that, since the Society's films do not include scenes of non-Christian festivities and rituals, or of the Fathers' and Sisters' domestic life, the Society's amateur film-makers skilfully avoided recording details of the personal lives of Christian missionaries working across the British Empire. This omission brings to mind the choice made by John Grierson and Basil Wright almost a decade later when working together on the final cut of Cargo from Jamaica (Basil Wright, 1933). On this occasion, they decided to exclude a scene of an indentured labourer, 'which Wright had planned to use in order to underline a theme of exploitation', and included instead one of bananas being unloaded (Low 1979: 60). Racial contentions and the colonial exploitation of labour forces were not fashionable topics in interwar Britain with the imperial (and religious) propaganda deliberately oblivious to such sociopolitical conflicts. The Mill Hill missionary film-makers' preference for topics common to interwar popular visual narratives of the British rule in India, and to those found in contemporary travelogues, documentaries and newsreels, make the Saint Joseph's Missionary Society's early amateur films function both as visual manuscripts of a particular religious promotional campaign and as unsophisticated, raw visual accounts of everyday life in India. This grants them an ideological and poetic licence that recalibrates their documentary legacy and, as in the case of HSBC's *Lemon Grove* TV commercial, encourages a new and pertinent reading of their role in authenticating specific social and cultural imperial/global networks – the type of key 'sociological and aesthetic functions of film-making' applauded and encouraged by John Grierson (Aitken 2013: 145).

In order to test the thesis proposed in this chapter, that both the Saint Joseph's Missionary Society's early colonial films made in India and the banking corporate philanthropic agenda of HSBC's *Lemon Grove* operate outside their original ideological frameworks, the following sections of this chapter will present a dual critical analysis while gauging the relevance of these films in support of Grierson's first principles of documentary film-making. In Grierson's opinion 'the ruling élites had a commitment to inform and educate those over whom they held "stewardship"' (Swan 2008: 5). This was a belief that inspired him to regard film-making as one of the key instructional and social tools available to his contemporaries. 'I want to look upon the cinema as a pulpit, and use it as a propagandist', remains one of Grierson's most quoted statements (Beveridge 1978: vii). It was within this intellectual framework that Grierson hypothesised the first three principles of documentary film-making – the epitome of 'socially useful cinema' (Aitken 2013: 91), and 'an instrument of social persuasion' (Tudor quoted in Aitken 1998: 48). These principles stipulated that the films should 'photograph the living scene and the living story', that the 'original (or native) actor, and the original (or native) scene, are better guides to a screen interpretation of the modern world' and, finally, that 'stories . . . taken from the raw can be . . . more real in the philosophical sense' (Aitken 1998: 83). Most importantly, Grierson emphasised a feature common to amateur and ethnographic films when noting that '[s]pontaneous gesture has a special value on the screen' (Aitken 1998: 83) and, consequently, the immediacy of social interactions between the film-maker and his or her subjects can also be experienced by proxy by the viewers. Grierson's aesthetic principles and the core theoretical agenda that buttressed his work for and with British, and later Canadian and Australian government departments and corporate sponsors, were also observed to some extent by most members of the British Documentary Movement, including such as Basil Wright, Arthur Elton, Edgar Anstey, Stuart Legg, Paul Rotha and Harry Watt.

'THEY BELIEVE THAT WE BELIEVE'

The prima facie evaluation of the two case studies discussed here, . . ./o14 *India* and *Lemon Grove*, considers their specific contexts of production and distribution alongside their role in fostering visual narratives of immediate relevance to their audiences, whether interwar British Catholic congregations or mid-2010s consumers of corporate advertising. The use of visual aids in religious proselytising and in commercial advertisements has often relied on the long-lasting effects of visual priming and the deep emotional engagement experienced by audiences. Paul Rotha, one of the key British documentary film-makers who worked for the EMB Film Unit beside John Grierson and Basil Wright, remarked that 'an audience must be emotionally involved before it will absorb [an] argument, let alone facts and opinions' (Rotha in Aitken 1998: 160). In tune with Rotha's opinion, but from the pulpit of religious propaganda and about a few decades earlier, *Ministry – the International Journal for Pastors* advertised the use of pictorial aids for Bible study and endorsed the views that '[e]very evangelist, Bible instructor, lay evangelist, and personal worker will be materially helped by using this teaching aid'(Anderson 1956), and that '[t]he interest of our hearers is strengthened, and they have more confidence in us. They believe that we believe what we are preaching when we present visual evidence'(Froom 1947).

Using film in educating young Christians had already become an educational norm in Britain by the late 1940s with best-practice manuals made widely available and national, regional and corporate film libraries offering a variety of film genres for loan. For instance, *Films for Church and Youth*, a slim volume published in 1947, highlighted for young Christians the importance of using 16mm copies of documentary films in lectures (Edinburgh House Bureau for Visual Aids 1947). One of the examples included in this volume was *Made in India*, a film 'produced in 1941–42 by Indian photographers and craftsmen' (ibid.: 8). In this case, it was recommended that the priest/lecturer could engage the audience at the end of the projection by recounting the final caption of the film – 'If poverty is abolished, agriculture scientifically organised, and industry well planned, India's future as a great nation is assured' – before asking his audience 'Are we satisfied that this will meet all India's needs? What about her religious and social divisions?' (ibid.). This juxtaposing of economic, social and faith-based challenges and contradictions is also found in the Saint Joseph's Missionary Society's amateur productions, which included similar thematic and stylistic models to those found in contemporary instructional, documentary and religious films. It is plausible to suggest that some of the Society's amateur film-makers in the 1920s and 1930s would have been familiar with the films produced by the Salvation Army at the initiative of and under the direction of Commander Herbert Booth, who believed that the use of films can 'feed the imagination of the poor and attract them to his sermons on salvation' (Lindvall 2007: 7).

Like the Salvationists, or the British interwar documentary film-makers keen on recording social and religious networks across the Empire, the Mill Hill amateur film-makers relied on the marketing rhetoric employed by advertisers of imperial products – a strategy also evident in HSBC's recent commercials and particularly in *Lemon Grove*. The bedrock of such media productions remains the process of visual priming although there is a strong overlap between the evangelist tone of commercial advertisements and the marketing strategies of religious propaganda.[11]

A detailed account of the theories of perception, persuasion and psychology defining the process of visual priming is not the subject of this chapter. However, it is important to note that at its core is the relationship between cognitive systematic processing, which is 'contemplative, analytic, and responsive to the argumentative quality of the message', and heuristic processing, which 'occurs whenever an individual

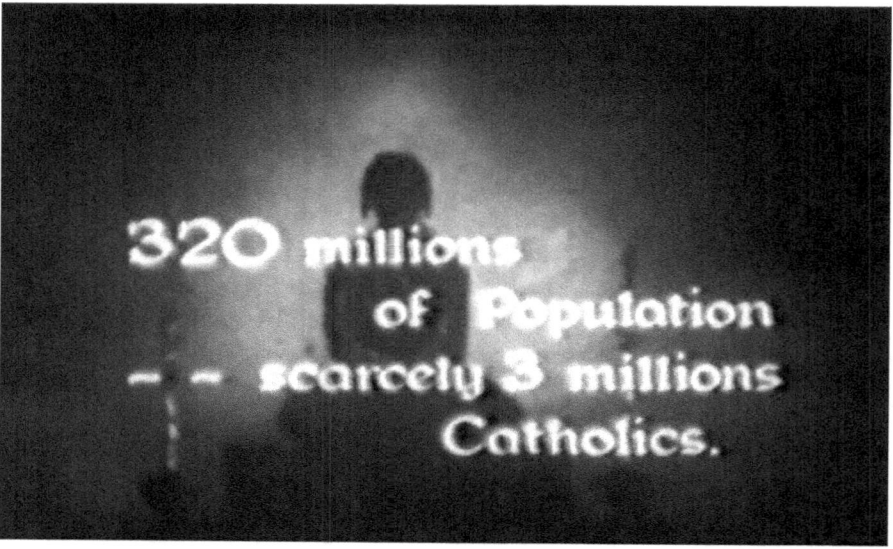

Figure 6.1: *Saint Joseph's Missionary Society Collection*, India, 1928–32 © BECM, screen capture.

relies on some short-cut decision-making rule to construct an attitude towards the persuasive advocacy' (Dillard and Peck 2000: 462). Moreover, the process of visual priming and by its inherent manipulative strategies discussed, for instance, by Stéphane Doyen, John A. Bargh and Wendy Gardner, is often achieved through a strategically efficient, recurrent and prolonged production and dissemination of particular sets of visual discourses. It is thus possible to argue that visual records such as those discussed here mediate between different constructions of social reality and of individual, community and national identities across historical times. They also often complement or contradict traditional research practices and recurrent cultural assumptions. For instance, the Mill Hill Fathers' amateur films of their work in India in the late 1920s and early 1930s, as seen in . . ./o14 *India*, cover a range of general topics also common to interwar travelogues, documentaries and newsreels, topics such as tribal craftsmanship, children at play, women displaying traditional jewellery, agricultural practices, ruins, village life and street scenes.

The imperial ideological dimension of their amateur missionary films was mostly evident in their inter-titles while the sponsorship campaign in support of the Society's works in India was underlined in newspaper headline-like titles (Figure 6.1). Audiences viewing this film, whether in interwar Britain or in any of today's multicultural and politically correct societies, would first react by relying on the cognitive heuristic process: they would let the effect of visual priming summarise the narrative and message of the film. As such, . . ./o14 *India* becomes just another imperial, unethical visual record marked by the rhetoric of the West's racial and cultural supremacy. So, white European Catholic missionaries in this film vouched for a God-sent and Empire-endorsed civilising and redeeming mission, while Indian people were represented as culturally and socially immature, as obedient recipients of much-needed medical, educational and spiritual help. Any of the interwar British or American Empire films would have endorsed a similar narrative based on the contemporary collective conscience and popular perceptions of race and colonial hierarchies.[12] However, in this context, the film's affiliation to visual ethnography is one of its intrinsic methodological redeemable features: amateur films, when not staged, can secure visual records of authentic ethnographic fieldwork. It is from this perspective that . . ./o14 *India* deserves to be analysed within the framework of cognitive systematic processing and so avoid a short-cut heuristic and pejorative interpretation of the film.

HSBC's *Lemon Grove* presents another example of how the effects of visual priming can obscure the intrinsic message of a film. Most

Figure 6.2: *Lemon Grove*, India, 2013 © HSBC, screen capture.

audiences of this TV commercial, whether in cinema halls or online, also rely on the heuristic process when securing an immediate reading of *Lemon Grove* as a coherent and easy-to-relate-to story of the friendly, fair trading of goods between three young entrepreneurs – an American girl who buys organic lemons locally sourced by an Indian girl and then sells them to her distributor in France, a young boy running a lemonade stand (Figure 6.2). The soundtrack in *Lemon Grove* is designed to be enchanting and uplifting in spite of its presumed risqué connotations. The message, at face value, endorses the undisputable benefits of well-structured international business opportunities, which in the words of Andrea Newman, HSBC's global head of advertising and marketing communications, were brought to 'life with a sense of warmth, simplicity and optimism to inspire growth' (McCabe 2013).[13] Consequently, it could be argued that HSBC's *Lemon Grove* TV commercial refers strictly to the network of the financial US–Indian–French interconnectedness that its own banking system aims to facilitate at a global level. However, when analysed in greater detail, this short advertising featurette discloses thematic and stylistic patterns common to British interwar imperial narratives of trade and race.

Assessed from the interpretative angles proposed by the effects of visual priming and its implicit heuristic process, both case studies discussed here fit the assumptions common to their contemporary popular imperial/global cultures and corporate interests – i.e. mid-twentieth-century British missionary amateur films as products par excellence of imperial ideologies of race and Christian evangelism; twenty-first-century TV commercials as entertaining and socially engaging examples of corporate publicity and philanthropic networks. The thematic gap between these films remains wide open unless John Grierson's core principles of documentary film-making and cognitive systematic processing are employed as primary analytical tools. It is in this theoretical framework that . . ./o14 India and Lemon Grove acquire a different artistic legacy, while entering into a direct ideological dialogue of meaning and style.

VISUAL RHETORIC AND A THEORETICAL 'ABOUT-FACE'

A preacher in his youth, 'the modern-day prophet of cinema' (Evans 1991: 3), John Grierson believed in the moral code decreed by the Bible, embraced religious morality as the cornerstone of social and political engagements and integrated such core ideas in his theories of documentary film – a genre 'ideally suited to represent the interconnectedness of social relationships' (Aitken 1998: 38). He was a supporter of film productions made on location rather than in a studio since, in his opinion, the resulting images 'revealed a greater quantity of information about the empirical world, and about the interdependence of social and individual relations' – the cornerstone of a film-maker's moral engagement and responsibility (Aitken 2013: 99). Grierson's beliefs echoed to some extent those of earlier Christian apostles as well as of twentieth-century religious film producers and apologists – and these beliefs also inform successful marketing campaigns in which the meme of reciprocal altruism buttresses the long-lasting tradition of visual evangelism (Blackmore 1999), whether in TV commercials such as those produced by HSBC, in British interwar poetic documentary films or in early missionary productions.

Recent theories of perception and cognitive processes directly affected by visual literacy have highlighted the proposition that, to secure proficient communication systems, 'the greatest altruism [persuasive charity] should be shown to those who are capable of being convinced' (Rose in Blackmore 1999: 189). Scholars of religious studies often anchor this visual and moral rhetoric in the three key reasons given by Saint Bonaventura's (1221–74) for using images when preaching the Gospel. In his august opinion, images, first, 'were made for the simplicity of the ignorant [to be able to] read . . . more open Scriptures'; second, he believed that 'emotion is aroused more by what is seen than by what is heard [the sermon]'; and third, he asserted that 'those things which are only heard fall into oblivion more easily than those things which are seen' (Bonaventura 1941: 194). Saint Bonaventura's opinion was echoed, for instance, in the early 1900s when the *Congregationalist* journal published a note on how 'the motion picture business would prove a worthy effort for "social justice" and universal brotherhood' – words that rung true thirty years later when Grierson announced his principles of the documentary film (Lindvall 2007: 8).

This visual evangelism and its intrinsic process of visual priming concerning issues of social awareness and engagement, religious and commercial networks and corporate marketing campaigns for imperial products – summarised by Grierson in his first (three) principles of documentary film – help us redefine the interpretation of the Saint Joseph's Missionary Society colonial amateur film . . ./o14 India and HSBC's *Lemon Grove,* within reversed and, thus, paradoxical cultural legacies. First, by testing . . ./o14 India against Grierson's theoretical triad proposed as the aesthetic and ideological foundation of the British documentary film movement, it can be argued that rather than being a clear-cut example of imperial and religious propaganda this missionary amateur film functions as a valid and unswerving visual document of social and cultural interconnectedness. Despite sharing a set of thematic strands with most colonial ethnographic and travelogue films as well as with ethnofiction productions . . ./o14 India's immediate visual dimension endorses Grierson's 'first principles'.[14] It shows the 'living scene and the living story', the 'original/native' people and the 'original/native' scenes (Figure 6.3) and, according to Grierson, it allows the viewer to have access to 'raw [visual and cultural] material' before being guided on how to read these images by way of inter-titles, an approach that raise different theoretical and ideological issues. Hence, . . ./o14 India is defying its intrinsic imperial stereotypification of race and colonised people and, paradoxically, echoes the social engagement and documentary film-making poetics advanced by Grierson.

Furthermore, although produced at the high noon of missionary–educational–civilising rhetoric . . ./o14 India escapes the visual narratives specific to imperial popular culture and the colonial anthropological discourse of late colonial times by offering access to 'raw' images documenting social, racial and cultural interrelations between the Mill Hill missionaries and Indian people. It is in this context that this film, and several other Saint Joseph's Missionary early amateur films, challenge the preconceived post-colonial assumptions of being just an example of imperial ideology and religious fundraising. Without attempting an over-arching comparison, it is possible to propose that, despite their prescribed promotional agenda for making . . ./o14 India, the Mill Hill

Figure 6.3: *Saint Joseph's Missionary Society Collection*, India, 1928–32 © BECM, screen capture.

amateur film-makers who recorded scenes of Indian men and women working and living in their villages appear to have had a similar interest in promoting social and cultural awareness to most of the British Documentary Movement's film-makers or twenty-first century visual anthropologists.

Thus, examined from the critical angle proposed by Grierson's theories of the documentary film, and taking into account a more cognitive and detailed quality of the visual message, . . ./o14 *India*'s scenes of group or individual portraits of Indian potters and tailors and of Indian women living in impoverished rural communities become thematic and methodological counterparts to filmed scenes of inter-war British men and women shown in various instances, whether at work or at home, as in, for instance, *Drifters* (John Grierson, 1929), *Housing Problems* (Arthur Elton and E. H. Anstey, 1935), *Coal Face* (Alberto Cavalcanti, GPO Film Unit, 1935) or *Industrial Britain* (Robert Flaherty, 1933) – key productions of the British Documentary Movement. In this particular aesthetic and thematic framework such films, compatible in their historical period and yet divided by their original purpose and audiences, are nevertheless cohesive examples of 'socially useful cinema', of 'more open scriptures', and of interdependent social networks (Aitken 2013: 90).

Second, by replicating the same theoretical exercise of analysing non-documentary films based on Grierson's procrustean theoretical framework, it can be argued that HSBC's *Lemon Grove* functions like an EMB production rather than a modern, politically correct and postcolonial advertisement for global entrepreneurial networks and fair trade. Despite relying on a scripted storyline and employing actors rather than the 'raw material' of native scenes and people, *Lemon Grove*'s visual narrative and its implicit advertising agenda subscribes to Grierson's appeal for socially engaging films that 'deal with issues of choice and action in social environments' (Aitken 2013: 98). Moreover, the belief shared by Grierson and others working for the EMB (1926–33) was that:

> [all that they] wanted to sell was the idea of the Empire as a co-operative venture between living persons interested in each other's work, and in each other's welfare. [Their] task was not to glorify the power of the Empire but to make it live as a society for mutual help, a picture of vivid human interest, as well as of practical promise. (Amery in Aitken 2013: 94)

Following the standards of prestige advertising, this HSBC TV commercial banks on the core theme of interconnectedness and on its ubiquitous power of persuasion: the mutual altruism of 'co-operative venture' of 'a society for mutual help and welfare' – an ideological meme borrowed from earlier evangelical discourses. Moreover, *Lemon Grove* calls for social interaction at local and global levels across a visual and narrative pattern that perpetuates a well-preserved colonial ideology of race and of imperial (global) trade hierarchies. It offers a clear sense of the legacy of violent racism in scenes that, at a first glance, indicate cooperation within a unified gender, race and age framework. Also, the core visual tropes defining the interaction between the two (American and Indian) girls restore the narrative undercurrents specific to the imperial racial supremacy of white Western people over their non-white Eastern partners. The relation between these two entrepreneurial girls, united by age and entrepreneurial impetus but separated by race and continents, is presented as having an implicit long-established, unilateral outcome: the lemonade is sold to and appreciated by

Western customers only. Thus, early and mid-twentieth-century imperial (fair) trade rhetoric is re-enacted in a 2013 TV advertisement that echoes, for instance, *Cargo from Jamaica*, and its storyline dyad of colonised peoples and lands as providers of raw materials and cheap labour, and of colonialist entrepreneurs and markets as sole beneficiaries of the end product, be it exotic commodities or highly marketable organic lemonades. Finally, HSBC's *Lemon Grove* echoes John Grierson's praise of imperial documentary films, which succeed in representing contemporary social realities by 'guid[ing] the spectator into an understanding, cum acceptance, of the status quo' of their historic and economic times (Aitken 2013: 99).

CONCLUSIONS: UNILATERAL ALTRUISM AND IMMUTABLE RACIAL HIERARCHIES

It is often the case that audiences are subjected to images that are difficult to decode as authentic accounts of historical contexts and ideologies. As discussed in this chapter, some colonial missionary films such as the Saint Joseph's Missionary Society's early promotional films are not always examples of crude imperial credos and religious civilising endeavours – by the sheer force of the medium (film) and genre (amateur film) they can instead document to a great extent racial interactions and social networks. Also, twenty-first-century corporate TV advertising might not always be fine-tuned to contemporary political correctness and, by relying on the effects of visual priming shown by their focus groups/audiences, can often propose a racially reductive narrative common to the long tradition of imperial popular culture.

This chapter has proposed a hypothetical analytical framework in which John Grierson's first three principles of documentary film can help redefine the role and place of two case studies, . . ./o14 *India* and *Lemon Grove*, within post-colonial studies of race and free trade. It has been argued that, in following Grierson's aesthetic and film production codes, the Saint Joseph's Missionary Society's early amateur film made in India in the mid to late 1920s could be classified as an *avant la lettre* documentary, while HSBC's second TV commercial in its *Lemon* series could join the list of the EMB Film Unit's productions from the late 1920s and early 1930s. Thus, neither of these two films remain fixed in orthodox theoretical assumptions about their place and meaning within colonial or contemporary popular cultures. As a result, the colonial missionary amateur film . . ./o14

India is paradoxically resisting deep-rooted imperial stereotypes of race and colonised people by echoing the social engagement, narrative patterns and documentary film poetics proposed by Grierson as key features of cinematographic engagement: an engagement based in expressive richness, interpretative potential and the representation of social relationships within empirical representation (Aitken 1998: 41). In this case, scenes filmed by an amateur film-maker challenge imperial ideology with images rich in social-realist rhetoric and confer upon . . ./014 *India*'s thematic and stylistic framework a Griersonian dimension of theoretical and social engagement, and empirical detail. A similar paradoxical reattribution of meaning is offered by HSBC's *Lemon Grove* TV commercial and its idyllic-rich representation of international trade and gendered unified story. Although originally produced to advance corporate capitalism in a playful and uplifting manner, with Western consumers made to believe ('buy') a fair(ytale) trade of entrepreneurial networks and goods outside exploitative business strategies (Kapoor 2013), this TV advertisement perpetuates imperial corporate philanthropic strategies on the robust ideological scaffolding of social stereotype, economic inequality and advertorial campaigns.[15] Lastly, a key feature that unifies . . ./014 *India* and *Lemon Grove* ideologically is the concept and illustration of direct or implicit charity – the time-honoured veneer of imperial racism, from Catholic missionaries treating leprous patients in India (Figure 6.4) to Indian–American lemonade sold by French entrepreneurs (Figure 6.5).[16] In both films the meme of unilateral altruism functions at full power and so disseminates the 'civilising mission' of imperial educationalists, entrepreneurs and missionaries. From this perspective, the Mill Hill Sister cleaning the wounds of a leper patient and the American business-girl buying fresh lemons from her newly accredited Indian 'supplier' share the rhetoric of charitable aid work within the visual and ideological narrative of the West always/still assisting the East in its development. This is acutely relevant today when celebrity philanthropy and Messiah/saviour complex programmes are buttressed by a vast amount of illustrations promoting global networks of dutiful social engagement – an advertising model that often testifies to the stubborn legacy of imperial visual literacy.[17] There are nevertheless numerous recent examples of reversed economic and racial frameworks in which white Western people work for or rely on the benevolence of non-white employers, from Singapore to Paris and via Washington – free individuals seen as active agents of change, rather than as 'passive recipients of dispensed benefits' (Sen 1999: xiii).

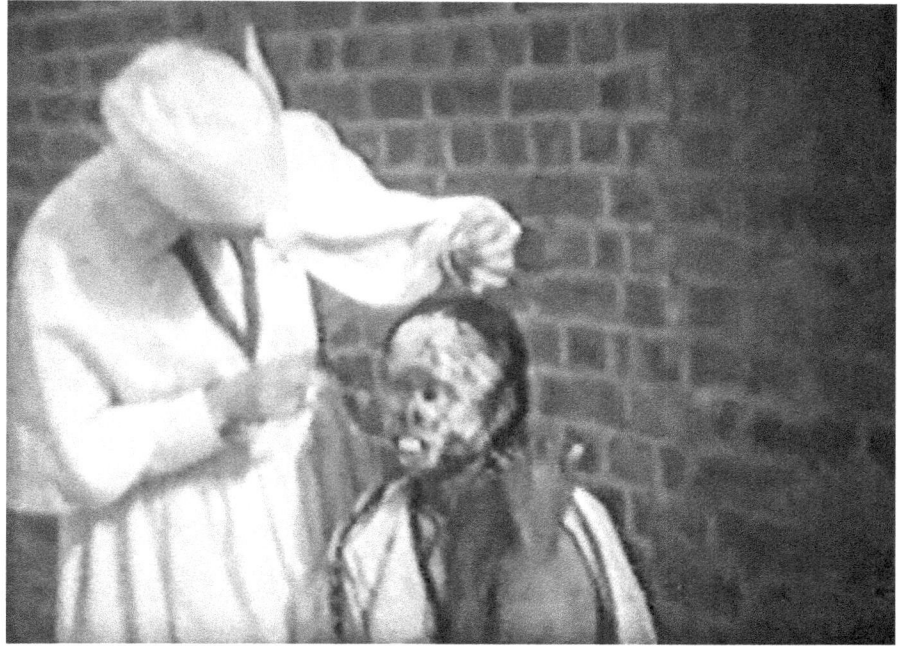

Figure 6.4: *Saint Joseph's Missionary Society Collection*, India, 1928–32 © BECM, screen capture.

However, the ever growing and reassuring statistics confirming this new dynamic cannot yet fully reshape the unrelenting tradition of racial discrimination and stereotyping. This is a distinctive feature of . . . /o14 India and Lemon Grove, which the former film's visual and social engagement rhetoric escapes by echoing John Grierson's principles of documentary film, while the latter film has its elan of multicultural, gender empowering and political correctness punctured by its unwitting exercise in doubly patronising race and gender interrelations.

Although ideologies and historical interpretations could easily be misconstrued, observable behaviour, whether recorded as such or performed for the camera, remains relevant and revelatory. Theories of perception, visual priming and of documentary film-making can often help elucidate how and why some of the early twentieth-century colonial (missionary) amateur films and mid-2010s expensive TV commercials denote unrelenting patterns of ideological and cultural affinities defining the pervasive cruelty of a global, well-hidden and highly active racism. In the light of this, it is possible to suggest that not all colonial

Figure 6.5: *Lemon Grove*, India, 2013 © HSBC, screen capture.

(non-fiction, amateur) films anchored in imperial social, educational or religious proselytising agendas are devoid of an authentic documentary merit, one that transcends their propagandistic function.[18] Equally, it could be argued that not all films produced in a spirit of global philanthropy and corporate political, racial and gender awareness and correctness are free from 'contamination' by racism and cultural stereotypification; most such films continue to risk perpetuating visual memes common to colonial times. Hence, although produced almost a century apart and for allegedly opposing purposes, . . ./o14 *India* and *Lemon Grove* function harmoniously within and beyond a fixed historical and cultural framework. Finally, when assessed as primary research sources within unconventional theoretical frameworks such as the one employed here – John Grierson's principles of documentary film and theories of visual priming – these films operate as interchangeable visual records that call for new, extra-curricular perspectives on South Asia's role in shaping modern cultural and racial dynamics.

NOTES

1. https://www.youtube.com/watch?v=3TuLF7UogIo. Links given in the first seven notes in this chapter were last accessed on 30 April 2016.
2. https://www.youtube.com/watch?v=DhH7Ln79Liw.

3. https://vimeo.com/117041899.
4. http://www.about.hsbc.co.uk.
5. https://www.youtube.com/watch?v=4mNJx_LX9bE.
6. https://www.youtube.com/watch?v=yOcto5ANPC4.
7. See, for instance, Christian Jensen, 'The Adgenda: "Lemonade" ads are a smart move from HSBC' (http://www.newstatesman.com/business/2013/04/adgenda-lemonade-ads-are-smart-move-hsbc), and Spectrum Insight, 4 June 2013, at http://www.spectruminsight.net/spectruminsight-study-reveals-twitter-based-insight-can-deliver-significant-benefits-over-traditional-market-research/2013/06/.
8. The former British Empire and Commonwealth Museum (BECM, Bristol, UK) held ninety-seven film reels on 16mm and 8mm and glass plates dating from early 1900s to the mid 1960s. Bristol City Museum and Bristol Record Office now hold the BECM Collections.
9. For convenience, this film will be identified in this chapter as .../014 India.
10. For instance, *Panorama of Calcutta* (Warwick Trading Company, 1901), *Gibraltar* (Rosie Film Company, 1911), *India* (Eastern Exploration Company, 1927) or *The Kendal/Vernede Collection* (BECM, 1997/153/021).
11. On the theme of Christian parallels in Bollywood films see note in *Internet Evangelism Day*: 'If you like film, understand and love the Indian culture, and can present the Gospel in culturally appropriate terms to those of a mainly Hindu background, here is a God-given strategy to touch the rapidly growing numbers of online Indians, both in India itself and around the world.' Accessed on 3 June 2015 at http://www.internetevangelismday.com/bollywood.php.
12. For instance, *Sanders of the River* (Zoltan Korda, 1935), *Lives of a Bengal Lancer* (Henry Hathaway, 1935), *The Charge of the Light Brigade* (Michael Curtiz, 1936), *The Four Feathers* (Zoltan Korda, 1938) or *Gunga Din* (George Stevens, 1939).
13. See http://www.campaignlive.co.uk, accessed on 30 April 2016.
14. For instance, Alfred C. Haddon's *Torres Strait* film of the 1898 Cambridge expedition, Robert J. Flaherty's *avant la lettre* ethno-fictions *Nanook of the North* (1922), *Moana – A Romance of the Golden Age* (1926) and *Man of Aran* (1934), F. W. Murnau's *Tabu* (1936) or Luis Buñuel's *Las Hurdes: Tierra Sin Pan/Land Without Bread* (1934).
15. An advertorial is 'a newspaper or magazine advertisement giving information about a product in the style of an editorial or objective journalistic article' (*Oxford Advanced Learners' Dictionary*).
16. See 'Is lemonade legal? Testing the limits of silliness in East Texas', *The Economist*, 11 July 2015, p. 41 for a discussion on replacing traditional low-key trade practices with cottage-food charity tactics.
17. Several charities promoting community-based corporate philanthropy as a form of international corporate social responsibility are endorsed by Oprah Winfrey, Madonna, Gwyneth Paltrow, Richard Gere, George Clooney, Kim Kardashian, Scarlett Johansson, or by the 'I am African' campaign (http://www.keepachildalive.org/i_am_african/i_am_african.html). Moreover, racist narratives are still found in allegedly unbiased advertisements such as the 2009 Cadbury Milk chocolate *Big Plant Cocoa Farm*, which includes a series of anthropometric portraits of Ghanaian people (TC: 02:09) (https://www.youtube.com/watch?v=2ktLtvinZBs), or the Thai commercial for *Black Herbal Toothpaste*

(https://www.youtube.com/watch?v=moNU9KULHO8). All links accessed on 30 April 2016.
18. Of note, these films' propagandistic function remains nevertheless a valuable feature, rich with historical data relevant to most scholars of media and social anthropology.

REFERENCES

Aitken, Ian (2013), *Film and Reform: John Grierson and the Documentary Film Movement*, London: Routledge.
Aitken, Ian (ed.) (1998), *The Documentary Film Movement, An Anthology*, Edinburgh: Edinburgh University Press.
Anderson, Roy Allan (1956), 'A new visual aid for evangelism', *The Ministry*, May, accessed 1 March 2015 at https://www.ministrymagazine.org/archive/1956/05/a-new-visual-aid-for-evangelism.
Bargh, John A. (2006), 'What have we been priming all these years? On the development, mechanisms, and ecology of non-conscious social behavior', *European Journal of Social Psychology*, 36, 147–68.
Beveridge, James (1978), *John Grierson: Film Master*, London: Macmillan.
Blackmore, Susan (1999), *The Meme Machine*, Oxford: Oxford University Press.
Bonaventura (Saint) (1941), *Liber III, Sententiarum: Dist. IX, Art. I, Quaestio II, Opera Theologica Selecta*, Florence: ex typographia Collegii S. Bonaventura, p. 194.
Dillard, James Price, and Peck, Eugenia (2000), 'Affect and persuasion: emotional response to public service announcements', *Communication Research*, 27, 461–95.
Doyen, S., Klein O., Pichon C. L. and Cleeremans, A. (2012), 'Behavioural priming: it's all in the mind, but whose mind?', *PLoS ONE*, 7: 1, accessed on 5 February 2015 at e29081.doi:10.1371/journal.pone.0029081.
Edinburgh House Bureau for Visual Aids, Films for Church and Youth (1947), *A selected list of 16 mm background films for use in churches and youth groups*, Conference of Missionary Societies in Great Britain and Ireland, London: Edinburgh House Press.
Evans, Garry (1991), *In the National Interest: A Chronicle of the National Film Board of Canada from 1949–1989*, Toronto/London: University of Toronto Press.
Froom, Fenton E. (1947), 'Visual evangelism and visual aids', *The Ministry*, October, accessed on 1 March 2015 at https://www.ministrymagazine.org/archive/1947/10/unknown.
Gardner W., Gabriel, S. and Lee, A. (1999), '"I" value freedom, but "we" value relationships: self-construal priming mirrors cultural differences in judgment', *Psychological Science*, 10, 321–6.
Grierson, John [1926] (1979) 'First principles of documentary', in Forsyth Hardy (ed.), *Grierson on Documentary*, London/Boston: Faber & Faber, pp. 35–46.
Kapoor, Ilan (2013), *Celebrity Humanitarianism: The Ideology of Global Charity*, London: Routledge.
Lindvall, Terry (2007), *Sanctuary Cinema: Origins of the Christian Film Industry*, New York: New York University Press.
Low, Rachel (1979), *The History of the British Film 1929–39: Documentary and Educational Films of the 1930s*, London: Allen & Unwin.

McCabe, Maisie (2013), *HSBC Shows the Power of International Connections in 'The Lemon Grove'*, 4 March, accessed on 23 February 2015 at http://www.campaignlive.co.uk.
Russell, Patrick (2007), *100 British Documentaries*, London: British Film Institute, pp. 55–7.
Sen, Amartya (1999), *Development as Freedom*, Oxford: Oxford University Press.
Swan, Paul (2008), *The British Documentary Film Movement, 1926–1946*, Cambridge: Cambridge University Press.
Winston, Brian (2014), 'The Griersonian tradition postwar: decline or transition?' *Journal of British Cinema and Television*, 11: 1, 101–15.

CHAPTER 7

Conversion, Salvation and the 'Civilising Mission': Christian Missions and Documentary Film in India (1900–60)

Emma Sandon

The large missionary film collections held in various British archives attest to the extent of mission activity in parts of the world where British missionaries travelled to proselytise Christianity.[1] Many missionary societies used film as well as other visual media, including photographs, lantern slides and filmstrips, in the first half of the twentieth century. In order to understand how Protestant and Anglo-Catholic organisations adopted film to convert and recruit, and to raise funds for the spread of the Christian faith, this chapter will look at examples of documentaries from these film collections that were made in India between the 1900s and the 1950s, and will also discuss related films mentioned in catalogues and missionary literature but of which there are no copies in the various archives. India was a key site for British missionary activities in the British Empire. It became a British Dominion of the said empire, and was named the Empire of India in 1876, after the British East India Company had transferred its rule to the British Crown in 1858. The film collections cover the period from the turn of the nineteenth century up until the decade after India's independence from Britain in 1947.

The films that will be discussed here draw on styles of early actualities, travelogues, films that constructed a sense of travel and showed tourist views of places, and popular ethnographic dramas that involve staging and filming scenes of the everyday life of people from another culture. Subjects include farming, fishing, hunting, culinary methods, craft and building techniques, ceremonial performance and religious activities, as well as familial relations, social structures and governance.[2] The films also fall under categories such as travel, educational and instructional documentary, as well as drama-documentary or documentary-drama, broadly defined as hybrid forms of film-making that re-enact and reconstruct actual events through characterisation and actuality footage. The films cover a range of missionary work, including proselytising and converting Indian subjects to Christianity, and church activities promoting the introduction of Western health and education as part of a 'civilising mission'. They also portray the building and expansion of churches, mission stations, hospitals and schools. The films were made to envision missionary work overseas for British audiences and were circulated to raise funds and encourage the recruitment of staff from Britain to work in the missions. Some missions also screened their films widely in the regions in which their missionaries worked, including in schools and during religious services, in order to convert and recruit indigenous people to assist in running these religious educational and health establishments. Missionary organisations competed for influence in different parts of the British Empire and the films illustrate how rural village communities in India were often regarded as particularly fertile recruitment grounds for Christianity, and how they were targeted through the provision of schools and hospitals.

The growth of British missions overseas has a long and complex history and a complicated, often conflicting, relationship with imperial interests.[3] Scholarly work on the global spread of Christianity has recently begun to examine the role of media technologies in the dissemination of Christian religious beliefs and ideas. Some attention has been given to the involvement of Christians in the cinema industry (Bottomore 2005, Lindvall 2007, Lindvall and Quicke 2011, Machin 1992). There are, however, few studies of the widespread use of documentary film by missions in religious teaching in education and social improvement contexts. Missionary films have sometimes been described as amateur films or home movies, as a number of societies, for example the London Missionary Society (LMS) and the Methodist Missionary Society (MMS), used 16mm film, a format that was originally introduced in the 1920s for amateur use as an alternative to the more cumbersome 35mm equipment.[4] However, the use of 16mm cannot be regarded as indicative of a purely amateur purpose. By the

1930s, 16mm as a semi-professional format had entered the educational market that had begun to flourish as an alternative to theatrical film exhibition, although some missionary productions still continued to be shot on 35mm film.

Assumptions have also been made about the marginality of missionary films' circulation compared to mainstream cinema-going and therefore to everyday film-viewing experiences. Francis Gooding argues that films made by mission societies in effect preached to the converted, reflecting churchgoers' ideas about the mission field and the importance of the work of their missions, in order to raise funds and support and attract volunteers (Gooding 2010). However, besides the centrality of Christianity in public and domestic life in British society in the first half of the twentieth century, there is also evidence that these films, circulating through non-theatrical screenings in churches, schools and educational circuits, were seen by more people than has previously been recognised. This chapter also argues that missionary films were clearly influenced by instructional and educational film practices that have recently become of interest to film scholars (Acland and Wasson 2011, Orgeron et al. 2011). The films are more sophisticated and more professionally produced than many amateur and home movie films, being well shot and edited and often filmed by experienced cinematographers such as Henry Howse, who worked on newsreel and feature films in Britain, South Africa and America; Deane Henry Dickason, an American director and producer of travel films; and Norman Spurr, who worked for the British Colonial Film Unit.[5] In addition to these there were also missionaries who trained themselves, including such as T. H. Baxter, Lieutenant Colonel Roussel, Robert O. Latham and Wilfred Le Cato Edwards, who worked for the Salvation Army (SA), the Church Missionary Society (CMS), the LMS and the MMS, as well as for interdenominational bodies, such as the Missionary Film Committee (MFC) and the Religious Film Society.

In terms of storytelling and their use of documentary styles, missionary films are arguably equivalent to other documentary films of their period, particularly those shot in the 1920s and 1930s. They reflect particular approaches to documentary using hybrid drama-documentary styles popular at the time with British documentary and colonial film-makers. They create narratives and representations found in colonial films, counterpoising images of 'primitivism' with 'civilisation', as well as using Christian tropes, metaphors and rhetorical strategies such as 'darkness' and 'light', the embodiment of the saviour, the healer and the sick or the unwashed 'heathen'. Some denominations did not initially approve of the popular medium of film and not all mission societies were keen to use this new technology of communication. The archival collections provide the evidence however, that societies such as the CMS, the Church of Scotland (CoS), the LMS, the MMS, the SA, and the Saint Joseph's Missionary Society, were quick to adopt and use film for the purposes of evangelism.[6] This chapter will discuss a selection of documentaries to examine what British missionary societies were producing for educational and religious non-theatrical exhibition.

THE SALVATION ARMY: SOCIAL WORK AND SALVATION FOR TRIBAL COMMUNITIES

The Salvation Army church showed an early awareness of the power of the new film medium with its first films being made in 1903. Cox attributes the SA's use of cinema, adopted alongside that of lantern slides, to its love of showmanship, in which the SA staged celebrations, festivities and pageants involving fireworks, processions and drama (Cox 2008: 238). *Commissioner Higgins visits Ahmedabad Girl's School* (SA, 1904) is one of thirteen films shot in India between 1903 and 1906. It covers the farewell tour of Commissioner Edward Higgins before he retired from his post as resident International Secretary of the SA for India. Lieutenant Colonel Roussel filmed the girls of the industrial school performing a dance drill with flowers for the visiting party of Higgins and his small group of accompanying male and female Salvationists in two wide tableaux shots. The girls are dressed in traditional saris, as is their teacher, Captain Karmala Bai, who conducts their dance. The missionary women in the visiting party are also wearing saris, in keeping with SA practice of adopting indigenous attire and clothing, as well as pith helmets (Fletcher 2015: 59). According to Tom Rice, the film promotes the Army's work in education. At the time, the SA was running 415 day schools and eleven industrial boarding schools.[7] Roussel also shot other films for the SA depicting the Army's social service and welfare work in the compulsory vocational re-education of ex-prisoners, their hospitals, rescue homes for women, homes for children orphaned by famine; and processions of SA officers. In addition to this, Roussel also shot films on the 'Christianisation of villages' by the SA, events that involved acts of destruction of Hindu temples and what the SA referred to as 'heathen idols' (Fletcher 2015: 63–4). The SA claimed in 1904 that they had over 2,000 outposts in India and Ceylon, the majority of which had established SA corps.[8]

The SA, however, closed its Cinematograph Department in 1908, as it joined an anti-obscenity campaign in Britain, led by the National

Social Purity Crusade (renamed National Council of Public Morals in 1910), against the 'immoral' behaviour of people in public social spaces. The campaigners claimed that anti-social conduct was encouraged by film exhibition taking place on Sundays, and through the representation of 'disreputable' or criminal behaviour, including those involving sex, drinking, fighting, violence and killing (Rapp 1996: 183). The SA did not, however, abandon film-making immediately but phased out its use of the medium over the following few years. Tony Fletcher lists some of the cinematograph shows and film lectures given by the SA between 1907 and 1912 in India and described in their paper, *War Cry*, shows and lectures that attracted thousands of people at a sitting (2015: 78). By 1914 the SA had, however, ceased its cinema services and closed its film library, and made few films after that date.

One of the films the SA did, however, produce after 1914 is *From India's Coral Strand* (SA, 1925), sections of which are held at the National Film and Television Archive, BFI Collections, and listed on the Colonial Film website as *Salvation Army Work in India, Burma and Ceylon* (SA, 1925). The film presents the SA work with villages that the British imperial government had designated as populated with 'criminal tribes'. 'Criminal tribes' was a legal designation for peoples from low castes and tribal communities created by the Criminal Tribes Acts of 1871 and 1911, Acts that effectively criminalised people from birth. Fakir Singh (the Indian name adopted by Salvationist Frederick de Lautour Tucker, later Booth-Tucker) was at the forefront of SA work with the 'criminal tribes'. The mission began to establish what were known as 'criminal settlements' from 1908, the responsibility of which was delegated to SA by the Indian colonial government, which had failed to run them successfully. The SA built settlements in different regions of British India, for example, the first settlement established was in the United Provinces (now Uttar Pradesh and Uttarakhand), for the Dommara in Gorakhpur, followed by the Hewittpur settlement for the Haburahs.[9] In the Punjab, they set up the Sir Louis Dane Weaving School and Industrial Home (named after the Lieutenant Governor of the Punjab who provided government funds for it) and the settlement Changa Manga for tree-felling labour for the Forest Department (Cox 2002: 240–1). One of the scenes in this film features the SA officers converting Bhil peoples of Rajasthan, also registered as a 'criminal tribe'. A female Salvationist encourages a Bhil woman to remove her traditional bracelets on the grounds that spirituality does not require material possessions (see Figure 7.1). Conversion was not the only aim of Salvationists, as they believed that converts needed to achieve full sanctification or holiness, a state of unworldliness, through abstinence and lack of material possessions.

CONVERSION, SALVATION AND THE 'CIVILISING MISSION' 153

Figure 7.1: *Salvation Army Work in India, Burma and Ceylon* (1925, 35mm, Salvation Army). Inter-title: 'The Salvation Army stands for definite conversion and separation from the things of the world'. Courtesy of BFI.

This film also shows scenes of the Catherine Booth Memorial hospital in Nagercoil, Kanyakumari, Madras Presidency (now Tamil Nadu). Bullock carts and the new 'Motor Ambulance' bring in sick and injured patients to the hospital. British and Indian medical orderlies are seen at work treating patients, administering medicine, dealing with maternity needs of women and weighing babies. The film then presents the different departments, 'The Dental Department' with shots of people having extractions and denture fittings, and 'The Ophthalmic Department' where, according to the inter-titles, 'these men came to the hospital quite blind and have since received their sight'. No further detail about the cause of their blindness is given, but the implication is that modern medicine can perform miracles. These scenes of hospitals and medical personnel administering to patient needs are common to many of the films made by different missionary societies.

From India's Coral Strand was exhibited in Britain in 1926 and an accompanying brochure was also issued. The film was shown as part of a live musical show performed by Ellen Olsen, a Swedish missionary known by her adopted Indian name of 'Khushi', who had first gone to India in 1914. She toured the show in halls in Britain over an eight-month period with her party of eight girls from the Satara Girls' School, Maharashtra. The film was made to raise funds for SA work in India and Ceylon, although it was not altogether a financial success, partly due to the SA having already distanced itself from film production by this time (Fletcher 2015: 86). The cinematograph was part of the entertainment strategy used by the SA to attract both adults and children from the working classes in Britain and rural audiences in India to their proselytising events. They did this in the early days of film, before cinemas became commercially established as places for entertainment. Once the Salvationists decided that cinemas and the showing of commercial film could be sinful, the question of their producing and screening films also became compromised, and they eventually stopped making documentaries about their mission activities, moral dramas about abstinence and sin, and showing films of Bible stories in their lectures and meetings. While the SA's use of film for purposes of evangelism lasted for only a short period of time, it certainly served to draw public attention to the SA, and drew significant numbers to their proselytising events.

THE METHODIST MISSIONARY SOCIETY: EDUCATION AND CONVERSION IN ADIVASI COMMUNITIES

The MMS also used film alongside other media and forms of performance, including lantern slides and filmstrips, photography, plays, music and broadcasting on radio. The MMS was formed in 1932 from a merger between the Wesleyan Methodist Missionary Society (WMMS), foreign missions of the United Methodist Church (which had already brought together a number of Methodist missions in 1907); and the Primitive Methodist Church.[10] The Society made films consistently from the late 1920s up until the late 1950s, although before that the WMMS was also involved in various interdenominational film collaborations. The MMS also published articles and photographs of film events in their magazines, *Foreign Field* and *HOD* (Home Organisation Department), for supporters. *HOD* advertised films to be shown in churches or cinemas for two to three evenings at a time. The MMS was committed to advancing the education of women and attracted women missionaries to teach in the overseas mission schools in their recruitment drives. They were also keen to recruit from the local communities in India to join their missions and take up positions as lay preachers (evangelists who preach but are not ordained) and ordained clergy.

One of the films the MMS produced, *Lakshini the Santal Girl* (MMS, 1930) was filmed in the Bankura district in West Bengal, where the mission ran a school and a hospital. It was made by Reverend W. Le Cato Edwards, who shot a large number of films for the MMS, the LMS and for interdenominational missionary bodies set up to produce films.[11] *Lakshini the Santal Girl* is about a girl from the Santal tribe, who is taken from her family to be educated at Sarenga Methodist Girls' School.[12] The theme of 'primitiveness' informs the first inter-title, 'Depicting life among the Santals, an aboriginal people living in and around Sarenga, Bengal'. This is followed by another inter-title: 'A Santal Village', which accompanies a shot of men and boys herding their cows and water buffalos along a path, past huts and people, towards and past the camera. They are followed by women carrying wood bundles on their heads, and by one woman who balances pots while holding a child on her hip.

Using an ethnographic style popular at the time the film then establishes how Lakshini lives with her brothers and parents through presenting their activities on the verandas in the courtyard of their mud-structured house. The older brother is playing with a bow and arrow while Lakshini helps her mother with the housework, giving the sick younger brother water to drink from a bowl, and grinding and sifting grain to make flour. We are shown the mother going to collect water from the river with other women, while the father and elder son go hunting, inter-titles reminding us that this is a pre-modern culture: 'The Santals are among the few races who still hunt with bow and arrow.' We see a staged scene with one of the men killing a wild boar. The next scene is of Methodist missionaries visiting the village, bringing with them a gramophone, a scene which draws on the trope of images of 'primitive' peoples' encounters with modern technologies in colonial films. A missionary visits Lakshini's home to suggest that she should be educated, and her parents agree to this. She walks for some miles to reach the boarding school at Sarenga accompanied by her father and brother, who carry the bed she will sleep on. On route they stop for refreshment, lighting a fire using a traditional method of friction between two pieces of wood.

The film then moves to the story of Lakshini's progress to civilisation, pre-empted by the inter-title: 'Now see Lakshini developing under modern educational methods.' The film shows Lakshini at the school. Whole scenes are devoted to her, dressed in school uniform, learning to read, write and understand the Bible (Figure 7.2).

The older girls work in the rice fields and later all the girls visit the Sarenga Methodist Church. The documentary shows the architecture

Figure 7.2: Lakshini at school learning Bible stories (1930, Methodist Missionary Society). Courtesy of BFI.

of the buildings and surroundings, contrasting this to that of the village and the home Lakshini has left. Lakshini's progress in education is symbolised through shots of her sitting for examinations. During her time at school she becomes ill and is taken for treatment to the Sarenga Methodist Hospital. While Lakshini's illness is performed for the benefit of viewers, who, through that illness, are able to see the hospital at work, the film also documents the arrival and treatment of a man who is badly injured, to further reinforce the positive role played by the missionaries. Lakshini recovers and then walks back to school while the injured man, now bandaged, is taken by cart back to his village. Finally, Lakshini wins a scholarship to the secondary boarding school in the city and the film closes with her, now a mature girl, being waved off by fellow students, and she is no longer on foot, but transported by vehicle to her new life.

This film uses the story of Lakshini to illustrate the achievements of the mission in providing education and health care. The mission's approach to proselytising among tribal or Adivasi communities, who were outside of the caste system, was one that many mission societies advocated. The MMS was also keen to convert young women whom they perceived might be influential in the future in their communities and did this through first recruiting young girls, removing them from their homes, and then educating them in both western ways of living and the values of Christianity. The film's emphasis on the Indian teachers at the school and the Indian medical staff working at the mission hospital implies that Lakshini will return with professional training and join the mission staff as a nurse or teacher. This film showcases the mission institutions and the social work that the Methodist church was providing for people in India. Contrary to the SA films, in which army-style discipline leads to salvation, this Methodist narrative is more about how education and Christianity can provide long-term benefits to marginalised indigenous groups, better enabling them to enter modern life in India. Hardiman comments that missionaries also had a strong presence in educational and medical work in many Adivasi areas because the Adivasis were thought to be more reachable than those within the caste system: 'adivasi society ... was seen as being free from the stranglehold of caste'. This however, is qualified by his observation that conversions in these communities were actually few in number (Hardiman 2006: 144).

The MMS film collection includes a range of films that addressed different audience tastes. Apart from social improvement stories using popular ethnographic drama-documentary styles, there are other films that use themes of biblical significance, such as the stories of disciples and their conversion to Christianity. Two drama-documentaries that Le Cato Edwards filmed for the MMS were on the difficulties of converting people to Christianity in villages divided by different castes and sub-castes; a subject that missions in India were particularly concerned about. New evangelical missions often also advocated the abolition of caste among Indian Christians, in contrast to those missions operating in South India in the earlier part of the nineteenth century, which had not. For example *Through Fires of Persecution* (MMS, 1935) is presented as 'A True to Fact Story from the Trichinopoly District of South India' about 'outcast' villagers who want to convert to Christianity.[13] The film depicts elders discussing their problems with an Indian minister, the outcome being that four convert to Christianity. These men are then subject to persecution by their Brahmin overlords, who send their servants to assault the men and their wives, smashing the water pots they are filling at the river and burning the wood they have collected for fuel. When, however, the converts stand firm against their persecutors, others follow their example and convert to Christianity and the film reinforces this with shots of people being baptised by the minister and attending the church in large numbers at Dharapuram. *Trial and Triumph: The Story of Vekata Rao of Hyderabad, South India* (MMS, 1944) has a similar theme about a man from an unnamed 'caste' who becomes a Christian and is ordained. He is beaten and persecuted by his fellow villagers, yet nonetheless succeeds in winning his family over to become baptised as Christians. The message of these two films is that Christians should stand firm in their faith in the face of opposition and persecution, and that Christianity will benefit those who convert and be ultimately rewarding, as, in the eyes of the Christian God, everyone is equal.

Not all MMS films used drama-documentary. A later yet notable documentary in the MMS collection is *Fighting Leprosy in India: The Work at Dichpali*, (MMS, c. 1945), one of a number of missionary films made about leprosy asylums. The film is about the treatment of this biblically associated disease and the redemption of sufferers through Western medicine and Christian faith. It was made at the Methodist Victoria Treatment Hospital, originally set up by Isabel Kerr, a Scottish medical missionary with the Wesleyan mission station at Dichpali, near Nizamabad, in the princely state of Hyderabad under the British Raj (now Andhra Pradesh and Telangana) in South India.[14] Dr John Lowe, who took over the running of the Dichpali hospital from Kerr, reported between 1925 and 1943 on his work there in *Foreign Field*, the Methodist in-house magazine on its overseas missions. *Fighting Leprosy in India* picks up on these reports, visually showcasing the 'hydnocarpus oil treatment' used at the hospital. The film opens with shots of the layout of the buildings at Dichpali. There are private wards, which house people from all over India, an inter-title claims, while another tells us that the film offers a glimpse of the 820 patients, while 1,462 others were regretfully refused admission. This information is intended to act as an appeal to viewers for funds. The camera then shows British missionary nurses treating patients with injections, Indian medical staff looking at samples through microscopes, and shots of women patients collecting hydnocarpus seeds from trees for use in treatments. Scenes show how the colony is, as is claimed, self-sustaining through the labour of patients, whom we see digging, building and harvesting. Further scenes demonstrate how well treated people living in the asylum are, with food being provided by the mission and shots of an Indian hospital sister giving out rations of rice to assembled patients.

A key sequence shows large groups of patients gathered for the occasion of the film production. They sit or stand, facing the camera. Then a missionary enters the frame and the camera pans with him as he walks alongside the crowds. He motions to some of the boys to jump up and down for the shot, a tactic designed to demonstrate their recovery. Another striking sequence shows the physical recovery of 'individual patients'. They are framed one by one, through a device of a centred camera that moves in a 180 degrees semi-circle to film each person in turn. None of the sixteen boys and men are named as they are revealed face-to-camera in mid-shot, bare to the waist, portrayed to represent types from all over India in a manner similar to that of colonial, scientific photographic practice. The men smile or stare at the camera, one salutes it. This kind of treatment of leprosy in India was soon to be replaced. Already, by 1945, it was known that the treatment with refined oils developed by Western medicine from traditional Indian medicine and used widely during the 1920s and 1930s was often ineffective, extremely uncomfortable and painful to those who were administered the injections, and even caused harmful side-effects such as ulcers (Shankar 2006: 283–4).

Fighting Leprosy in India, and previous films mentioned, demonstrate the wide range of drama-documentaries and documentaries the MMS made to promote its mission work in India. Unlike the SA, who used film to draw large audiences to their evangelising events, the MMS used film more as an educational tool and developed policy to promote its use in schools and religious teaching. This recognition of the power of film to persuade also ensured Methodist interest in interdenominational collaborations in film production. While depictions of the 'primitive' are embedded in the MMS films, drawing on tropes found in popular ethnographic colonial films and other representations, they more consistently nevertheless emphasise the mission's modernisation programme of educational and health work.

THE LONDON MISSIONARY SOCIETY: PREACHING TO THE CONVERTED AND ECUMENICAL WORK

Another missionary society that used film extensively was the London Missionary Society (LMS).[15] Thirteen LMS films made in India between 1930 and 1950 are deposited in the collections of the National Film and Television Archive, BFI. These documentaries promote the LMS mission hospitals and schools in South India. Howard Diamond, the LMS assistant treasurer, writing for the *Chronicle: A Magazine of World Enterprise*, in 1936, reported that there were two cameras that rotated between the LMS missions, and footage was sent for editing to London before the films were released for screening all over Britain (Diamond 1936: 254). Gooding (2011) has written about LMS filmmaking activities, and this chapter will, therefore, not elaborate in any detail on their films; other than to highlight the seriousness with which the LMS engaged with film in order to promote their educational and health work in India (Gooding 2010, 2011). Gooding acknowledges that the LMS had a considered policy towards film based on an active programme of film-making which lasted from the 1930s up until the late 1950s, and consisted of educational and religious films distributed through their film library. Gooding also suggests, however, that the films were not particularly effective, or well made. He, for example, quotes a 1946 review in *The Church's Guide to Films for Religious Use* that did not regard the LMS films as sufficiently well made.[16]

Yet the Indian films made for the LMS by Le Cato Edwards between 1930 and 1939, were, arguably, of a more professional quality than others made by LMS.[17] After the end of the Second World War, the LMS also occasionally appointed other experienced film-makers to work on films, most notably Deane Dickason, an American producer and director of travel films, who made *Health for India* (LMS, 1946). Apart from its own productions about LMS missions in India, Africa, Papua New Guinea and Samoa, the Society was also committed to ecumenical film production, and was involved in, for example, the International Missionary Council project entitled the Bantu Educational Kinema Experiment, which made films for African audiences (Gooding 2011: 248–53).[18] By the 1950s, however, it could be said that LMS had reverted back to more amateur film production for use within the Society. The role of the LMS photographer and film-maker was taken up by Reverend Robert O. Latham. He wrote the voice-over script for *India Mission* (LMS, 1950) and published guidance on how to run follow-up discussions with the screening of films, and on the importance of reciting prayers at the beginning and the end of the session. By this time, however, LMS was no longer leading ecumenical initiatives in developing film for educational needs.

THE CHURCH OF SCOTLAND: CHRISTIANITY UNITES ALL ETHNIC COMMUNITIES AND CASTES

In contrast to the LMS, there are fewer examples of films made in India by the CoS, and those in the archives, additionally, only date from the 1950s onwards. The CoS Foreign Mission Committee first sent missionaries to India in the 1830s but the CoS then experienced a major split when people left to set up the Free Church of Scotland. This scission had an impact on the CoS's overseas mission activities, and, as a result, the church only began establishing stations and building churches and colleges in India from the 1870s onwards. The CoS and Free Church

CONVERSION, SALVATION AND THE 'CIVILISING MISSION'   161

of Scotland reunited again in 1929 and then withdrew from India in 1948, after the declaration of the independence of India. The CoS was also influential in the emergence of the United Church of Northern India, formed in 1924 from a union of Congregational (American) and Presbyterian Churches.

Kalimpong (CoS, 1953), produced by James Ballantyne for the CoS Foreign Mission Committee, represents a pivotal moment in the history of the CoS.[19] The documentary is about the United Church of Northern India, based at the MacFarlane Memorial Church, in West Bengal, Darjeeling, and named after the Reverend William MacFarlane, who opened schools in the 1870s for the CoS, first in Darjeeling, then in Kalimpong. The film presents the history of the CoS in the area by adopting a travelogue style. There are scenes of everyday life, with many shots of people in groups and of individuals working and at leisure. An inter-title states that the church converted many Lepcha, the indigenous tribal peoples of the area, and also Nepali, who migrated to the area during the time of British rule as Kalimpong developed into an important commercial trading post for furs, wool and grain. There are portraits in the film of ministers, pastors and plainsmen from the Lepcha, Nepali and Oraon communities; as well as from Sikkim, a neighbouring state. The film emphasises the Church's ability to accommodate, and indeed 'unite', all the different ethnic and cultural traditions that coexist in Kalimpong, including refugees from China, Tibet, the Soviet Union and Mongolia; all of whom are portrayed. The film also includes children, and attempts to show things from a child's point of view, such as when a portrait of a boy playing with a toy is accompanied by the inter-title, 'my turn next'. Other inter-titles address the audience directly, with statements such as 'beggars from Tibet' alongside group portraits of children facing the camera, or with questions such as 'Can we meet their greater need?' *Kalimpong* shows a wide range of images of the bustling life of the town and its importance as a trading centre through shots of its markets, playgrounds, fairgrounds and street scenes.

Ten minutes into the film, its political purpose is also broached when the famous Buddhist monastery Zang Dhok Palri Phodang in Kalimpong is shown. The monastery and the town became an important centre for Buddhism, particularly after 1950, when the government of the People's Republic of China sent troops to occupy Tibet, declaring that the territory would become part of China. While implicitly critiquing this, however, the film also promotes Christianity as a better alternative to communism than Buddhism. Using the attractions of a travelogue style, the monastery building and flags waving in the wind are filmed, and there are long shots of mountain landscape views, followed by close-ups of male priests and their acolytes (young boys) in the Tibetan red and yellow robes, playing traditional musical instruments. The film here even attempts to belittle their beliefs and practices in order to bolster a stronger representation of Christianity. Scenes of Buddhist devotion by men and boys are contrasted with scenes of the large numbers of local women going to attend a service at the United Church of Northern India. Shots of different ethnic groups mingling outside the church are also followed by shots of ministers from the different communities of the Lepcha and Nepali. Inter-titles inform us that the church schools in the area are teaching literacy in native languages. Through close-ups, we also see girls learning to act, sew and make crafts at the Kalimpong Girls' High School, and boys running and playing sports at the Boys' High School.

Three British Woman's Guild missionaries are also filmed who, we are told, have been in service for thirty years at the Charteris Hospital, which first opened in 1893, and the film inter-title then asks, 'who will succeed them?'; a recruitment and funding ploy to draw in audiences to consider what their own role might be in the future of the hospital. The film then tours the medical block and the maternity wards, before showing the isolation blocks for tuberculosis and an Indian medical officer at a table outside, seeing a line of patients and prescribing them medicine. The film documents nurses training, children being weighed at the Kalimpong welfare centre, and finally shows the leper hospital buildings in which treatment, injections, remunerative work and recreation take place as part of the leper therapy. Inter-art college students are presented as the future leaders for the church and the community. Indigenous Christian preachers from many different ethnic backgrounds are shown to lead evangelism in the future India. Liladhar, a Brahmin converted into an evangelist, is shown preaching (Figure 7.3). This shot highlights the success of the United Church of Northern India in attracting Brahmins, a caste of priestly status in Hindu society who developed their theological teachings on points of convergence between Christian and Hindu thought. A further success is claimed with footage of the Reverend Tharchin La, the first Tibetan preacher to be ordained. Inter-titles declare at the end of the film that the Young Men's Guild Mission that sponsored this work has now closed and emphasise that it is important that Indian and Scottish missionaries work together to counter the threat of Chinese communism on the borders of Kalimpong. This can be achieved, the last statement in the film declares, by establishing the need for Christianity in the new, independent India. This documentary was made some years after the CoS had left India and attempts to make a claim to its historically established and continuing influence in the region through its support of the United Church of Northern India.

CONVERSION, SALVATION AND THE 'CIVILISING MISSION' 163

Figure 7.3: Liladhar, the convert Brahmin, now evangelist (*Kalimpong*, 1950, copyright, Church of Scotland). Courtesy of the Scottish Screen Archive.

CONCLUSIONS: FILMING THE 'CIVILISING MISSION' OF CHRISTIANITY IN INDIA

This chapter has set out to describe and contextualise a number of films made by British missionary societies in India, and to locate them as part of broader colonial documentary practices. The examples are drawn from the archives of Protestant missions – SA, MMS, LMS and CoS – to demonstrate the wide and varied nature of documentary production for religious purposes. This chapter has also discussed how the SA used film in its infancy for a brief period as part of its performative and spectacular approach to evangelisation and conversion, at the high point of its popularity in Britain and as it established corps across parts of the empire. The CoS documentary production is an example of how the church produced films more strategically, linked to its efforts to retain its presence in places where former colonies, Dominions and Protectorates had become independent from British rule. The MMS and LMS, who produced films over a number of decades, created consistent policies to use film as part of their evangelist strategy during the twentieth century. These three societies, the CoS, LMS and MMS, were also involved in ecumenical initiatives in film production with other mission societies which did not make their own films; societies such as the Church Missionary Society (CMS). Seven missions were represented on the MFC, which was established by the Conference of British Missionary Societies, a Protestant interdenominational organisation, to actively promote filming activities and improve the film production values of missionary films.[20]

Film-making served the different missionary organisations in a number of ways. Documentary film was recognised by missionary societies as a persuasive form and was used to spread Christian values and to recruit personnel by linking Christianity with progress and modernity through education and science. Looking at examples of documentaries made in India, there is also a remarkable similarity between those films made by different societies in their promotion of Western education and health as part of the Christian mission. They all, for example, draw upon aspects of contemporaneous documentary film approaches such as the travelogue style, the ethnographic view, the spectacle of the human body and other animated, illustrative, mapping and visual means that organised space and time in the documentary film then. The films also visualise the history of the mission in the foreign field, making claim to a Christian presence in India over a long period of time. They attempt to create a legacy of the benefits of Christianity and Western civilisation for India in relation to the activities of the mission, particularly in those films made after Indian independence. These films also familiarised audiences in Britain with Christian perspectives on civilisation, development, progress and modernity, through educational and religious distribution and exhibition. The uptake of film by missions, and specifically their use of documentary film, was, as this chapter has argued, mainly for the purposes of evangelising and promoting the 'civilising mission' of Christianity. The films show how churches and missionary societies established their missions across the empire through the provision of social work, hospitals and schools. This spread of Christianity was not, however, necessarily as successful as the films purport that it had been, as there is evidence that the missions met with resistance both from the marginalised communities they targeted and from the broader cultures and societies they attempted to convert. This adds a degree of complexity to any attempt to assess the evangelical influence of these films.

ACKNOWLEDGEMENTS

With special thanks to Jacqueline Maingard.

NOTES

1. National Film and Television Archive, BFI Collections, London; Bristol Museum, British Empire and Commonwealth Museum collection (BECM); School of Oriental and African Studies special collections; see *Colonial Film: Moving Images of the British Empire* (http://www.colonialfilm.org.uk, accessed on 30 April 2016) for a catalogue of some of these collections; also see Scottish Screen, Glasgow, for Church of Scotland films.
2. For a discussion of popular ethnographic styles and 'dramas of native life' see Sandon (2000: 108–47).
3. Robert E. Frykenburg argues that 'Christian movements in India seem to have been most successful when least connected to empire. Movements of conversion occurred not because of, but despite, imperial expansion, in places removed from imperial control' (2006: 492).
4. There were, however, a number of compact 35mm cameras in use, for example the Debrie 'Le Parvo', developed in France by Joseph Jules Debrie in 1908.
5. The Colonial Film Unit was set up by the British Ministry of Information in 1939 to produce propaganda and instructional films for African audiences to be shown by mobile cinema units in the British colonies in Africa. It was disbanded in 1955. See http://www.colonialfilm.org.uk/production-company/colonial-film-unit (accessed on 30 April 2016) for further details and references.
6. The films of the Saint Joseph's Missionary Society in the BECM collection are currently not available for viewing at the Bristol Museum whilst cataloguing is underway, with the exception of one film on the *Colonial Film* website.
7. Rice (2009: 1) quotes these figures from the SA report *Social Gazette*, 14 May 1904.
8. Rice (2009: 11) quotes this figure from the SA paper *War Cry*, Summer, 1904.
9. The Dommara, better known as Dom, a semi-nomadic ethnic group originating from the Middle East, live in various parts of north and south India, working often as street musicians and performers. The Haburah lived near Moradabad, northeast of Delhi, and at the time were associated by the mission and colonial authorities with thievery. The Salvation Army trained the Haburah women in this settlement to make uniforms for the military during the First World War.
10. The Methodist Union, as it was known, reunited the Methodist Church by bringing together the key secessionist sectors that had split from the Wesleyan Methodist Church during the nineteenth century, once it had become a non-conformist church with its own ordained ministers. Methodism originally began as a movement in the Anglican Church of England led by John Wesley (1703–91).
11. Wilfred Le Cato Edwards (1894–1986) was born in Sandwich, Kent, the son of Ebenezer Edwards (1859–1955), a missionary in the Bahamas. From 1921 to 1945, he was Principal of the Boys' High School in Secunderabad and then in charge of training at Aler, Hyderabad, India. Between 1947 and 1955, he was Methodist Missionary Representative to the Church of South India.
12. The Santal or Santhal tribe is the third largest tribe in India. In British India, the community resided in the British provinces of Bengal, Assam and the princely state of Nepal (currently Jharkhand, West Bengal, Bihar, Orissa, Assam, Nepal and Bangladesh). Historically, they resisted British rule during the nineteenth century, waging war against British settlement.
13. 'Outcast' is used by the MMS to describe people who were socially stigmatised and who did not have any status in the caste system.

14. Dr Isabel Kerr (née Gunn) (1875–1932) was born in Scotland and graduated in medicine at Aberdeen in 1903. In 1907, she accompanied her husband, Reverend George M. Kerr to Nizamabad, India, where he was superintendent of the Wesleyan Mission Station, while she was in charge of its hospitals. They set up the hospital at Dichpali for the treatment of leprosy in 1915, with land and maintenance funding donated by the Nizam (local Muslim sovereign). She launched the treatment of leprosy with hydnocarpus oil from 1921 and ran a leprosy clinic in Hyderabad, which was financed by the Government of India. In 1923, she was awarded the Kaiser-i-Hind Gold Medal by the British monarch for distinguished services to the British Raj.
15. The London Missionary Society was a non-denominational missionary society, Congregationalist in outlook, that was formed by non-conformists and evangelical Anglicans in 1795 to enable evangelists to spread the gospel through overseas missions.
16. *The Church's Guide for Film for Religious Use*, London: Church of England Films Commission (1946: 54) (Gooding 2011: 254, note 34).
17. Their films include: *Union Boys' High School at Bishupur No. 17* (1930), *Erode* (1937), *Salem* (1937), *LMS at Work in the Jiangari Field of South India* (1939), *LMS at Work in the Tamil Field of South India* (1939) and *LMS at Work in the Telugu Field of South India* (1939) (all 16mm).
18. See also the entry on the Bantu Education Kinema Experiment (BEKE) on the *Colonial Film: Moving Images of the British Empire* website, accessed on 30 April 2016 at http://www.colonialfilm.org.uk/production-company/bekefilm; Aboubakar Sanago (2011) 'Colonialism, visuality and the cinema: revisiting the Bantu Educational Kinema Experiment' and Aaron Windel (2011) 'The Bantu Educational Kinema Experiment and the political economy of community development', both in Lee Grieveson and Colin MacCabe (2011); Burns (2002) and Reynolds (2015).
19. Ballantyne also directed other films for the Church of Scotland Foreign Mission Committee: *In His Name: the Epic of ITU Leper Colony* (James Ballantyne, 1950) on the Church of Scotland treatment colony in Nigeria and *Sheikh Othman* (James Ballantyne, 1954) on the Church of Scotland's Boys' Brigade Mission and the Keith-Falconer hospital in Aden.
20. The seven missions were the Baptist Missionary Society, the Church of England Zenana Missionary Society, CoS, CMS, LMS, the Society for the Propagation of the Gospel and WMMS.

REFERENCES

Acland, Charles R. and Wasson, Haidee (eds) (2011), *Useful Cinema*, Durham, NC: Duke University Press.

Bottomore, Stephen (2005), 'Religious filmmaking', in Richard Abel (ed.), *Encyclopedia of Early Cinema*, London/New York: Routledge, pp. 549–50.

Burns, James M. (2002), *Flickering Shadows, Cinema and Identity in Colonial Zimbabwe*, Athens: Ohio University Press.

Cox, Jeffrey (2002), *Imperial Fault Lines: Christianity and Colonial Power in India, 1818–1940*, Stanford: Stanford University Press.

Cox, Jeffrey (2008), *The British Missionary Enterprise since 1700*, New York/London: Routledge.
Diamond, Howard (1936), 'Films in Britain', *The Chronicle: A Magazine of World Enterprise*, November, London: London Missionary Society, 254.
Fletcher, Tony (2015), *The Salvation Army and the Cinematograph 1897–1929: A Religious Tapestry in Britain and India*, London: Local History Publications.
Frykenburg, Robert E. (2006), 'Christian and religious traditions in the Indian empire', in Sheridan Gilley and Brian Stanley (eds), *The Cambridge History of Christianity: World Christianities c.1815–c.1914*, vol. 8, Cambridge: Cambridge University Press, pp. 473–92.
Gooding, Francis (2010), 'Missionary societies', accessed on 21 June 2015 at http://www.colonialfilm.org.uk/production-company/missionary-societies?page=1.
Gooding, Francis (2011), '"Of great use at meetings": the film-making principles of the London Missionary Society', in Lee Grieveson and Colin MacCabe (eds), *Empire and Film*, London/New York: Palgrave Macmillan, pp. 247–60.
Grieveson, Lee and MacCabe, Colin (eds) (2011) *Empire and Film*, London/New York, Palgrave Macmillan.
Hardiman, David (ed.) (2006), *Healing Bodies, Saving Souls: Medical Missions in Asia and Africa*, Amsterdam/New York: Rodopi.
Lindvall, Terry (2007), *Sanctuary Cinema, Origins of the Christian Film Industry*, New York/London: New York University Press.
Lindvall, Terry and Quicke, Andrew (2011), *Celluloid Sermons: The Emergence of the Christian Film Industry, 1930–1986*, New York/London: New York University Press.
Machin, G. I. T. (1992), 'British churches and the cinema in the 1930s', in Diana Wood (ed.) *Studies in Church History*, vol. 29, 'The Church and the arts', Oxford: Ecclesiastical History Society by Blackwells.
Orgeron, Devin, Orgeron, Marsha and Streible, Dan (eds) (2011), *Learning with the Lights Off: Educational Film in the United States*, Oxford/New York: Oxford University Press.
Rapp, Dean (1996), 'The British Salvation Army, the early film industry and urban working-class adolescents, 1897–1918', *Twentieth Century British History*, 7: 2, 157–88.
Rice, Tom (2009), 'Commissioner Higgins visits Ahmedabad Girls' School', April, accessed on 21 June 2015 at http://www.colonialfilm.org.uk/node/1555.
Sandon, Emma (2000), 'Projecting Africa: two British travel films of the 1920s', in Elizabeth Hallam and Brian V. Street (eds), *Cultural Encounters, Representing 'Otherness'*, London/New York: Routledge, pp. 108–47.
Shankar, Shobana (2006), 'The social dimensions of Christian leprosy work among Muslims: American missionaries and young patients in colonial northern Nigeria, 1920–1940' in David Hardiman (ed.), *Healing Bodies, Saving Souls, Medical Missions in Asia and Africa*, Amsterdam/New York: Rodopi, pp. 45–68.

PART III

Documentary Representations: Projections, Idealised and Imaginary Images

CHAPTER 8

Screening the Revolution in Rural Vietnam: Guerrilla Cinema Across the Mekong Delta

Thong Win

On 24 December 1948 on the banks of a common waterway in the province of Đồng Tháp Mười (Plain of Reeds), the Southern (Communist) Party Conference was held at the store of revolutionary military leader Dương Văn Dương. Within twenty-four hours of the conference, graphic artists, musicians, painters and military leaders descended upon the site in the Mekong River Delta in order to finalise and set up their displays for the conference. Among the conference participants were Mai Lộc, Khương Mễ and other members of the region's military cinema division, who were editing the final moments of their documentary, *The Battle of Moc Hoa*, from their makeshift post-production laboratory on a small dinghy. Their exhibit was to be housed in a small temporary building on the site and would use a precariously balanced film projector powered by a portable generator. Khương Mễ, a founding member of the film unit, recounts that local villagers arrived in their dinghies throughout the day of the conference. In spite of a lack of advertising for the clandestine film showing rows of moored dinghies were evident, just as there would be bicycles outside popular picture palaces for a film premier in Saigon (Khương 1997). For many of the local farmers and families from nearby villages it was their first experience of cinema. The attendees were directed into the building where the first guerrilla film screening was staged. Khương and fellow film-maker Mai Lộc formed a protective perimeter around the projector and generator. If the projector toppled or the projection lamp were to become extinguished it might have meant that the screening would be cut short and a day-long trip to Saigon to procure replacement parts would then have to take place. For the twenty-minute newsreel depicting the Battle of Moc Hoa, Khương and Mai were given a standing ovation. The next morning, Khương found that the exhibition space had been stripped apart by overeager attendees who had arrived in the unfulfilled hope of seeing repeated screenings of the film (ibid.). This story of the first film screening by guerrilla film-makers at Đồng Tháp Mười was compiled from various accounts of the event, and these, together with other scant sources available provide a context for examining how film-making and exhibition practices informed Vietnamese revolutionary ideology and established support for the revolutionary cause. These fragments also provide a basis for assessing how guerrilla cinema was folded into a cultural vanguard to recruit support in the rural regions of South Vietnam following the start of the First Indochina War.

This chapter explores the beginning of Vietnam's revolutionary cinema in 1948 by addressing competing conceptions of Vietnamese modernity. In mapping the sites of guerrilla exhibition, the essay will focus on war zone 8 South Vietnam, which is often referred to as the birthplace of guerrilla cinema and the site of the first screening held in Đồng Tháp Mười. This context for film exhibition was to eventually become a significant popular counterweight to European picture palaces in Hanoi and Saigon, despite its location in the hinterlands. As here, guerrilla screenings more generally were necessarily staged outside the cultural and political centres, and, in addition to attracting a Vietnamese audience, these events, crucially, were also magnets for disparate communities across the Mekong Delta that came together to form an emerging 'geo-body', to use the term coined by Thongchai Winichakul; and one that also reinforced anti-colonial imperatives (Tongchai 1994: 17). The history of guerrilla exhibition in the Mekong Delta is, therefore, a regional history that demonstrates the material and ideological struggle South Vietnamese cultural resistance engaged in against French colonialism. The entanglements of guerrilla cinema were also congruent here with an emerging cultural policy directed from Hanoi, although, and as will be described later, that cinema also existed in a parasitic relationship with French colonial modernity in Saigon. All of this implied a varied and vibrant process of exhibition.

MAPPING THE 'GEO-BODY' OF THE VIETNAMESE REVOLUTION

In his work on the transformation from the kingdom of Siam to the modern nation of Thailand in the late nineteenth century, Thongchai Winichakul uses the term 'geo-body' to refer to the ensemble of technological operations that constitute a territoriality which in turn spatialises a conception of nationhood. Focusing on cartography, Thongchai makes a case for how, in areas with overlapping sovereignties, maps allowed for a reconception of feudal space into bounded territory that marked the shift from indigenous imaginings of space to a 'geo-body' as precursor to the geographically bounded nation. According to Thongchai, the nation is preceded by the binding of multiple localities under an imagined conception of shared space, time, language and culture made possible by the circulation of media and other influences. In evoking the notion of the geo-body, this chapter will suggest reading guerrilla film exhibition in the Mekong Delta as binding disparate localities under an imagined nationalist community. As part of guerrilla activities in the region, the exhibition of films throughout the war zones bound the zones together into recognisable administrative bodies and likewise provided a crucial link between the populations of each zone and an emerging national body. The circulation and exhibition of guerrilla films within the countryside constitutes what Thongchai, in the Siamese context, calls the 'positive identification of the realm of Our Space', and a way of laying claim and inscribing a new communist Vietnamese nationalism to contested territory (Tongchai 1994: 191).

While French colonial maps segmented Indochina into three protectorates – Tonkin (1884), Annam (1884) and Cochinchina (1862) – the revolution for Vietnamese independence, whose military resistance against French colonialism began with the August Revolution of 1945, effectively remapped Vietnam into organised war zones. Each zone established its own system of local governance, which coordinated guerrilla efforts in tandem with other zones at the behest of Hanoi. For the revolutionary government, this newly imagined cartography was projected against French colonial strategies of territorial amalgamation which worked in the interests of the colonisers. The military strategy of segmenting and renaming Indochina as part of different war zones rather than relying on colonial distinctions can also be understood as an act of resistance and reclamation, and, through this strategy, the leadership in Hanoi sought to shape policies in favour of eventual national unification for the provincial regions along the Mekong Delta. Relatively disconnected from the general and other aspects of the polity of the North, these policies generated a shared goal and imagined space for revolutionaries in South Vietnam. For example, in a 1949 letter to citizens working for the revolution in provincial areas, Ho Chi Minh argued that the revolutionary struggle against French colonialism and the foundation for a post-colonial Vietnamese society would depend not only on the revolutionary leadership in Hanoi but also on peasant forces operating in the rural communities of Vietnam, and, in order to realise this, Ho Chi Minh directed cadres active in rural communities

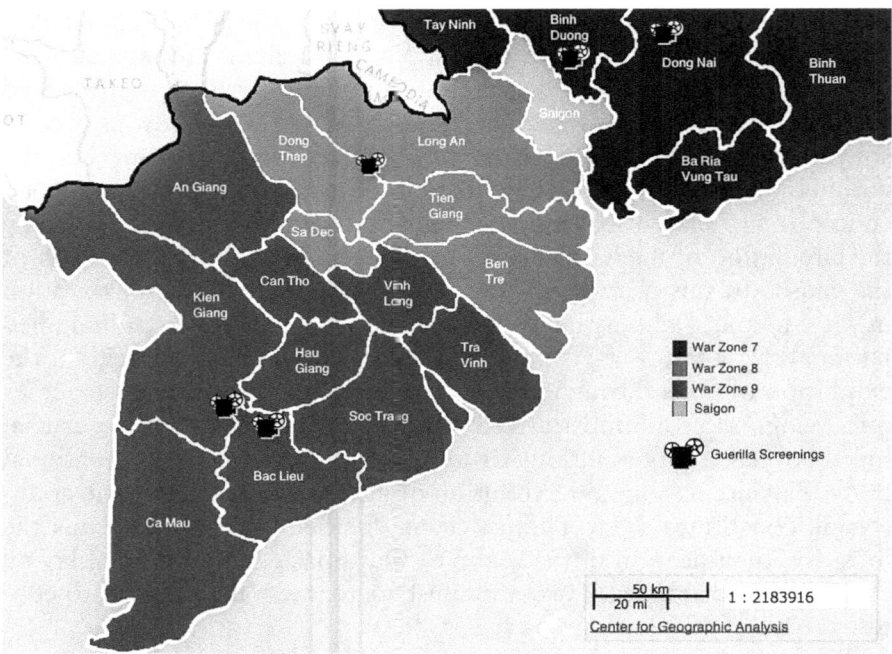

Figure 8.1: Map of the Mekong Delta's three guerrilla war zones and their notable film screenings (original graphic).

to take it upon themselves to proselytise the revolutionary agenda to their own and remoter regions of the country.[1] Ho Chi Minh's letter here emphasised the importance of the extension of the revolutionary idea throughout the outlying provinces, in contrast to such extension within the urban areas, and, as part of this, and through a distribution network for the exhibition of revolutionary films, the government in Hanoi traversed across political cultural and geographic lines using the film to create a nationalist space that remapped a revolutionary political imaginary cinematically (Figure 8.1).

Guerrilla film screenings were canonised in state-sanctioned narratives of Vietnamese film history through the multiple heroic accounts that featured the role of film-makers producing and exhibiting films in the war zones.[2] For instance, Nguyễn Đức Dương, the former Head of the Research Office at Viet Nam Feature Film Studios, described the documentary-realist ethos during the revolutionary period as being one where '[film-makers] brought revolution and resistance to the people through newsreels [that] went deep into the national liberation revolution by fostering an awareness of social events' (Nguyễn 2008: 466).

These generalised accounts did much to establish a nationalist connection between guerrilla activities and Hanoi. However, they also tend to favour the repetition of established narratives without reference to how these narratives were bounded to larger political discourses. Generally, these accounts situate and characterise guerrilla film-making as an imperfect and transitory moment in the evolution of Vietnamese revolutionary film-making. This imperfect and transitory aspect was in part seen as related to Hanoi's distance from and political relationship to the Mekong Delta, a distance and relationship which meant that it was not a simple task to dictate the terms and ideology of the revolution to local communities. The transmission of such information would for example have to circumvent the material challenges posed by attempting to reach provincial areas patrolled by French colonial forces, negotiating with the pro-French-leaning native communities and overcoming issues related to the dissemination of these messages to a largely illiterate peasant population. In order to overcome these difficulties, the expanding relationship between Hanoi and the war zones included the circulation of guerrilla film units in the Mekong Delta, and these activities forged a crucial link in the ideological formation of a conception of a unified Vietnam.

In aligning Hanoi's policies with peasant audiences in the Mekong Delta, Saigon served as the epicentre for film activities in South Vietnam, and this context for distribution reframed the production and exhibition of counter-colonial film and ephemera in the revolutionary imagination. Though exhibition practices and revolutionary politics conflated and disaggregated outside the boundaries of Saigon in various ways, these guerrilla practices cannot be thought of as existing entirely beyond the orbit and influence of Saigon. In keeping with guerrilla practices of clandestine mobility and piratical subterfuge, the established infrastructure for colonial exhibition in Saigon was also necessary in order to develop the web of revolutionary exhibition within the war zones. Large urban film theatres were open every night and the more luxurious venues typically charged more than smaller theatres. The prohibitive ticket prices at the larger urban film theatres favoured the patronage of French colonial society and middle-class urban Vietnamese civil servants. Despite the possible existence of working-class film exhibition spaces in Saigon, the opportunity to attend a screening was determined not only by price but distance from the theatres as well. As a result, farmers among others who lived outside of the cities would rarely step into a movie theatre.[3]

The urban focus of colonial exhibition and limited expansion of such exhibition into the rural areas of Indochina allowed guerrilla film exhibition to exploit the gap opened up by this and attract large audiences, particularly after the August Revolution of 1945. Opportunities to mobilise a large neglected rural portion of the population into a resistant political body entailed developing exhibition practices that could canvass the difficult terrain without attracting attention from colonial authorities in Saigon or at the regional military outposts, and this was in part why the strategy of mobile film exhibition was adopted to connect regional communities to the war front. Thanks to a parasitic relationship to the colonial infrastructure for exhibition, guerrilla cinema activities relied on film-making and exhibition equipment acquired in Saigon to establish a shadow network of mobile screenings. Memoirs by Khương Mễ, Mai Lộc and other historical accounts of the guerrilla cinema trace the circuitous and often difficult ways in which guerrilla film-makers would procure French cameras and projection equipment, film stock, technical manuals and spare parts through local shops in Saigon. Those with contacts at production houses and theatres could occasionally obtain gallons of chemicals used to develop film. Even incidental material needed in the production of films such as ice had to be obtained in Saigon and its outlying towns. Materials obtained in Saigon would then be smuggled out of the city and into the countryside by small dinghies that doubled as mobile post-production laboratories (Văn 1997). As one may expect, trips into Saigon to replenish materials and obtain new parts for cameras and film projectors were also a necessary risk for guerrilla film-makers. Recycling, conservation and 'making do' became the mantra for guerrilla film-makers, who then became mythologised within the folkloric history of revolutionary cinema. The material working conditions and scarcity of available resources dictated not only the way that films were produced but also framed the exhibition experience as a rare opportunity. Within this, Saigon was important, and the movement of materials, films and personnel across the Mekong Delta depended on the city. Saigon was, in effect, a source of materials, and a nodal point in a matrix of exhibition practices which reached well beyond the colonial spatial economy for film exhibition.

SCREEN ENCOUNTERS IN THE RE-IMAGINED DELTA: CULTURAL POLICY FINDS AN AUDIENCE

If Saigon was the organising force for materials used in film-making practices throughout the Mekong Delta then it was Hanoi and its emerging cultural policy in the late 1930s and throughout the revolution that reorganised the map of film exhibition in South Vietnam. Trường Chinh, who was second in command behind Ho Chi Minh during the

First Indochina War (the War of Resistance in Vietnam, 1946–54), was the leading Party theoretician who provided the theoretical parameters for an emerging cinema in the Mekong Delta.[4] Writing after the 1930s, Trường Chinh's contributions to the communist-oriented publication *Su Thuat/Truth* devised a skeletal framework for a cultural front that advocated the mobilisation of all art forms in service of the revolution and the socialist state. Though Trường Chinh never addressed film-making as a political tool in his recommendations for a cultural front, he eventually folded it into the nationalist agenda. Though not explicitly referenced in official discourse, guerrilla film-making existed as a satellite experiment for the diffusion of revolutionary politics. Its success led to its expansion not only as part of the revolutionary credo but as an enduring narrative considered central to revolutionary efforts. Memories of those involved in guerrilla cinema in the Mekong Delta however point to a fruitful alliance between film-making experiments outside Hanoi, and the revolutionary objective of mobilising peasant populations in the countryside. The historian Kim N. B. Ninh has remarked that the core of Trường Chinh's cultural policy 'emphasized that it was important to remember that the ideological struggle could not be separated from the political, military, and economic struggle, especially when the French colonial authorities and their Vietnamese collaborators continued to mesmerize the masses with their degenerate culture' (Ninh 2002: 45). Trường Chinh's concern with French cultural production and its influence over the Vietnamese masses equally questioned the effectiveness of Vietnamese cultural production in winning support for the revolution. Trường Chinh's revision of the arts for a free socialist Vietnam was drawn along the three axes of nationalisation, popularisation and scientific orientation (Ninh 2002:63). According to Trường Chinh, the task for revolutionary intellectuals was to disconnect their work from centuries of traditional, superstitious and bourgeois sentimentality and to reorient their work along newly established lines. If Vietnamese intellectuals were in the process of defining a modern Vietnamese character both politically and within the arts, the emergence of a new popular art form as separate from centuries of traditionalism was undoubtedly appealing, since the production and reception of film could be tailored to meet Party demands during wartime. As an art form whose formal and aesthetic qualities were still being negotiated, cinema was granted a privileged position within the Party in a cultural struggle against colonial and imperial forces.

Though film screenings were meant to be didactic, they were also framed as informal events where local communities could gather and exchange stories (see Figure 8.2). As an element of political work among rural peasants, the informality of the film screening as a social event was a mixture of novelty, curiosity and political discussion. These makeshift film theatres appeared to a wider audience and became a political vehicle for the Communist Party's nationalist agenda. By exposing audiences to the 'truth', it was believed, a truth revealed by the 'objective eye' of the documentary camera lens, the heroic righteousness of the revolution might be revealed. Such exposure to truth would, according to the logic of the cultural policies elaborated, convince those in attendance to join the revolution. Audience reception in the formation of nationalist impulses gestures to the ethos of guerrilla film exhibition as its participants remember it. Though historical details are certainly lacking, surviving testimonies in memoirs and interviews emphasise the overwhelming folkloric romanticism bestowed by audiences on film-makers, viewed as important figures who helped establish a unified Vietnam. Rather than amounting to a uniform model of screen encounters in the region, the mobility of guerrilla cinema was characterised by varied intensities based on its geographical relationship to the flow of material channels and French colonial outposts. The concerted effort by revolutionary film-makers and exhibitors operating in both the Mekong Delta and in Hanoi was thus central to disseminating a sense of nationalist modernity in the cause of the revolution.

Figure 8.2: The crowd gathers around the screen to watch *The Battle of Moc Hoa* at the Đồng Tháp Mười screening on 24 December 1948.

In the light of Trường Chinh's cultural programme, the first guerrilla screening in Đồng Tháp Mười in war zone 8 could be understood as a politicised classroom whose experimentation with film was intended to create the desired revolutionary audience. Though the screening of *The Battle of Moc Hoa* was only an exhibit incorporated into the larger context of the conference, it marked a desired shift to a populist model of film exhibition. With Saigon firmly under French colonial control and more sympathy to be found in rural war zones, Trường Chinh wrote that 'The towns, which were formerly cultural centres, are now occupied by the enemy . . . By contrast, the countryside, formerly a dark backward place, is now becoming civilized' (Trường 1994: 124). Every guerrilla screening within the Mekong Delta could be considered as a mobile classroom that attempted to mould provincial populations into the desired form of national subject. Bringing the technology and skills acquired in Saigon to the countryside, guerrilla film exhibition literally functioned as the 'civilising' force in Trường Chinh's reformation of artistic practice.

A significant portion of the film footage from the revolutionary period has been lost or is deteriorating in Vietnamese film archives. The footage that remains has been the focus of historical projects hoping to excavate and preserve this early moment in Vietnamese film history.[5] One of these projects is the French documentary film, *Gao Rang/Grilled Rice* (Claude Grunspan, 2001), which returns to modern Vietnam in order to interview former members of the guerrilla cinema movement. The film itself is an act of preservation as hinted at in the title, given that members of the guerrilla film units would store and preserve their footage in grilled rice. The rice would protect and insulate the footage from moisture, an ever-present problem in the region. By naming the documentary *Gao Rang*, Grunspan both draws upon this revolutionary method of film preservation to define his own work as a type of preservation. The film incorporates interviews and archival footage with film-makers' commentary to contextualise the film-making and exhibition conditions of early revolutionary cinema in Vietnam. In order to demonstrate the context in which guerrilla films were screened, *Gao Rang* stages a film screening for a local community in the jungle using the equipment then available to guerrilla film-makers. Under the direction of Mr Xuong, one of Vietnam's first film projectionists, they erect a makeshift screen out of bamboo and cloth. Mirroring the construction of the jungle screening, the film-maker intercuts excerpts from the 1978 documentary *Những người mang ánh sang/People Who Bring the Light*, which depicts members of a guerrilla cinema unit building their own jungle screening theatre.

A local man at the jungle re-enactment sings a song praising Ho Chi Minh as the father of the nation prior to the screening, a ritual we are led to believe was common practice. The reconstruction of the jungle screening here provides insight into the political utility of the guerrilla cinema units and the traditional framing of the cinematic image. While the title of the documentary film *People Who Bring the Light* reflects the physical process of film projection, it also plays upon the metaphor of light (*ánh sáng*) as a source of illumination and knowledge (i.e. *ánh sáng trong bóng tối*, a light in the dark). The invocation of Ho Chi Minh and the reunification of the nation prior to the screening also link the revolutionary cause with both meanings. In other words, it was the revolution led by Ho Chi Minh and Trường Chinh that would guide Vietnam through the colonial 'darkness' (i.e. ignorance, apathy). Attitudes towards attending a guerrilla film screening were also characterised by its pedagogical dimension and such attendance was conceived of as being synonymous with consumption of educational cinema and news. Unlike colonial film screenings in the urban centres, guerrilla cinema exhibited in the rural regions of the Mekong Delta was often a primary source of news (Tran and Nguyen 2007: 102–4).

Returning to Trường Chinh's newly defined cultural policies, the pedagogy of guerrilla cinema was not only limited to the projection on-screen but the screen encounter itself was an educational moment for rural audiences – what was being taught was not just the policies of the Party but actually lessons in how to be a post-colonial subject. Attending a film screening was like attending an introductory course on the new cultural character of a liberated Vietnam. With the target audiences of cultural output shifting from bourgeois intellectuals in city centres to rural peasants with limited formal education, it was necessary for revolutionary artists to adapt messages and genres through film to this new audience. In Trường Chinh's view, the cultural objective of mobile cinema was to reach the audiences that were either passed over or were unable to consume more traditional forms of media because of a lack of formal education. In pursuit of an egalitarian culture, Trường Chinh wrote that 'In order to serve the Fatherland and the people, cultural workers must create works which are simple and well-adapted to the level of the people, who for the most part are illiterate or have only little education' (Trường 1994: 125). As we have seen, in colonial Saigon, the democratising power of cinema's visuality was bounded by its middle-class urban constituency. Guerrilla cinema, as conceived within the context of

Trường Chinh's notion of artisitic production was free to the public. It contrasted significantly with the colonial exhibition context in Saigon and the exclusionary pricing practices of French colonial film distribution and exhibition companies such as La Société Indochine Films et Cinémas and Société des Ciné-Théâtres d'Indochine (Wilson 2007: 60–116).

A crucial component of Trường Chinh's 'new democratic culture' for a post-colonial Vietnam emphasised *khoa học hóa* (scientific orientation) as the vehicle for cultural and industrial modernisation. A scientific tradition, understood as a prerequisite to the development of a modern nation, was a concern for a revolutionary government that found itself simultaneously dependent on and shackled by the technological advancements introduced into Indochina by colonial powers. At a disadvantage and feeling outpaced by the rapid development of other nations, Trường Chinh's emphasis on science as a tenant for post-colonial Vietnam required a radical break with long-standing tradition. Trường Chinh wrote in his programme for a scientifically inflected culture:

> We learn from the advanced cultures of the world, yet take a critical view of and censure its reactionary elements. We search for and study literary and artistic works bequeathed to us by our forefathers, but we put them under the microscope, criticize them and pick out only the positive traditions . . . The Vietnamese new democratic culture must be scientific in character as opposed to the backward, corrupt, and feudal, but condemns superstition, idealism, mysticism . . . all those habits that are irrational and retrograde. (Trường 1994: 251–2)

Cinema's position as a key cultural form privileged in this newly configured culture seemed all but guaranteed. Despite the technological challenges of producing and exhibiting films, the imagined objective recording of reality dovetailed with Trường Chinh's call for scientific objectivity. When in proper hands (i.e. revolutionary hands), cinema ostensibly documented the world with scientific precision. Guerrilla screenings such as *The Battle of Moc Hoa* in Đồng Tháp Mười existed as scientific spaces whereby 'reality' was mechanically reproduced for the audience. As a means to pervade modern technologies, revolutionary ideologies and modern nationalism, screenings such as the one held in Đồng Tháp Mười, were beacons with which to establish a conduit of communication and popular support between Hanoi and rural Vietnam.

When asked why war zone 8 Cinema was created, in a 1987 interview, Lieutenant General Tran Van Tra – a military commander of the Zone – responded:

> All people must fight. If you want to win a war you need to combine strength . . . Whoever has a sword should use a sword, whoever has a gun should use a gun. Whoever does not have a gun should use a hoe/space . . . Uncle Ho had called for this. Because of this [assertion] the first film-makers, like Mai Loc, Khuong Me, Vu Son . . . of course carried their machines into the war zone. (Bảo 1997: 8)

Tran's response revealed the totalising conception of the Vietnamese revolution that cultural production and military production could in no way be divorced from one another. Revolutionary tools would be mobilised across all sectors in the country. The opening credits to *The Battle of Moc Hoa* echo both Ho Chi Minh and General Tran's revolutionary call for total warfare. The opening credits feature a spinning globe and when Vietnam revolves into view a soldier armed with a rifle emerges and walks forward. As the globe fades out, the soldier's rifle is replaced with a camera and the logo for the National Guard Cinema Crew of zone 8 appears. This footage was a figure that pointed in and of itself to the transformation of the rifle into a camera as a synecdoche for revolutionary politics and the cinematic apparatus. The rifle as camera suggested a relationship of equivalence that underscored its political and operational uses but also referred to a cultural struggle fought on screens across Vietnam. During the revolution, Vietnamese film-makers reframed the cinema as a weapon to rally support for their cause. For guerrilla cinema, the battle would be won on makeshift screens in villages as much as on the battlefield.

CONCLUSIONS: GUERRILLA CINEMA AND THE NATIONALIST PROJECT

In 1951 the guerrilla cinema operations in war zones 7, 8 and 9 were once again reorganised into a more centralised entity, known as the Southern Resistance Cinema. Though operating in similar fashion prior to being combined, this reorganisation streamlined coordination efforts across the southern territory. The combination of the three zones into a regional cinema area would once again be subject to reorganisation on 15 March 1953 when Ho Chi Minh signed decree 147/SL, which established

Vietnam's National Cinema and Photography Enterprise within the Ministry of Information and Propaganda. The decree formally institutionalised and consolidated Viet Minh film activities throughout the country under the auspices of the Communist Party and likewise formally drafted its services in the cause of the ongoing anti-colonial revolution against France and later the United States.

The popularity of guerrilla screenings became fertile territory for an emerging cultural policy dictated by Hanoi, whose formal properties were harnessed by the Party, not only to proliferate the revolutionary cause but also to unify the various regions into a coherent geo-body. Trường Chinh's programme for revolutionary arts dovetailed with pre-existing guerrilla activities occurring within the Mekong Delta. However, it was through Trường Chinh's cultural policies that guerrilla film-making activities were given political legitimacy and institutional support. The combined efforts of guerrilla film-makers and Trường Chinh's cultural policies provided a cultural space to foster the nationalist imaginary of the revolution in the rural areas of Vietnam. Rural populations were linked to the revolutionary government and the military front through the circulation and exhibition of guerrilla films throughout the Mekong Delta. Through these films, populations were indoctrinated into the newly defined character of the revolutionary government.

Cinema's role within the Communist Party's cultural policy post-1953 was the seemingly inevitable result of the intersection between Trường Chinh's writing on Vietnam's new democratic culture and the emergence of guerrilla cinema in the Mekong Delta. The nationalisation of the film industry in 1953 would also define the cultural relevance and purpose of Vietnamese revolutionary cinema for the next three decades. The movement of Vietnamese revolutionary cinema from zone cinema to national industry paralleled and participated in the construction of Vietnam as a modern geo-body, and, although cultural and political satellites in the Mekong Delta were associated with Hanoi's cultural policy, guerrilla cinema also allowed rural audiences to reimagine themselves in relation to other local communities and to gain an emerging conception of a Vietnamese nation, guided every step of the way by shadows flickering across makeshift screens.

NOTES

1. In a letter instructing revolutionary cadres on how to spread the revolutionary message, Ho Chi Minh urged, 'Provincial cadres must go to districts and villages.

District cadres must go to villages and hamlets': Ho Chi Minh (1949/2007), 'To Peasant Cadres (November 1949)', in Bello 2007: 70.
2. For examples of state-sanctioned narratives of Vietnamese film history see Trinh (1983), and two volumes of *History of Vietnamese Cinema*: Hoàng et al. (2003), and Vũ et al (2003).
3. Despite the sparse archival documentation available on colonial exhibition in Indochina catering to middle class elites, there is even less available on local theatres whose patronage was from the urban working class. La Société Indochine Films et Cinémas dominated the exhibition market with one hundred theatres in Indochina in all three regions prior to the 1945 August Revolution. In his research about colonial theatres in Indochina Nguyễn Van Ky counts twenty-eight theatres in Tonkin, eighteen theatres in Annam and thirty-three in Cochinchina with the majority of the theatres in large cities such as Hanoi, Hai Phong, Nam Dinh and Saigon – costing anywhere from 5 xu to 2 hao (between one-hundredth and one-tenth of a piaster). To put these ticket prices into perspective a ten-hour working wage for a mineworker was 3 hao and a farmer would typically not exceed 2 hao for a day's work. See Nguyễn 1995: 181–91.
4. Trường Chinh is a pseudonym that means Long March. His real name was Đặng Xuân Khu. An admirer of Mao Zedong, his pseudonym is the Vietnamese cognate for Long March and is a reference to Zedong's rise to power in the 1930s.
5. During a recent research trip to Ha Noi, Vietnam, I was able to view digitised copies of this footage at the Viet Nam Film Institute (VFI). For the past decade, the institute has gone to great lengths to preserve and digitise the remaining footage before it succumbs to humidity and poor archival conditions. Though the amount of footage digitised is respectable, one is constantly reminded of the footage that has been lost.

REFERENCES

Bảo Định Giang (1997), 'Lieutenant General Tran Van Tra on the decision to create zone 8 Cinema', in Hoà Bắc Nguyễn (ed.), *Kỷ Yếu Điện Ảnh bưng biền/Guerrilla Cinema*, Ho Chi Minh City: Nhà Xuất Bản Văn Nghệ T. P., pp. 7–9.
Bello, Walden (ed.) (2007), *Ho Chi Minh: Down With Colonialism!*, London/New York: Verso.
Hoàng Thanh, Ngọc Trương Phạm, Bảo Bành, Quang Chính Vũ, Mạnh Lân Ngô and Phan Bích Hà (2003), *Lịch Sử Điện Ảnh Việt Nam: Quyển Một/The History of Vietnamese Cinema*: vol. 1, Hanoi: Cực Điện Ảnh Xuất Bản.
Khương Mễ (1997), 'The first film screening in Dong Thap Muoi', in Hoà Bắc Nguyễn (ed.), *Kỷ Yếu Điện Ảnh bưng biền/Guerrilla Cinema*, Ho Chi Minh City: Nhà Xuất Bản Văn Nghệ T. P., pp. 59–61.
Nguyễn Văn Ky (1995), *La Société Vietnamienne face à la Modernité, Le Tonkin de la fin du XIXe siècle à la Seconde Guerre Mondiale*, Clamecy: Nouvelle Imprimerie Laballery.
Nguyễn Đức Dương (2008), 'Methods of social realism in Vietnamese movies', in Vũ Dũng Phạm et al. (eds), *Vietnamese Cinematography: A Research Journey*, Hanoi: Thế Giới Publishers.
Ninh, Kim N. B. (2002), *A World Transformed, The Politics of Culture in Revolutionary Vietnam, 1945–1965*, Ann Arbor: University of Michigan Press.

Thongchai Winichakul (1994), *Siam Mapped: A History of the Geo-body of a Nation*, Honolulu: University of Hawaii Press.
Tran Thanh Tung and Nguyen Thi Thuy Nga (2007), 'Revolutionary cinema between the wars', in Philippe Dumont and Kirstie Gormley (eds), *Vietnamese Cinema*, Lyon: Asiexpo, pp. 96–116.
Trường Chinh (1994), *Selected Writings* (New Impressions), Hanoi: Thế Gioi Publishers.
Văn Dĩ (1997), 'Delivering guerrilla cinema', in Hoà Bắc Nguyễn (ed.), Kỷ Yếu *Điện Ảnh bưng biền/Guerrilla Cinema*, Ho Chi Minh City: Nhà Xuất Bản Văn Nghệ T. P., pp. 95–8.
Vũ Mạnh, Quang Chính, Lân Ngô et al. (eds) (2003), *Lịch Sử Điện Ảnh Việt Nam: Quyển Hai/The History of Vietnamese Cinema*: vol. 2, Hanoi: Cực Điện Ảnh Xuất Bản.
Wilson, Donald Dean, Jr (2007), 'Colonial Viet Nam on film: 1896 to 1926', PhD dissertation, City University of New York (unpublished).

CHAPTER 9

Ho Chi Minh in France: An Early Independence Newsreel

Dean Wilson

On the eve of his exile in 1814 to the Tuscan island of Elba, the Emperor of France, Napoleon Bonaparte, abdicated power and bade farewell to his ministers in a ceremony at the Château de Fontainebleau, a sprawling complex of residences and gardens roughly thirty miles southeast of Paris. The palace had been expanded, decorated and preserved since the twelfth century under successive French monarchs. During the Second World War, Nazi officers occupied Fontainebleau and after the war it became an official residence of the North Atlantic Treaty Organization (NATO) command. An extraordinary artefact of European cultural and political history, Fontainebleau was also the setting, in July 1946, for a paradigm shift in South-East Asian documentary film history, for it was here that two Vietnamese immigrants living in Paris preserved on film a conference between delegations from the newly established Democratic Republic of Vietnam (DRV, 1945–76) and from the government of the Fourth French Republic (1946–58). The film focuses on President Ho Chi Minh, who sought independence for Vietnam but left the Château de Fontainebleau that summer with only a modus vivendi for future talks with the French government that never occurred. Three months later, the First Indochina War (1946–54) erupted.

This chapter sets out the social and film-historical context of the three short films produced that summer and projected as newsreels in rural areas of Vietnam prior to the outbreak of hostilities. These three films were later combined and repurposed to form the feature-length documentary *Ho Chi Minh in France* (Mai Thu, 1946). Several versions of the resulting film are held by the Vietnam Film Institute archives in

Hanoi and these include voice-over narration, graphics and additional footage from later periods in history, including scenes of war. The original version, however, appeared in short newsreel segments that were used to heighten awareness of the events at Fontainebleau among the peasantry in Vietnam and alert them to the imminent conflict, which erupted in the ensuing months. These three newsreel segments of early independence material ushered in the era of state-sponsored documentary film production and launched the period of national cinema in Vietnam.[1]

THE SOCIOPOLITICAL CONTEXT PRIOR TO FONTAINEBLEAU

The Japanese occupation of French Indochina began in September 1940, during the schism that broke out when the Third French Republic (1870–1940) was dissolved after the defeat of France by Nazi Germany. Following the defeat, two French governments vied for prominence: one aligned with the Nazi occupation of France and located in the city of Vichy under Marshal Philippe Pétain, the other based in London and aligned with Britain and other Allies under the leadership of General Charles de Gaulle. The colonial administration in French Indochina remained loyal to Pétain, and the Imperial Japanese Army (IJA) met with no significant resistance when it invaded the port city of Haiphong with a disproportionate show of military force, and then entered the colonial capital of Hanoi. Although the IJA had swiftly taken over the transportation infrastructure, the French colonial administration continued as it had for the past half century. In this way, the occupation was unusual, for there were essentially two occupying systems of foreign power coexisting simultaneously until March 1945, when the IJA command reacted in panic to Allied advances in the region by forcing the French out. The Japanese sense of urgency led to the pre-emptive military seizure of French colonial offices and the abrogation of all French claims to the Vietnamese territory. In a ceremony whose documentation was signed by the Japanese emperor, the IJA granted full independence to Vietnam and restored the monarchy of the Nguyen Dynasty, established in 1802, to political power under the traditional emperor Bao Dai (1913–97).[2]

The Japanese government's acknowledgement that a geographic and linguistic space called Vietnam was possible fuelled nationalist hopes among resistance groups in the Vietnamese territory. Since the consolidation of French Indochina in 1887, no such national entity had existed. Instead, the geographical territory now known as the unified Socialist Republic of Vietnam consisted of three distinct areas within French Indochina: the protectorate of Tonkin bordering China in the north, the protectorate of Annam in the central region and the colony of Cochinchina in the south (bordering today's Cambodia and the South China Sea). The Japanese surrender to Allied forces in August 1945 resulted in a power vacuum that opened a window of opportunity for the establishment of the DRV as a viable political entity. The new government was comprised of nationalist groups dominated by communists and motivated by the desire for the distinct territorial restoration of Vietnam to its pre-colonial borders. Action to this end had been planned months before the surrender and was coordinated by the League for the Independence of Vietnam, known as the Viet Minh (1935–55), and the clandestine People's Committees of the Indochinese Communist Party (ICP, 1930–45), in rural areas where the IJA had a minimal presence. In a major development, upon the Japanese emperor's announcement of surrender by public radio address, Ho Chi Minh quickly ensured the written legal abdication and transfer of power in Vietnam from Bao Dai to himself. Throughout the Vietnamese territory, paramilitary forces loyal to Ho Chi Minh were then able to rapidly seize control of important facilities and referred to their endeavour as the 'August Revolution'. On 2 September 1945, while the formal surrender of Japan was enacted aboard the battleship USS *Missouri*, Ho Chi Minh addressed an enthusiastic crowd in excess of one hundred thousand people to proclaim the national independence of the DRV.[3] The complexity and nuances of this period far exceed the ability of this chapter to set out an exhaustive account of them. A briefer account of the historical background will, nonetheless, be attempted here in order to later establish how documentary cinema developed in French Indochina within a context of colonial occupation and anti-colonial resistance; and also how the production and reception of *Ho Chi Minh in France* can be situated within that development and background.

A variety of indigenous groups too numerous to mention had pursued the ideal of national unity for Vietnam for quite some time.[4] The historical continuity of resistance in Vietnam also included an awareness and even appreciation of Japan's successful imperialist exploits long before the occupation of Vietnam. The catalytic representative of Vietnamese nationalism in the early twentieth century, Phan Boi Chau (1867–1940), for example, looked to the Meiji Restoration (1868–1912) in Japan[5] and the IJA triumph in the Japan–Russo War (1904–5) for inspirational models of national unity in Vietnam. Phan was the first to systematically educate and arm young people for revolt, in an attempt to restore the Vietnamese territory to the dynastic unity it enjoyed prior to the introduction of the French colonial presence. The aura of imperial Japan was, therefore, an important influence here, and would also animate nationalist debates among Vietnamese intellectuals and royalists for years to come (Sinh 2009: 32).[6]

After the First World War (1914–18), Ho Chi Minh lived in France and used the name Nguyen Ai Quoc when he joined the French Communist Party in 1920 as a founding member.[7] He later organised the first incarnation of the Viet Minh in the mid-1930s while living in China as a Communist International (1919–43) consultant for the Red Army. Non-communist Vietnamese nationalists were unable to commit to a sustained united front against the French, however, and the Viet Minh group's cohesion frayed, as members left (Duiker 2000: 244–7). Although they lacked military training and weapons, the remaining elements of the Viet Minh eventually received paramilitary support from the United States and Chinese nationalists with the aim of sabotaging Japanese army positions in northern rural areas from 1941 onwards (Duiker 2000: 284–5).[8] Despite frequent disputes, Ho Chi Minh then succeeded in merging the Viet Minh with the Indochinese Communist Party (ICP, 1930–45), which had been actively recruiting and organising for independence throughout the Vietnamese territory with increasing success following the precipitous annulment of French colonial authority by the Japanese in March 1945 (Marr 1971: 113–16). The cumulative efforts by disparate groups over time, therefore, had, by 1946, established the social context in which *Ho Chi Minh in France* was to be screened with a sense of climactic urgency, particularly after the disastrous famine of early 1945 that killed millions of farmers (see Gunn 2011).

Following the Japanese surrender in early August 1945, the abdication of Emperor Bao Dai helped to consolidate visions of national unity and conferred a public aura of legitimacy upon the presidency of Ho Chi Minh. This proved its worth when Ho delivered his declaration of independence speech to a rapt crowd of new citizens; and it also enabled him to enact a legal provision that both the French and Japanese occupying regimes had used to exploit the Vietnamese territory and its inhabitants (Marr 1971: 117). In March 1946, as Chinese, Indian and British troops repatriated the IJA under Allied supervision, Ho Chi Minh was forced to negotiate with the French authorities, who aggressively moved to regain power in the territory. Ho signed a tentative agreement to insert the DRV within a new legal entity called the French Union, which would essentially maintain the five areas of pre-war French Indochina with limited degrees of independence, pending further negotiations, as French troops re-entered Hanoi and the French High Commissioner in Indochina established a separate state in Cochinchina. Tensions were extraordinarily high because the French knew that Ho Chi Minh had widespread national support and that military enforcement could trigger a large-scale armed revolt by the Viet Minh or any number of other political, religious or paramilitary groups. The Fontainebleau conference was scheduled as a continuation of talks begun with high French officials in Vietnam, during which the DRV also sought recognition from the United Nations and the United States. As the talks in Vietnam continued, an atmosphere of scepticism gathered momentum, and daily violent skirmishes, mistrust and exasperation increasingly affected relations between the DRV and the French Fourth Republic (Duiker 2000: 366–83; Irving 2010: 146–8; also Cooper 2001: 179; Hammer 1955: 91–2).[9]

COLONIAL FILMS, WAR PROPAGANDA AND THE STRUGGLE FOR INDIGENOUS FILM-MAKING

Prior to *Ho Chi Minh in France*, there had been no real local tradition of documentary film-making and viewing in French Indochina. While the cinema arrived in Indochina in 1896 with the first wave of Lumière operators demonstrating the portable *cinématographe* – a camera cum printer and projector – factors such as illiteracy, poverty and distance from urban centres prevented films being shown to most rural native inhabitants. To make matters worse for years to come, the French also imposed strict control over film activities through censorship, restricted ownership permissions and police surveillance; in order to set limits on indigenous development of the medium, even among the highly educated Vietnamese cultural elite, which had enjoyed long-standing ties to Europe, Japan and China through trade. Although Indochina had appeared on movie screens in large public spectacles such as the Universal Exhibitions of Paris, beginning in 1900, few colonial subjects in Indochina had seen or understood how French cinematography portrayed them to foreign viewers.[10]

When, however, the Japanese Navy crushed the Russian fleet in the Tsushima Straights, ending the Japan–Russo War with a decisive victory in 1905, the rapid proliferation of reportage and films documenting the war augmented the popular fascination with the new medium and also fuelled the aspirations of colonial subjects under the yoke of oppression in Asia and Africa. Anti-colonial nationalists like Phan Boi Chau acclaimed the 'Asian triumph' of Japan and enthusiastically embraced the power of the film medium at one and the same time. But while the French industry profited from Japanese cinema's expansion, Indochinese subjects were, as previously mentioned, more often than not kept away from film by various official means (Desser 2000: 10–12; Nornes 2003: 2–12).[11]

In addition to such exclusion, the French colonial authorities also attempted to use film as propaganda. Near the end of the First World War, the governor of Indochina initiated an institutional framework for documentary film with the Mission Cinématographique/Cinematographic Mission, an extension of the French army photographic unit, stationed in Hanoi, which toured rural areas in the northern provinces, erecting enormous travelling outdoor screens thirty metres high to project war footage sent from the European front. Films of military parades and naval exercises appeared in the programme, drawing crowds in the thousands who were overwhelmed by the amplified sound and the industrial sophistication of weaponry and sheer violence depicted in towering grandiosity. The mission incorporated aspects of documentary film production that included camera operation, film processing, editing, printing and screening, and the short documentary films made were then also shipped back to Europe for purposes of both economic gain and propaganda. On rare occasions, these reportage films would also appear on screens in cinemas within Vietnamese territory, and were attended by audiences drawn from the colonial elite and local francophone Vietnamese community with sufficient disposable income to pay the price of admission. In general, however, the mission contributed to the further diminishment of a Vietnamese culture already compromised and marginalised by exploitative colonial policies. And yet, what the mission also achieved at the international level, starting in 1917, was that it proved to be a significant precursor to the cultural policy launched at the first meeting of the League of Nations on 16 January 1920, and influenced that organisation's emphasis on documentary cinema throughout the 1920s. The ostensible humanitarian purposes of the institutional frameworks for screen culture represented by the mission and the League nevertheless, however, also perpetuated the colonial myth that film reception should involve a form of moral instruction for colonised peoples; and the French vigorously promoted their civilising mission through film as a veiled means of governing their colonial subjects, and, in addition, stemming the economic influence of Hollywood (see Druick 2008: 66–75; Bloom 2008: 125–39).

During the interwar years, French reportage and newsreels increasingly depicted members of the Nguyen Dynasty royal family, who resided in the imperial citadel of Hue in Annam. Vietnamese reactions to these newsreels suggested two main currents of indigenous reception. On the one hand, because the revolutionaries sought social change and modernisation, they regarded the monarchy as a continuation of a feudal culture that had been overturned under French colonialism and that the French now wished to reinvent as a part of the ongoing process of colonial subjugation. While he was in France during the early 1920s, Ho Chi Minh had been an acerbic critic of the powerless emperor Khai Dinh (1885–1925), Bao Dai's father, who often appeared in newsreels with heavy make-up and elaborate apparel (see Thanh 2003: 27; Wilson 2007: 86). On the other hand, the films were better received by royalist intellectuals like Pham Quynh (1892–1945), who revered the royal family and saw the future of authentic Vietnamese governance in Bao Dai, who in fact spent most of his childhood in Paris and also remained there for most of his life. A similar bifurcation occurred when a French company attempted a film adaptation in 1924 of the eighteenth-century Vietnamese literary classic *Truyen Kieu*, written by Nguyen Du (1766–1820) and publicly reproduced in 1820. The film, entitled *Kim Van Kieu* (A. E. Famechon, 1924), was hailed as a triumph by the colonial press but languished in the theatres and was never released in France. This film was, furthermore, the subject of ridicule in the writings of several prominent Vietnamese-language journalists, such as Nguyen Van Vinh (1882–1936) (see Thanh 2003: 22).[12]

When Khai Dinh died in 1925, a self-taught Vietnamese photographer from Hanoi, Nguyen Lan Huong, requested permission to film the spectacular funeral with his own Paillard-Bolex camera. This person was thoroughly investigated by the French police and found to be a willing collaborator, therefore permission to produce this film was granted and for the first time, in 1926, a colonial subject of French Indochina produced a documentary film. Nguyen produced two short films covering both the funeral and the enthronement of ten-year-old Bao Dai. They were delivered to the colonial authorities, who subsequently distributed them through Gaumont for placement in European newsreels.[13] The films were screened for a short time in Vietnamese cities with much celebration from the official press, but their monarchic focus was also increasingly out of step with the times; as anticolonial intellectuals openly and widely questioned the relevance of the royal family and the institution of the monarchy. Not long after the enthronement of Bao Dai, *Pathé Revue No. 45* – a newsreel from January 1927 with a segment depicting riots among migrant workers of various nationalities, including Vietnamese, in France – was confiscated from theatres in Indochina and sent back to France with official scorn and reprimands that it could incite upheaval among labourers in the colonies.[14]

Progressive documentary film-making in French Indochina was doomed to fail before the August Revolution of 1945 because of the previously mentioned controls that the colonial government had enacted over film production and reception, and only print authorship promised a degree of autonomy for Vietnamese dissidents seeking the freedom to express themselves. The shared experience of documentary as a form of cultural knowledge that could influence and shape the social context was, therefore, disproportionately one-sided, and remained so even as some colonial policies changed – enabling native theatre groups to attempt a small number of fiction film co-productions – and other Asian cinemas emerged (Thanh 2003: 36–50). Given the brutal punishments meted out by the colonial police and military, unauthorised production or exhibition that strayed from the authoritative colonial line would have been impossible until the cumulative efforts of resistance organisations reached a critical mass following the Japanese surrender of August 1945.[15]

By 1940, the newsreel form invented by Pathé and conventionally understood to be short, informative and sequential – an audio-visual extension of print media – had embraced a number of rhetorical devices derived from the political and advertising realms. Reportage and the recording of historical events, including discoveries of nature, science and ethnology, had, for example, evolved into sensationalised instruments of ideology and nationalistic rhetoric on a grand scale.[16] Since the 1920s, documentary film output in Europe had merged with the rhetoric of mass communication for a variety of purposes, including nationalist political propaganda, economic development initiatives and educational programmes related to medical science and other topics (Druick 2008: 75–87). In reciprocal fashion, Japanese documentary newsreel production served the expansion of the Japanese Empire in the years of conquest leading up to the Pacific War (1941–5). During the war, the film industry of Japan reinforced the institutional objectives of the IJA and in June 1940, just after the invasion of French Indochina, the Japanese Minister of Foreign Affairs announced the imperial goal of a self-reliant 'bloc of Asian nations led by the Japanese and free of Western powers' in a radio broadcast describing the benefits of the Greater East Asian Co-Prosperity Sphere. This was the official source of the phrase 'Asia for Asians' included in Japanese propaganda films screened outdoors by mobile projection teams in Indochina during the occupation (see Thanh 2003: 52; Nguyễn 1998: 9).[17]

Yet the occupiers did not banish the newsreels of Western nations or exert pressure on French authorities to modify the system of controls that had been put in place since the first movie theatres were built in 1910. Additionally, all the major American newsreel productions continued to appear on movie screens in Indochina, much as they always had. Despite French colonial officials having developed cinema policies to favour the French industry, and despite the opposition of leftist dissenting film-makers in Japan, most notably the remnants of the influential Prokino group,[18] as late as March 1942 – three highly consequential months after the bombing of Pearl Harbor – Paramount newsreels appeared on visa rosters alongside those of Gaumont, Pathé and Éclair, the three major French documentary studios by then subjected to co-productions with German partners under supervision of the Nazi central film office (Nationalsozialistische Deutsche Arbeiter-Partei). Remarkably, American, Vichy French and Japanese newsreels, the latter being the *Nippon News*, appeared on movie screens in Vietnamese territory until spring 1942.[19] But shipments of motion pictures to Indochina were rapidly declining due to maritime conflicts, and had become sparse by the summer. French and Chinese distributors in Indochina then resorted to showing older films from their collections, including documentaries from the 1930s, made before cinema rosters approved for screening became dominated by Japanese and Éclair Nazi propaganda newsreels from late 1943 onward.[20]

At the beginning of the Pacific War, there were more than fifty urban movie theatres and dozens of entrepreneurs approved for mobile projections operating in Vietnamese territory.[21] By 1943, their numbers had diminished significantly and films were also scarce. Even so, the majority of the Vietnamese population anyway lived in agricultural hamlets and villages where film screenings were rare. Here, the Viet Minh had also effectively established printed and spoken messaging systems to organise resistance activities with greater impact than the imperial propaganda of the IJA, whether filmed or written propaganda. All this inhibited the introduction of IJA propaganda films into the hinterland, and, in addition, the Viet Minh were also able to make their own propaganda film when the newsreel-like documentary film *Ho Chi Minh in France* appeared in the fall of 1946. Here, suddenly, was the president of the new republic himself being welcomed with fanfare and confronting the colonial authorities in their gilded halls with an unwavering entreaty for independence. His presence and actions, as shown by the film, revealed a degree of confidence that came through strongly. This was also the first set of newsreels to be delivered in the Vietnamese language.

TWO VIETNAMESE FILM-MAKERS IN PARIS

Just as the Universal Exposition of 1900 and the Cinematographic Mission of 1918 had circulated ethnographic representations of colonial subjects in the service of French military and economic policy, the International Exposition of Art and Technology in Modern Life, held in Paris in 1937, presented a spectacle of motion picture images from the colonies. The setting escalated ideological antagonism among those attending exhibits presented by the Nazis, the Soviets and the Fascists of Italy and Spain, and also exacerbated divisions within the fragile coalition of the French Popular Front, which hosted the event (see Fiss 2010: 131). At the time, a growing community of immigrants resided in France, many from the traditional aristocracies or educated

Figure 9.1: Mai Trung Thu, June 1946, courtesy of the artist's family.

classes of Indochina, while others from Indochina had arrived to accommodate labour shortages or to pursue economic opportunities. Among them were the two film-makers who produced *Ho Chi Minh in France* and the titular figure himself, before he had become the president of the DRV.

The older of the two Vietnamese film-makers, Mai Trung Thu (1906–80), was born in the northern port city of Haiphong and raised in a highly educated family (see Figure 9.1). In 1930, while in his early twenties, he graduated from the inaugural class of the Indochina College of Fine Arts in Hanoi. He emerged as an insightful painter of the human form using gouache on silk, and took advantage of his status, while teaching in the imperial city of Hue, to depart for the 1937 Paris Exposition. Mai Thu was affected by this experience, most importantly by the strong positive response he received for his visual art from critics, art dealers and other artists. The opportunities he then found in France caused him to remain there for the rest of his life, and he became, among other things, a fixture of the polemical Autumn Salon, which had famously inaugurated Cubism and other avant-garde movements.[22] Also an accomplished traditional Vietnamese musician, Mai Thu moved among the intellectual class of artists, ethnologists and performers affiliated with the newly established Musée de l'Homme/Museum of Man upon his arrival in Paris, frequently performing concerts and radio broadcasts.[23] He served briefly as a volunteer in the French Army from 1940 to 1941, and also taught himself photography and film-making, using portable cameras and sound recording phonographic disks.[24] Mai Thu embraced the Vietnamese independence movement, but he was not a political activist. As the main producer and director of *Ho Chi Minh in France*, he contributed sophistication and personal flair to the project, rather than political insight.

These relatively privileged circumstances contrasted starkly with those affecting the life, and particularly the early life, of Pham Van Nhan (b. 1920), the second contributor to *Ho Chi Minh in France*. Born in the northern city of Ha Dong, Pham, at the age of nineteen, had mastered the French language to such a degree that he was recruited as an interpreter for the Non-specialised Workers programme (Ouvriers non spécialisés, ONS), which sent 20,000 young Vietnamese men to work in French armament factories to replace citizens mobilised for the Second World War. Pham departed for France in November 1939 and found himself in work camps with thousands of other unpaid colonial subjects, moving from site to site on short-term assignments across the country. The overwhelming victory over France by German forces in May 1941 then brought the French arms industry to a halt, leaving the foreign conscripts isolated and trapped in their camps. None could return home because the British fleet had blocked maritime routes to the colonies. Once German forces had taken over the southern territory of France the following year, Pham relocated to Paris to continue his work as a translator for the Indigenous Workforce section (Main-d'œuvre indigène, MOI) of the collaborationist Pétain government. He stayed in a room at the SA and like many ONS workers found himself adrift without rights, even learning to survive on the streets after marching in labour protests and losing his job as a consequence. Once the Americans arrived, he was able to work as an electrician and also enrolled in a photojournalism correspondence course. By early 1946, Pham had developed a reputation in the Vietnamese diaspora community as a resourceful photographer. Thanks to his press credentials, he also became an ideal collaborator for Mai Thu's plan to document the Fontainebleau Conference and Ho Chi Minh's return to France.[25]

The two young men used handheld, hand-cranked, 16mm motion picture cameras, a Ciné Kodak Special (pictured in Figure 9.1) and a Paillard-Bolex H-16 Leader Reflex. These were among the first generation of portable film cameras developed in the 1930s. Mai Thu met Ho Chi Minh in Biarritz when his flight landed there and then travelled with him to Normandy and other locations in France, while Pham Van Nhan filmed events in Paris and Fontainebleau. Putting to use his experience as a photojournalist, Pham also managed the processing of the footage and edited the first versions of *Ho Chi Minh in France* at Mai Thu's home. Inserted among shots of the president and his delegation on their itinerary were newspaper clippings and still photographs from the French press, reflecting at first the optimism projected by French public officials, then ceding to strident statements from Pham Van Dong, the second most prominent member of the Vietnamese delegation, who objected to concurrent French measures taking place in Dalat that sought to extract Cochinchina from the unified Vietnamese state – essentially sabotaging the purpose of the Fontainebleau conference. Mai Thu recorded Ho's speeches in several locations using a phonographic disk recorder, and these segments played out with fixed camera positions in the film in order to depict Ho's remarks as delivered in a fluent, assured manner. Ho's unassuming and plainspoken demeanour appeared uncontrived, down-to-earth and calm. Speaking in the Vietnamese language before a seated audience of Vietnamese émigrés in Paris, the crowd was noticeably moved by his sincerity. In his itinerant formative years, Ho had worked on menial jobs, participated in socialist and communist activities and published an anti-colonial journal called *Le Paria* with dissidents from other countries seeking their fortunes in Paris. In the newsreel series *Ho Chi Minh in France*, he was welcomed on-screen by some of his earliest confidants from that time. Ho had in fact lived most of his life abroad and had used several different names as alibis. He had been imprisoned more than once, and had spent some years in Moscow as both a student and teacher. When he appeared on-screen in the fall of 1946, therefore, it was the first time many rural Vietnamese had seen him.[26]

HO CHI MINH IN FRANCE: SHAPING VIETNAMESE NEWSREEL FILM-MAKING AND RECEPTION

Ho Chi Minh in France consists of three short segments, each edited to present the central action as clearly as possible and at an unhurried pace. At screening events, a *benshi*-like narrator presented the events on screen in the Vietnamese language through a portable amplified sound system (see Thanh 2003: 52).[27] The original version of the film had considerable impact due to the fact that Ho Chi Minh himself appeared in it, and could also be seen to be celebrated with official fanfare in Paris, the capital of the colonial power. As the film also shows, when Ho arrived at Biarritz Airport, a truly impressive diplomatic welcome awaited him. In the presence of French military and government officials, large organised crowds of Vietnamese immigrants appeared, waving banners declaring 'Ho Chi Minh forever'. Wherever Ho addressed crowds in the film, the new national flag of the DRV, with its single yellow star in the centre, was prominently displayed. Ho posed for photographs with French children and adults, interacted with diplomats and inspected French troops. He was escorted onto substantial French naval vessels accompanied by a retinue of officers, and travelled in a diplomatic motorcade attended by French police. *Ho Chi Minh in France*, with its images of the colonial capital, far surpassed the decades-old standards of the rural itinerant screen culture in Vietnam, which had previously included only silent entertainment attractions and the war propaganda films of the Cinematographic Mission that were used to sell French Army bonds to raise money in 1917–18. Vietnamese people had, in addition, never appeared on rural screens prior to this event.

Tinged with irony due to the escalating French military presence in Vietnam, and the countermeasures to this taken by the Viet Minh, the pacific images in this film nevertheless succeeded in overturning almost a century of colonial ideological domination by capturing real and effectual revolutionary events, and also by reinforcing the groundswell of support for resistance. In another sense, the film was also exotic and mysterious. In one scene, for example, a garden party prepared in the president's honour included an orchestra performance played out on the veranda of the Château de Bagatelle in the Bois de Boulogne of Paris, an elegant Romanesque house surrounded by flowers, trees and sculpted shrubbery. Here Ho Chi Minh conducted himself with unwavering detachment, although his appearance alongside the imagery of the colonial metropole also embodied a certain abstruseness and 'otherness'. In similar fashion, when the Fontainebleau negotiations collapsed after it was announced that a simultaneous conference was underway with purported members of the French Union in the southern city of Dalat to solidify the statehood of Cochinchina within a new governmental structure under Parisian control, his composure in the face of French intransigence was portrayed as enduring and determined. This film galvanised thousands of peasants north of the seventeenth parallel, in areas where the Viet Minh were poised to take up arms. The Viet Minh had appropriated the Trans-Vietnam Railway and operated the train themselves in October and November 1946 in order to screen *Ho Chi Minh in France* at all the coastal towns and hamlets south of Hanoi. They halted the train and projected the film outdoors on large screens, not unlike the Cinematographic Mission had done in 1918, returning inland by truck to delay the inevitable confrontation with French troops.[28] This itinerary was only possible in the brief period before hostilities erupted in December 1946. Despite this, however, *Ho Chi Minh in France* had a major impact.

CONCLUSIONS: NEWSREEL, SELF-DETERMINATION AND NATION-BUILDING

Ho Chi Minh in France inaugurated the national cinema of Vietnam and is still shown in various versions today, most frequently on television. At the time, the social context of cumulative resistance efforts and long-term organisation prior to the appearance of the film prepared a keen and willing contemporary audience for its visual qualities and ideological address. In terms of its aesthetic and filmic quality, it could be argued that *Ho Chi Minh in France* incorporated sound, portable camerawork and the montage techniques of photojournalism in the service of what was in the end an unassuming and liberal anti-colonial message, devoid of bombast. Other salient qualities of the film include its positioning of the camera within the independence movement itself, to provide the visual record of Vietnamese self-determination on French soil, and the film tour previously referred to. As a newsreel, the film's three parts provided an authoritative commentary on current political events for a general public desiring national independence, and introduced that public to the leader who would eventually expel the French colonial order.

NOTES

1. The original titles are as follows: 'Hồ Chủ tịch thăm nước Cộng hòa Pháp' ('President Ho visits the Republic of France'), 'Phái đoàn Chính Phủ Việt Nam Dân chủ Cộng hòa tại Hội nghị Phông-ten-nơ-blô' ('Government Delegation of the Democratic Republic of Vietnam at the Fontainebleau Conference'), 'Sinh hoạt của 25.000 Việt kiều ở Pháp' ('25,000 overseas Vietnamese living in France'). There are at least two versions of the reassembled documentary feature in the collection at the Vietnam Film Institute archives in Hanoi, and other versions have been created for television broadcast. For a low-quality version from 1976, see https://www.youtube.com/watch?v=3A01rYdryfQ, accessed on 25 March 2016. I initially viewed the films in Hanoi at the Vietnam Film Institute in 2003. Although the existing prints are attributed to a group called 'Sao Vang' (Yellow Star), there were no production credits on the original footage, and director Mai Trung Thu's company in Paris was called Tan Viet, which opened in 1945. Mai Thu never mentioned his collaborator, Pham Van Nhan, in interviews. For an example in the recent Vietnamese press, see Phuong Nga (2014), *Le Courrier du Vietnam* at http://lecourrier.vn/le-cameraman-du-president-ho-chi-minh-en-1946-en-france/112535.html, accessed on 20 February 2016.
2. The events of this period are the subject of numerous studies. For a detailed introduction, see Marr (1995); for the Japanese political view, see Nitz (1983), and for the French political view, see Grandjean (2004).
3. This series of events has been thoroughly studied from multiple viewpoints. For an introduction, see Marr (1995: 126). For background see Huynh (1971). Also see the US perspective in Patti (1980) and an interesting French perspective in McAlister and Mus (1970).
4. On the background of early resistance to French colonialism, see Marr (1971), and Zinoman (2000).
5. The Meiji Restoration of 1868 restored imperial rule to Japan under Emperor Meiji.
6. On the royalist independence movement, see Tran (2013).

7. Duiker (2000: 66–7) covers this period in considerable detail, describing debates between Ho Chi Minh, then going by the name Nguyen Ai Quoc, and the nationalist intellectual Phan Chu Chinh. Duiker also includes a translation of Ho Chi Minh's interaction with then Minister of Colonies, Albert Sarraut, who had twice been Governor of French Indochina, p. 69.
8. Also see Patti (1970) on his direct involvement and Cooper (2001), and Hammer (1955), for perspectives on the French military and political reactions.
9. Lockhart and Duiker (2006), provide multiple reference points for the Haiphong Incident (1946).
10. The Lumière operator Gabriel Veyre stayed in French Indochina for almost two years, from 1899 to 1900. His correspondence in Jacquier and Pranal (1996), describes his itinerary in detail. The French National Film Archives in Bois d'Arcy near Paris hold a number of unrestored early films from Indochina and my earlier research references that collection. For a sketch of the period, see Thanh (2003: 9–15). Regarding the French global film industry, see Crofts (2002: 26), and Thompson and Bordwell (2003: 34–5). On French film controls, see Centre d'Archives d'Outre-Mer (CAOM), Aix-en-Provence, Fonds de la Résidence Supérieure au Tonkin (1874–1945), RST NF 585, RST NF 590.
11. On diverse reactions to the Japanese victory, see Mishra (2012: 2–5), and Sinh (2009: 10–14). Also, see Da Silva (2014). Although the founding trust for Nikkatsu included a partner named M. Pathé, a company founded in 1906 by Umeya Shokichi, it was not a representative of the French firm, yet the rapid expansion of the Japanese film industry was largely due to French sales of equipment, chemicals and financial investment. Also see Komatsu (2005), and Abel (2010: 404).
12. *Kim Van Kieu* (A. E. Famechon, 1924). No known prints of this film exist, see Thanh (2003: 20–5). For extensive commentary in the colonial press, see CAOM INDO RST NF 589.
13. CAOM, INDO GGI 64383.
14. CAOM, INDO GGI 60025.
15. CAOM, INDO NF 282 and Zinoman (2014: 2).
16. Baechlin and Muller-Strauss provide an accessible introduction (1952: 9). For an accessible summary in French that includes Nazi co-production data, see Gaumont Pathé Archives, http://www.gaumontpathearchives.com/index.php?html=4, accessed on 3 March 2016. On the early ideological developments of Japanese newsreels, see Nornes (2003: 12–14) and his chapter on Prokino (pp. 19–25). The ideological developments of Soviet Cinema have been abundantly researched; see for instance Vertov (1995) and Barnouw (1993: 85–110). For insights on the Empire Marketing Board, see MacKenzie (1989: 192–210).
17. On the policy of Asia for Asians, see Swan (1996: 139–49).
18. Nornes (2003: 35):
    The Proletarian Film League of Japan was a left-wing film organization, known as Prokino for short, active in the late 1920s and early 1930s in Japan. Associated with the proletarian arts movement in Japan, it primarily used small gauge films such as 16mm film and 9.5mm film to record demonstrations and workers' lives and show them in organized events or, using mobile projection teams, at factories and mines. It also published its own journals.

19. CAOM, RST NF 585, RST NF 530.
20. Ibid.
21. CAOM, INDO GGI 60025.
22. On the origins and cultural significance of the Autumn and Independent Salons, see Lovgren (1971).
23. On the history and culture surrounding the Museum, see Conklin (2014: 58–100).
24. Official site of the artist, http://www.mai-thu.fr, accessed on 1 February 2016.
25. Personal correspondence with Pham Van Nhan (2004), and ONS archive, http://www.immigresdeforce.com/pham-van-nhan, accessed on 1 February 2016. The Compagnie Générale de Télégraphie Sans Fil (CSF) offered free training courses during the post-war reconstruction; see http://www.ece.fr/90ans/lecole-centrale-de-tsf-sinstalle-rue-de-la-lune, accessed on 22 February 2016.
26. Part of Ho Chi Minh's declaration of independence speech on 2 September 1945 was captured on film by an anonymous French cinematographer. The footage surfaced and was retrieved by the Viet Minh after hostilities erupted in December 1946. They later recorded his voice with the complete text of the speech and edited parts together for a number of political propaganda films, Duiker (2000: 209–10).
27. *Benshi*s were Japanese performers who provided live narration for both Japanese and foreign silent films.
28. Nguyen Kim Cuong, http://www.tinmoi.vn/phan-nghiem-nguoi-xung-dang-duoc-de-nghi-trao-tang-giai-thuong-ho-chi-minh-01885376.html, accessed on 1 February 2016.

REFERENCES

Abel, Richard (2010), *Encyclopedia of Early Cinema*, London/New York: Routledge.
Baechlin, Peter and Muller-Strauss, Maurice (1952), *Newsreels Across the World*, Paris: UNESCO.
Barnouw, Erik (1993), *Documentary: A History of the Non-Fiction Film*, Oxford: Oxford University Press.
Bloom, Peter (2008), *French Colonial Documentary: Mythologies of Humanitarianism*, Minneapolis: University of Minnesota Press.
Conklin, Alice L. (2014), *In the Museum of Man: Race, Anthropology, and Empire in France, 1850–1950*, Ithaca: Cornell University Press.
Cooper, Nicola (2001), *France in Indochina: Colonial Encounters*, New York: Oxford International Publishers.
Crofts, Stephen (2002), 'Reconceptualizing national cinema/s', in Alan Williams (ed.), *Film and Nationalism*, New Brunswick, NJ: Rutgers University Press.
Da Silva, Joaquin (2014) *Chronology of Japanese Cinema*, accessed on 20 February 2016 at http://eiga9.altervista.org/chronology/chronology1900.html.
Desser, David (2000), 'Japan', in Gorham Kinden (ed.), *The International Movie Industry*, Carbondale, IL: Southern Illinois University Press, pp. 7–21.
Druick, Zoë (2008), '"Reaching the multimillions": liberal internationalism and the establishment of documentary film', in Lee Grieveson and Haidee Wasson (eds), *Inventing Film Studies*, Durham, NC: Duke University Press, pp. 66–87.
Duiker, William (2000), *Ho Chi Minh* New York: Hyperion.

Fiss, Karen (2010), *Grand Illusions: The Third Reich, the Paris Exposition, and the Cultural Seduction of France*, Chicago: University of Chicago Press.

Grandjean, Philippe (2004), *L'Indochine face au Japon: Decoux-de Gaulle, un malentendu fatal*, Paris: L'Harmattan.

Gunn, Geoffrey (2011), 'The great Vietnamese famine of 1944–45 revisited', *Asia-Pacific Journal*, 9: 5, accessed on 3 March 2016 at http://apjjf.org/2011/9/5/Geoffrey-Gunn/3483/article.html.

Hammer, Ellen J. (1955), *The Struggle for Indochina 1940–1955: Vietnam and the French Experience*, Palo Alto: Stanford University Press.

Huynh, Kim Khanh (1971), 'Vietnamese August Revolution reinterpreted', *Journal of Asian Studies*, 30: 4, 761–82.

Irving, R. E. M. (2010), *Christian Democracy in France*, London/New York: Routledge.

Komatsu, Hiroshi (2005), 'The foundation of modernism: Japanese cinema in the year 1927', *Film History*, 17: 2/3, 363–75.

Lockhart, Bruce M. and Duiker, William J. (2006), *Historical Dictionary of Vietnam*, Lanham: Scarecrow.

Lovgren, Sven (1971), *Genesis of Modernism: Seurat, Gauguin, Van Gogh and French Symbolism in the 1880's*, Bloomington: University of Indiana Press.

MacKenzie, John M. (1989), *Imperialism and Popular Culture*, Manchester: Manchester University Press.

Marr, David G. (1971), *Vietnamese Anticolonialism, 1885–1925*, Berkeley: University of California Press.

Marr, David G. (1995), *Vietnam 1945: The Quest for Power*, Berkeley: University of California Press.

McAlister, John T. and Mus, Paul (1970), *The Vietnamese and their Revolution*, New York: Harper & Row.

Mishra, Pankaj (2012), *From the Ruins of Empire: The Intellectuals Who Remade Asia*, New York: Farrar, Strauss and Giroux.

Nguyễn Văn Sự (1998), 'Từ Đồi Cọ, Một Phần Ba Thế Kỷ', *45 Năm: Fafim Việt Nam & Hoạt Động Phổ Biến Phim*, Hanoi: Fafim, pp. 9–17.

Nitz, Kiyoko Kurusu (1983), 'Japanese Military policy towards French Indochina during the Second World War: the road to the Meigo Sakusen (9 March 1945)', *Journal of Southeast Asian Studies*, 14: 2, 328–53.

Nornes, Markus Abé (2003), *Japanese Documentary Film: The Meiji Era Through Hiroshima*, Minneapolis: University of Minnesota Press.

Patti, Archimedes L. A. (1980), *Why Viet Nam? Prelude to America's Albatross*, Berkeley: University of California Press.

Sinh, Vĩnh (ed. and trans.) (2009), *Phan Chau Trinh and His Political Writings*, Ithaca: Cornell University Press.

Swan, William L. (1996), 'Japan's intentions for its Greater East Asia co-prosperity sphere as indicated in its policy plans for Thailand', *Journal of Southeast Asian Studies*, 27: 1, 139–49.

Thanh, Hoàng (2003), in Nguyễn Thị Hồng Ngát (ed.), *Lịch Sử Điện Ảnh Việt Nam Quyển 1: Từ cuối thế kỷ 19 đến giữa năm 1975*, Hanoi: Cục Điện Ảnh Xuất Bản, pp. 9–52.

Thompson, Kristin and Bordwell, David (2003), *Film History: An Introduction*, New York: McGraw-Hill.

Tran My-Van (2013), *A Vietnamese Royal Exile in Japan: Prince Cuong De (1882–1951)*, London/New York: Routledge.
Vertov, Dziga (1995), 'On Kinopravda, 1924', in Annette Michelson (ed.) and Kevin O'Brien (trans.), *Kino-Eye: The Writings of Dziga Vertov*, Berkeley: University of California Press, pp. 42–7.
Wilson, Dean (2007), *Colonial Vietnam on Film: 1896 to 1926*, PhD dissertation, City University of New York (unpublished).
Zinoman, Peter (2000), 'Colonial prisons and anti-colonial resistance in French Indochina: the Thai Nguyen Rebellion, 1917', *Modern Asian Studies*, 34: 1, 57–98.
Zinoman, Peter (2014), *Vietnamese Colonial Republican: The Political Vision of Vu Trong Phung*, Berkeley: University of California Press.

CHAPTER 10

Archives of the Planet: French Elitist Representations of Colonial India

Camille Deprez

In 1908, French banker and patron of the arts Albert Kahn founded Les Archives de la Planète/Archives of the Planet as a depository for photographs and short films of everyday life in the contemporary world. Still located in Boulogne, near Paris, the archives include 72,000 autochrome slates and 183,000 metres of film produced between 1909 and 1931. In the context of the First World War and the interwar years, the purpose of this project consisted of using images to better understand the world and unite its people. These archives were also embedded in a larger network of institutions financed by Albert Kahn that were designed to build a sustainable model of world peace (Baldizzone 2002: 3). Kahn organised four missions to the East between 1914 and 1928. This chapter will more specifically focus on the footage shot in India between 1927 and 1928 by operator Roger Dumas, who was invited by Jagatjit Singh Bahadur – Maharaja of Kapurthala and a personal acquaintance of Albert Kahn – to photograph and film his golden jubilee in his princely state in Punjab (see Figure 10.1). Following this celebration, Dumas's journey through India continued to be mainly directed by various invitations from Indian dignitaries.

These films are located at the margins of the official colonial discourse and cinema in various ways, and as such they constitute a rare archival source to both complement and prompt a reassessment of existing colonial historiography. First, the films stem from the private endeavour of a French patron of the arts striving to avoid further military conflicts after the First World War and were not meant to directly propagate the official political message of the French government. Second, half of the territory in colonial India was directly governed by the British Crown, while the other half was governed by Indian princes or autonomous tribal councils.[1] The films studied in this chapter focus on the princely states of India, which remain marginalised in the academic literature on the colonial era or are treated generally as unique spaces of British indirect rule (Copland 1997; Ramusak 2007). Third, a French operator shot this footage. However, the French colonial presence in India was restricted to five establishments located in the south and east of the territory and therefore remained marginal compared to the influence of the British Raj (Deprez 2014). Fourth, the term 'documentary' came into specialised usage in the 1920s to identify films shooting actual people in their everyday environments in real time; yet this included a large variety of film practices and aesthetic features. The films sponsored by Albert Kahn more specifically borrowed from the traditions of the picturesque, travelogues and expedition films, as well as from the new disciplines of human geography and anthropology, which attributed a greater importance to instinctive, informal and field-based observation, but did not belong to any precise subcategory of the documentary film. Furthermore, the formal qualities of these film shorts – such as their minimal editing or the unusually long duration of the shots – differed from more mature documentaries and mainstream colonial feature films. Like avant-garde cinema of the same period, they also belonged to a kind of minority cinema. Finally, these films were not shown in regular theatres, but were restricted to private screenings organised for the guests of Albert Kahn in his private villa, at classes of his close collaborator, the human geography professor Jean Brunhes, at the renowned research institute the Collège de France in Paris, and at occasional overseas screenings. So they did not reach the general film-watching public, neither in the colonies nor in metropolitan France. I argue, however, that it is precisely because of their outlying status that Albert Kahn's films are able to reveal interstitial significance concerning issues of colonialism and colonial documentary film-making.

In-depth analysis of this small corpus of films (thirty short films in total, all held at the Musée Albert-Kahn in Boulogne) complements the existing literature on the Archives of the Planet and, more specifically, Paula Amad's concept of a 'counter-archive' of time, memory and history, which she defines as distinct from mainstream positivist discourses and images of the period (2008: 4–6, 21–3). Beyond the already discussed utopian message of universal humanism and the scientific record of a world transitioning from tradition to modernity, these shorts reveal complex sites of colonial domination and resistance and the limits of

FRENCH ELITIST REPRESENTATIONS OF COLONIAL INDIA 207

international cooperation between people, both of which are also demonstrated through intricate relations between tradition and modernity. Finally, I will argue that although these films shot in the princely states

Figure 10.1: Portrait picture of Jagatjit Singh Bahadur, Maharaja of Kapurthala, taken from a 1926 group photo of representatives of the Chamber of Princes exhibited at Imperial Hotel, New Delhi. © Philippe Lopez, 2016.

of India are distinct from official colonial moving images and discourses of the time, they nevertheless support the elitist European representations of the Other, the longing for French grandeur on the international scene, and reinforce the existing sociopolitical order in India, which was, in fact, bound to disappear after independence under the pressure of indigenous nationalism and Nehruvian socialism.[2]

A SUBTLE GAME OF PRESTIGE AND REPRESENTATION

With the acceleration of decolonising and fascist pressures in the 1920s, Western countries turned to Eastern counterparts in search of different ways of life and thinking, while ideas of universalism, shared public space, common strategies and reciprocity developed (Bridet 2014: 119). The institutions and films sponsored by Albert Kahn intended to reunite the West and the East for the progress of humankind and international freedom and peace.[3] However, the films shot in India between 1927 and 1928 demonstrate the limits of Kahn's ambitions, as well as internal ambiguities. The ambition to deliver the idealist message of productive cooperation between the British Raj and colonial India was paramount, yet details show that a power struggle was inevitable. At times, the British are shown in a dominant position, such as when the princes bow to the Viceroy and Governor General of India, Lord Irwin (in office from 1926 to 1931), who sits next to the Maharaja of Kapurthala during his jubilee celebrations and thus competes with latter's position of power over his own territory. But, at times, the Maharajas also exclude the Europeans from their activities – for example, during the religious celebration inside a Sikh temple or during the Tuladan ceremony, when the Maharaja is weighed against sacks of grain to determine his worth. Shared experiences are, it seems, limited to less imperious occasions of leisure, such as a garden tea party, a motorboat ride or hunting. Such unremarkable interactions indicate cordial relations, but do not demonstrate any harmonious political or socio-economic cooperation between the colonisers and the colonised. Furthermore, the Maharaja of Kapurthala's decision to commission a French architect to build his palace could be interpreted as a strategy to align himself with French influence and position himself as equal to the British, thus suggesting a potential gap between the British and the Maharaja's understanding of their respective sociopolitical roles in India. The films, therefore, uncover fissures, both in the perceived autonomy of the Maharajas and the supposedly well-balanced relationship with the British colonial administrators, who retained the right to intervene in the states and to remove rulers from power when necessary (Bhagavan 2001: 392).

Most Maharajas, Nawabs (Indian Muslim rulers) and other heads of princely states sided with the British during periods of conflict, including India's First War of Independence, also known as the Indian Rebellion of 1857 (a revolt that led to the Crown's direct colonial governance under the newly created British Raj), the two World Wars and the resistance against independence in 1947. The Maharajas of Kapurthala, Patiala, Alwar, Bharatpur, Udaipur, Mysore and Bikaner, as well as the Nawab of Rampur, all of whom appear in Dumas's films, received honorary titles and medals for their effort in support of the Crown. The British were mainly concerned with their military alliance with the princely states, as shown in the two *Revue militaire/Military Review* films (shot in Bharatpur and Bikaner in 1927 and 1928), in *Parade militaire/Military Parade* (shot in Jhansi around the same time) and in *Lord Irwin at the Maharaja of Kapurthala Palace* (1927), in which the Maharajas deploy their military forces under the supervision of the viceroy, European guests and other invited princes. But the remote locations of Kapurthala, Bikaner, Jhansi and Bharatpur in the Punjab and Rajasthan regions expose their non-strategic position within the British Raj and explain why the British seldom came to visit. Therefore, these films display a staged and misleading representation of power and autonomy. They constitute rare footage of exceptional occasions, and do not reflect the real character of the cooperation between the British and the Maharajas.

Because Kahn's films were screened in non-commercial venues, they did not need to conform to the prevailing 'actuality' view of the world based on recent facts and events and developed by leading French commercial film companies such as Pathé and Gaumont in their weekly newsreels. Instead, the main events covered in the films shot in the princely states focus on ostentatious celebrations, imposing architecture and lavish lifestyles and contribute to visually reinforcing the prestige of the Indian rulers. For instance, for Jagatjit Singh's golden jubilee, five to six hundred tents were installed in the palace's garden to host his guests. Several panoramic shots passing in front of the tents, with the palace in the background, emphasise the scale, as well as the meticulous organisation, of the event. The shorts also show the Maharaja parading before his people in the streets of Kapurthala on the back of a combat elephant – a symbol rather than a tangible sign of power. Most shorts include surreptitious images of servants in livery, from hunting assistants to drivers, guards, gardeners and nannies. Although the princely states eventually lost their sociopolitical power with independence, the films overstate such power in the name of idealism and pacifism – two strong currents of thought in European intellectual circles of the 1920s. The Maharaja of Kapurthala organised sumptuous and expensive events, such as a hunt employing elephants, a garden tea party or the unveiling of a memorial dedicated to the Viceroy Lord Irwin, to court the British and in exchange for honorific titles. For instance, the Maharajas of Kapurthala, Patiala, Alwar, Bikaner, Udaipur, Bharatpur, Mysore and Bikaner, as well as the Nawab of Rampur, clearly identified in the films (among many other Indian dignitaries), sat in the Chamber of Princes from its very creation by the British in 1921 in compensation for their contribution to the First World War and their subsequent call for more autonomy. This institution, which remained active until the independence of India in 1947, was supposed to offer a platform for legislative and political discussions and an international voice to the rulers of the princely states of India, but it was never allocated any tangible power. One of Dumas's films focuses on a *Reception at the Parliament in New-Delhi*. Lord Irwin, Viceroy of India from 1926 to 1931, inaugurated the opening of the House of Parliament in Delhi in January 1927 and a few months later invited a group of princes, mainly from Punjab and Rajasthan, to visit the building where the Chamber of Princes' sessions would henceforth take place. Although the Maharajas and Nawabs swagger in front of Dumas's camera, in reality they were unable to negotiate power with the viceroy. Moreover, several important figures, like the Maharajas of Baroda, Gwalior and Holkar, refused to join the institution – an act of opposition to the British that is not apparent in these cheerful images. Interestingly, after the First World War, filming 'events' slowly took the upper hand, yet Kahn's films also include sequences where nothing specific happens, such as when the camera mixes general and closer shots, static and panoramic views of the Maharaja of Kapurthala's gardens, as if tracking the operator's casual stroll in the premises. This kind of sequence, which appears in several shorts, not only contradicts the ambition of the Archives of the Planet to focus on the demonstrative power of images (Le Martinel 2002: 65), but more intriguingly presents the princely states as quiet and immaculate spaces, which were yet cut off from strategic decision-making.

As suggested by François de la Bretèque (2004: 137), considering that the screenings' commentaries did not reach us, Kahn's films should be related to publications emanating from his sponsored institutions (the 'extra-filmic' analysis) and/or other films in the archives collection (the 'inter-filmic' analysis). In the case of India, four publications provide relevant sources of information. The first is a transcript of Rabindranath Tagore's speech delivered before the Kahn's Circle in Boulogne in 1921 and published in the 'Comité national d'études sociales et politiques' bulletin the same year (Tagore 1921).[4] This transcript acknowledges the relations between Albert Kahn and the Indian poet and intellectual, who embodied Kahn's dream of harmonious cooperation between the East and the West and of a superior and unified humanity. His influence on the films shot in India should therefore be scrutinised. The Société Autour du monde/Around the World Society bulletins also include three reports on India published by three high school teachers of history and geography, who benefited from Kahn's travel grants. The first was published in 1914 by teacher Paul Cornuel and highlights unequal opportunities between Hindus and Muslims and how the strict denominational education had deepened the gap between the two communities. He analyses the increasing influence of two Hindu reformist movements: the Brahmo Samaj,[5] first launched in 1828, which he describes as a simple form of spiritualism for educated minds; and the Arya Samaj, founded in 1875, which he presents as a conservative interpretation of Hindu sacred texts. He warns against the latter's violent political activism, which shifted from an early anti-colonial to a later anti-Muslim position, which, he felt, threatened social harmony in India (Cornuel 1914: 22–43). The second report, written by teacher Marthe Antoine, dates back to 1915 and mainly praises the charity activities undertaken by Indian organisations to support the emancipation of women. She presents such activities as successful examples of association between Western concepts (the British tradition of charity work) and the Indian local context (Antoine 1915: 93–106). In the third report, published in 1927, teacher Étienne Dennery focuses on his visit to the Hindu holy city of Benares – a centre of Indian nationalism – and his meeting with Mahatma Gandhi.[6] He presents the clashes between Hindus and Muslims as a threat to the country's unity and places the blame for this on the British. He also criticises Gandhi's advocacy of the traditional homespun cloth (*kadhi*), developed as a tool for economic self-sufficiency (*swaraj*), for being backward-looking and closed to any form of cooperation with Europe (Dennery 1927: 19–33). Based on concrete and individual cases observed on location in India and in line with Albert Kahn's ideals, these three reports emphasise either instances of, or the need for, cooperation at the local and international levels.

Although Tagore was in favour of India's independence, he was not a supporter of the National Congress Party[7] as the principal vehicle of the Indian nationalist project and resigned from all nationalist committees. Following his family's involvement in the Brahmo Samaj movement, he wanted to bring about a revival of the pre-British Indian culture (Somjee 1961). In his speech before the Boulogne Circle in 1921, he critiqued the dominant use of the notion of 'nation' by the Indian nationalist movement because he believed it to be a foreign concept unsuited to the Indian context and the antithesis of all that the human spirit stood for. Rather, he pursued an ideal of universal humanism and exhorted the West to better understand the East. This position echoes Kahn's troubled relation to the idea of the nation: a structuring and fundamental principle of French identity under the Third Republic, yet a potential threat to his universalist ideal. In the princely states, Roger Dumas filmed India at a time when the local population had no sense of national belonging. During the Maharaja's parade throughout the streets of Kapurthala, the crowds pay their respects to their only recognised authority figure. The films also include several panoramic shots of outer city walls and closer static shots of gates, which possibly idealise the princely states as separate, protected enclaves from the rest of Indian territory. However, Dumas's films seem to cherry-pick Tagore's ideas, without embracing his entire philosophy. For instance, they put aside his belief in the spiritual ideal – rather than science – as the best way to achieve universal unity and peace. Although Marthe Antoine's report shares Tagore's trust in individual liberation through action in civil society, such actions are not represented in the films shot by Roger Dumas in the princely states. As demonstrated later in this chapter, the only social reforms that appear in the films emanate from the Maharajas and not from civil society. Finally, pursuing their idealist vision of India, the films do not address the travel grantees' concerns with the rising tension between Hindus and Muslims and the responsibility of the local and British rulers for this sectarian conflict, which threatened and eventually doomed the objectives of universal humanism and long-term peace in the region. On the contrary, Dumas shot the construction of a mosque within Kapurthala's vicinity, built under the auspices of a Sikh leader. By following the detailed movements of the workers making bricks, dipping them in water, carrying them on their heads or climbing a temporary ladder, Dumas records the construction of the mosque as an uncontested project and suggests a friendly cohabitation between different religious groups in the princely state. Further, the presence of Sikh and Hindu Maharajas as well as Muslim Nawabs during Jagajit Singh's golden jubilee celebrations suggests an interreligious camaraderie within the Indian traditional elite, which was ultimately jeopardised by Hindu nationalism, the Partition of India and the creation of Pakistan. By embracing Tagore's universal humanism rather than Gandhi's *swaraj* (self-sufficiency) or Nehru's imported concept of nationalism, Dumas's films favoured utopia over the pragmatic political struggle for independence, and the corollary Partition, and thus stood against the course of history that India actually took.

THE INTRICATE RELATION BETWEEN TRADITION AND MODERNITY

Aligned with the Third Republic's investment in secular education, Kahn believed in teaching future elites to better rule the world of tomorrow. He was probably attracted to the princely states because they were considered more progressive and welfare-oriented than the rest of British India. Instances of modern and progressive reforms appear in the films, such as an elementary school, a cadet academy or a library sponsored by the Maharajas. But these distinguished institutions should be understood as a strategy to decolonise India, rather than mimic the colonial rulers.[8] They appropriate the Western concepts of 'progress' and 'modernity' and demonstrate India's unique ability to blend modernity with local customs and conditions. The films further contradict the myth of the princely states as 'pure pockets of India' (Bhagavan 2008: 887–8), where religious culture and traditions survived, by showing how traditions and modernity coexist. The Maharajas ride elephants and drive expensive cars, wear traditional outfits as well as Western suits, exhibit their wives and mingle with European women. The existing literature on the Archives of the Planet emphasises the intention of showing and recording what remained of a traditional pre-modern world that was bound to disappear;[9] however, the films shot in the princely states of Punjab and Rajasthan show a certain fascination for the coexistence of tradition and modernity. Compared with static photography, Dumas's mobile camera could indeed capture change, yet the basic editing of sequences clearly shows the cohabitation of modernity and tradition. In doing so, Kahn's films distance themselves on the one hand from the Hindu fundamentalists, who considered the princely states as sites of India's imagined past of purity and the foundation for the future nation, and on the other hand from the British administrators, who invented the princely states as simplistic, religious backwaters to serve as a contrast to Western progressivism and modern, rational and religiously neutral British India (Bhagavan 2008: 888–91), and in order to justify colonialism.

These films were shot during the interwar years, at the peak of French colonial expansionism. The meetings organised by Albert Kahn in Paris every fortnight covered a wide range of current issues, including the status of the French colonies. Paula Amad has rightly noted that if the Archives of the Planet were not directly aligned with French colonial propaganda, they were embedded in the global colonial culture of their time (Amad 2008: 265). Indeed, when looking closely at the films shot in India, beyond the message of international peace and humanism endorsed by Albert Kahn, operator Roger Dumas still maintains a gaze often tinged with colonialism and Orientalism. Contrary to newsreels and the influence of the Lumière brothers' films, Kahn's operators also took the time to immerse themselves in their new environment and did not restrict their work to a distanced gaze. For instance, the Maharaja's change of outfits shows that the jubilee celebrations were shot over the course of several days, and this allowed both narrative progression and a sense of dramatic construction. By mixing long with middle-distance and closer shots, and by using a mobile camera, the operator reveals his deep involvement and close relationship with his subject. He does not simply record situations as they unfold, but constructs a favourable representation of the events filmed. This is particularly obvious in a sequence where an unidentified Indian woman approaches the camera (cut from a long to a middle-distance shot), then shows her back and turns around to face the camera in a medium close-up. Her movements do not appear spontaneous, but rather seem to follow the instructions of the operator. Thanks to Kahn's close relationship with the Maharaja of Kapurthala, Dumas gained rare, intimate access to Maharanis, some of whom lived secluded lives (*purdah*). As the Maharani plays with the *pallu* (or the loose end) of her sari to reveal or conceal parts of her body, her Oriental beauty and grace are commodified to display the Maharaja's somptuous lifestyle and social prestige. Furthermore, this scene is inserted between the reflection of a building in a European-style fountain and a frontal shot of a building's façade, as if her status was reduced to mere property and an external sign of opulence. Yet, if such proximity reveals a negotiation of domestic intimacy between colonial and indigenous ruling forces that was crucial to both British and French colonial ideology, by agreeing to perform for the camera (she even smiles directly at the viewer), the Maharani also appropriates the medium, asserts herself as an autonomous and distinct subject, and thus resists the controlling colonial gaze.

Between connivance and resistance, both parties play around with, and thus blur, the limits of Orientalist representations. Here again, the films correspond with the publications. Marthe Antoine's report betrays instances of colonialism and Orientalism when she critiques the local traditions of castes, women's hypergamy and widowhood, whilst praising the positive role of the British in inspiring social reform. She also analyses the condition of Indian women based on Western notions of 'progress', 'individualism' and 'nation', without trying to understand the possible unsuitability of such concepts in the Indian context. In doing so, she perpetuates the idea that the British necessarily provide the tools for India's emancipation, and that the East remains subordinate to the West. This ambiguity reveals the long-lasting impact of Orientalism, in spite of the fact that films and publications sponsored by Kahn were produced at a time when such stereotyped representations were officially considered to be declining in prevalence and currency.

PROMOTING ELITISM, THE INDIAN SOCIOPOLITICAL STATUS QUO AND FRENCH INTELLECTUAL GRANDEUR

Because Dumas lacked the necessary field experience in countries where the French did not have a major colonial presence, such as India, he relied on Kahn's acquaintances and started filming the lives of the latter's local correspondents. As a result, these films do not fit the encyclopaedic trend developed by major French film companies Lumière and Gaumont during this period and contribute little to their catalogue of views from around the world. Dumas's trip to India was prompted by Rabindranath Tagore's and the Maharaja of Kapurthala's initial invitations to Albert Kahn's home in 1921 and 1923 respectively. The films' foci are clearly oriented by the privileged relations Kahn developed with these two important Indian figures and map out their like-mindedness. Both Tagore and Singh grew up in family environments open to Western influences, received an English education both in India and abroad and travelled the world. Jagajit Singh was interested and involved in European politics, attending the signing of the Treaty of Versailles (signed in 1919 to seal the end of the First World War) and later representing the Indian princes at the Société des Nations/League of Nations, founded in 1920 in response to the formation of this treaty. Albert Kahn developed a strong interest in such enterprises, as they were directly connected to his ideal of building sustainable world peace. Invited to Jagajit Singh's golden jubilee, Roger Dumas came to meet other Maharajas and Nawabs, who in their turn invited him to visit their princely states and directed his tour of India, as when the Maharaja of Patiala guided his visit to the Golden Temple in Amritsar.[10] These personal connections with Indian traditional elites provide unique access to rare events and moments of intimacy. On several occasions, the Maharajas even appropriate the body language and social behaviours of the Europeans as they were represented in many expedition and ethnographical films of the same period, such as the many moments when princes acknowledge the presence of the camera by pointing at it with a knowing smile or when an Indian guest invited to the hunt organised by the Maharaja of Kapurthala waves at the camera as he is carried on the back of an elephant. The collusion goes further when the Maharaja is shown accompanied by European women (including Lady Irwin, the viceroy's wife) during the garden tea party, the hunt, the visit of his sponsored cadet academy in Phagwara, his military review in Jhansi or at the unveiling of a memorial dedicated to Lord Irwin. Jagajit Singh, much like other princes, had several wives, including Spanish dancer and singer Anita Delgado, whom he married in 1908, and the Czech Eugenia Maria Grossupova, whom he married in 1942. If miscegenation had been the subject of multiple colonial films, these were often nonetheless produced to reinforce the racial superiority of the colonisers (Chowdhury 2000: 205–10). Yet, in the films presented here, the intimacy between Jagajit Singh and European women suggests the exotic fascination of these foreign women for the princes' lavish lifestyle, as well as Singh's ambiguous endorsement of the European mystification of the figure of the Maharaja, despite his personal inclination for Western cultures and values. In order to please French operator Roger Dumas while galvanising their own self-image abroad, the princes collaborated with him to create an idealised version of their traditional lifestyle before the camera (a hunt on an elephant's back, a garden party, jubilee celebrations, visits to uninhabited palaces, military parades and so on), although these activities remained occasional.

But by focusing mainly on the princely states, these films eventually fall short of the initial plan of 'presenting the world of facts in an "incorruptible" manner' (Amad 2001: 143) and, in the case of India, of recording an accurate representation of the country as a whole.[11] A banker linked to international finance, industry tycoons, political and social leaders, the intelligentsia, as well as the media, Kahn was in fact an elitist. Yet relying on a small, privileged group to lead India successfully into the future contradicted his ideal of humanism as serving common human needs and improving the condition of the weakest. Although these shorts seem to fit de la Bretèque's 'commemorative' (for example, the jubilee and military parades) and 'patrimonial' (for example, the focus on architecture) film categories (2002: 143),[12] they do not result in any systematic approach, or achieve an element of representativeness, and as a result they provide only incomplete and biased images of India. As a token of Kahn's friendship, one of these films' objectives is clearly to present the Maharajas as positive and likeable figures. For instance, one of the shorts shows several mid-shots of Kanteerava Narasimharaja Wadiyar, Maharaja of Mysore, smiling at the camera, approaching it in a friendly manner and socialising with other Indian dignitaries around him. He is not performing any significant action and is quite unknown to the French public; however, his importance is emphasised in the film simply because he was one of Jagatjit Singh's closest friends. Similar representations of the Maharaja of Kapurthala reappear throughout this series of films. Supporting Paula Amad's thesis of the counter-archive, Dumas includes the ordinary, unofficial and anecdotal elements of the extraordinary people, places and events he encounters (Amad 2008: 24). However, by focusing mainly on the traditional privileged few of India, Dumas's films elude the general concerns and lifestyles of the wider society and thus do not provide the instruments of sociopolitical change to which the Archives of the Planet project was committed. Occasional shots of civilians mainly represent them as faithful soldiers, dedicated servants or unchallenging subjects.[13]

Furthermore, I would suggest a reconsideration of Amad's claim that 'individual films lacked any internal argumentative structure' and remained 'unincorporated into any wider persuasive or poetic narrative' (2001: 153). Beyond claims of intercultural understanding and cooperation, and beyond a project of universal archiving, these films also reveal a restrictive, subjective, predetermined and idealised representation of colonial India. Under the influence of Indian Maharajas, and by mainly recording exquisite places, people and events, these films surprisingly praise the culture of kingship and reinforce the established sociopolitical order of India, when as a French citizen, Kahn should, according to the values of the Republic, have been championing republicanism and questioning royalty. The films were based on direct on-site observation, yet they provided a certain amount of mystification vis-à-vis the genuine context of the events filmed, so as to fit the primary objectives of Kahn's project. Such exclusive representations of India not only avoid images of striking poverty and the critique of the Maharajas (or any other form of domination by a privileged minority) by Gandhi and the Indian Nationalist Movement, but also ignore possible solutions to social problems, despite the fact that these issues are mentioned in the travel grantees' reports. This partial depiction further contradicts the humanist ideal proposed by the Archives of the Planet. The project of mutual cultural, racial and religious respect is eventually restrained by the political, economic and social powers being centralised in the hands of a small and privileged group of people. In addition, through closer affiliation to Tagore and the uncluttered spiritualism of the Brahmo Samaj initiated by his father, Kahn supported an elitist group influenced by Christian missionaries and stereotyped conceptions of the East that did not reach the wider Indian population in any influential way. Thus, his films remained inevitably disconnected from the situation on the ground. Agrarian revolts and communal clashes took place in the states at the beginning of the 1930s (Cop and 1997: 130–1) and signs of rising tension were presumably already visible during Dumas's visit from 1927 to 1928, yet they remain completely absent from the films.

Albert Kahn and the philosopher – and his personal mentor – Henri Bergson, as well as human geographer and main collaborator Jean Brunhes, belonged to the post-1870 Franco–Prussian war generation, who dedicated their lives to re-establishing French intellectual grandeur as a competitive presence in relation to neighbouring Germany, and globally. Kahn's Société Autour du Monde fund, for instance, was administered by the Sorbonne to enable young teachers chosen from 'the intellectual and moral elite of the nation' to 'enter into sympathetic communication with the ideas, feelings and lives of other people' (Amad 2008: 32). In France, colonial expansion was still perceived as an important instrument to maintain French grandeur and power at political, economic and moral levels. At times, a leftist-oriented political intelligentsia could contest the modalities of the imperial endeavour, but not – or rarely – its principle (Deprez 2014: 32). The planetary ambitions of the Kahn archives were embedded in these French national ideals. This patriotic impetus reveals the complex relationship Kahn developed towards nationalism and his higher ideal of universal humanism. Yet, it also explains why Kahn's operator was keen on displaying – and perhaps he exaggerated – the French architectural influence on the Maharaja of Kapurthala, despite the fact that the latter mainly toyed with the French baroque style to visually display the flamboyance of his princely state and to symbolically assert his contested authority against the British. Thus, monuments were not only filmed as a 'spectacle for the eye' to 'magnify the spectacular' as argued by Paula Amad (2008: 234), but more specifically contributed to instilling a sense of French grandeur in exclusive European audiences back in Paris. Dumas allocated more time to shots of the main palace – completed in 1906 by French architect Alexandre Marcel and inspired by Versailles, Fontainebleau and Louvres châteaux – than any other edifice on the premises, although this and other palaces reveal the princes' eclectic interests in both Western and Oriental architecture.

CONCLUSIONS: A BIASED REPRESENTATION OF INDIA

The films shot in India from 1927 to 1928 were shaped by the personal vision of Albert Kahn and his operator Roger Dumas, who projected their utopian ambition of world peace and universal humanism onto their filmed subjects. Thus the initial intention of gaining an exact and comprehensive knowledge of foreign lands, advocated by human geographer and close collaborator in the Archives of the Planet project, Jean Brunhes, was necessarily distorted by the operator's subjectivity and personal experiences in the field. Despite the inclusion of discourses of accuracy and authenticity to legitimise these documentary films as respectable artistic, entertaining and educational forms (Amad 2008: 32), they remained irremediably subjected to the general objectives pursued by Kahn and the operator's appropriation of such objectives. As a result, with the active cooperation of the Maharajas and Nawabs of India, they provided largely staged and partial visual representations of the princely states.

The idea that a strategic withdrawal from British colonisation could come from the princely states was an illusion. They were too marginal to take on more powerful forces coming from within the Congress Party and the influence of Nehru's socialism. Even Mahatma Gandhi eventually had to align with the Congress Party; a compromise Rabintranath Tagore never accepted. By following Tagore's ideals, rather than primary anti-colonial positions in India, Kahn's films were inevitably disconnected from local circumstances. Although Kahn's motto in his essay *Droits et devoirs des gouvernements/Rights and Responsibilities of Governments* was to see in order to know, to know in order to predict and act upon social reality (1918: 9), he and Dumas, influenced by utopian ideals of universal cooperation and peace, clearly did not predict – or did not want to envisage – the end of the princely states in India. However, the project of a new, independent India did not accommodate these princely states, which were criticised by Gandhi and Nehru as pockets of despotic control, and they eventually lost their power with independence in 1947. Moreover, and as mentioned, the rising conflict between Hindus and Muslims does not appear in the films, although after the Partition of India and Pakistan in 1948, Hindus replaced Muslims in Kapurthala and nation states superseded multiculturalism. Thus, Kahn's films not only offered a counter-archive of history, but were also set against India's historical course. We know that neither bulletins nor films ever reached their targeted elite audience in time to be of immediate impact. Dumas's shorts shot in the princely states ultimately demonstrate that

Kahn's films were both embedded in and at odds with the time, and this ambivalence may also explain why the Archives of the Planet project eventually failed.

ACKNOWLEDGEMENTS

This paper is based on research funded by the School of Communication, Hong Kong Baptist University, project FRG1/13–14/047: 'The documentary film in India: film analysis and online knowledge transfer'. I would also like to thank Serge Fouchard, curator at the Musée Albert-Kahn in Boulogne, for facilitating access to the archives during the course of this research.

NOTES

1. The term 'Indian princes' was invented by the British colonisers to cover diverse practices of local governance and thus implies a colonial bias, as well as limited understanding of this issue at the local level.
2. Jawaharlal Nehru borrowed his vision of political, social and economic reforms from socialist ideals, while adapting these ideals to the specificities of the Indian context (including a mixed planned economy, an opposition to the caste system, an emphasis on secularism, a focus on decentralisation, cooperatives, and so on).
3. They included the Société Auteur du Monde/Around the World Society fund (1906–49), administered by the Sorbonne, which financed travel grants and organised conferences in Paris; the Comité national d'études sociales et politiques (National Committee of Social and Political Studies, 1916–31), also known as the 'Circle', which gathered distinguished individuals every fortnight in Paris to discuss various sociopolitical issues and published bulletins; the funding of Jean Bruhnes's new human geography chair at the prestigious Collège de France in Paris; and the Centre de documentation sociale/Social Documentary Resource Centre (1919–40), which organised seminars to make up for French tardiness in the human sciences.
4. See note 3 for more details about this committee.
5. It is interesting to note that the Brahmo Samaj was created by Raja Ram Mohun Roy and Debendranath Tagore, the father of poet and intellectual Rabindranath Tagore, with whom Albert Kahn met and shared similar political views. One might wonder if Albert Kahn or Jean Brunhes influenced Cornuel's reporting his firsthand observations of this organisation.
6. This possibly explains why Roger Dumas, whose Indian journey mainly followed invitations from various dignitaries in Punjab and Rajasthan, also shot footage in Benares. This footage, however, falls beyond the main objectives of this chapter.
7. Formed in 1885, the National Congress Party (or Congress Party) was the principal organised political force that dominated the movement for independence in India.

8. Other Maharajas, such as the Maharaja of Baroda, utilised this concept of being 'almost but not quite' like the Western colonisers (Bhagavan 2001: 387).
9. François de la Bretèque writes that Kahn wanted to show and record the remains of a pre-modern world that was bound to disappear, but without filming the 'eternal man', like Robert Flaherty in *Nanook of the North* (2002: 143). Paula Amad also mentions this general intention, while highlighting how the films recorded mainly 'shifting identities under the forces of modernity'; 'a perpetual flux between the traditional and the new' (Amad 2001: 150–1). In the case of the Indian princely states, I would argue that there was a simultaneous cohabitation between tradition and modernity, rather than shift or flux.
10. Besides the princely state of Kapurthala, Dumas also visited palaces in Patiala and Rampur in the state of Punjab, and Deeg, Alwar, Sariska, Bharatpur, Bikaner, Gajner and Udaipur in the state of Rajasthan, as well as surrounding areas.
11. The Musée Albert-Kahn in Boulogne holds thirty-seven films shot by Roger Dumas in India from 1927 to 1928, among which seven are rushes and thirty are edited films. Out of these thirty-seven films, only seven do not focus on the princely states, being shot in Benares, Delhi and Agra (the Taj Mahal).
12. Out of the thirty films shot in or about the princely states by Roger Dumas, twenty-one focus – either fully or partially – on architecture and typically include panoramic shots and general views of cities, palaces, forts, the Golden Temple in Amritsar and even a mosque under construction.
13. Only three shorts – two focused on the construction of a mosque and rural life in the vicinity of Kapurthala and the third shot in the streets of Rampur – describe the daily lives of local workers, farmers and shopkeepers in the princely states.

REFERENCES

Amad, Paula (2001), 'Cinema's sanctuary: From pre-documentary to documentary film in Albert Kahn's *Archives de la planète*, 1908–1931', *Film History*, 13: 2, 136–59.

Amad, Paula (2008), *Counter-Archive: Film, the Everyday, and Albert Kahn's Archives*, New York: Columbia University Press.

Antoine, Marthe (1915), 'Mon voyage autour du monde: Octobre 1912–Août 1913', *Bulletin de la société autour du monde*, 93–106.

Baldizzone, José (2002), 'Introduction et brève chronologie d'Albert Kahn', *Le Cinéma d'Albert Kahn: Quelle place dans l'histoire?*, *Les Cahiers de la Cinémathèque*, 74: Special Issue, 3–4.

Bhagavan, Manu (2001), 'Demystifying the "ideal progressive": resistance through mimicked modernity in princely states', *Modern Asian Studies*, 35: 2, 385–409.

Bhagavan, Manu (2008), 'Princely states and the Hindu imaginary: exploring the cartography of Hindu nationalism in colonial India', *Journal of Asian Studies*, 67: 3, 881–915.

Bridet, Guillaume (2014), 'L'Inde une ressource pour penser: Retour sur les années 1920', *Mouvements*, 1: 77, 119–30.

Chowdhury, Prem (2000), *Colonial India and the Making of Empire Cinema: Image, Ideology and Identity*, Manchester: Manchester University Press.

Copland, Ian (1997), *The Princes of India in the Endgame of Empire, 1917–1947*, Cambridge: Cambridge University Press.

Cornuel, Paul (1914), 'Les Indes', *Bulletin de la société autour du monde*, 22–43.
De la Bretèque, François (2002), 'Albert Kahn, d'un certain regard sur le monde et sa place dans l'histoire', *Le Cinéma d'Albert Kahn: Quelle place dans l'histoire?, Les Cahiers de la Cinémathèque*, 74: Special Issue, 137–46.
Dennery, Étienne (1927), 'Avec Ganchi à Bénarès', *Bulletin de la société autour du monde*, 31 décembre, pp. 19–33.
Deprez, Camille (2014), 'Colonial discourse and documentary film at the margins: the case of *Delhi grande ville de l'Inde supérieure* and *Dans l'État du Cachemire*, two early Pathé Frères films shot in India', *Studies in European Cinema*, 11: 1, 26–39.
Kahn, Albert (1918), *Des droits et des devoirs des gouvernements*, Paris: Self-published.
Le Martinel, Bertrand (2002), 'Le paysage des géographes français au temps d'Albert Kahn', *Le Cinéma d'Albert Kahn: Quelle place dans l'histoire?, Les Cahiers de la Cinémathèque*, 74: Special Issue, 63–8.
Ramusak, Barbara N. (2007), *The Indian Princes and their States*, Cambridge: Cambridge University Press.
Somjee, A. H. (1961), 'The political philosophy of Rabindranath Tagore', *Indian Journal of Political Science*, 22: 1/2, 134–45.
Tagore, Rabindranath (1921), Speech transcript (untitled), *Bulletin du comité national d'études sociales et politiques*, 2–11.

CHAPTER 11

'Sufficient Dramatic or Adventure Interest': Authenticity, Reality and Violence in Pre-War Animal Documentaries from South-East Asia

Timothy P. Barnard

In late 1926 William Douglas Burden, an American explorer, returned from South-East Asia with two of the rarest animals in the world. They were Komodo dragons, and their presence in the Bronx Zoo created a sensation throughout New York City, meriting coverage in the leading newspapers of the day. However, the stir they created only lasted a few months. The two animals died – one in October, the other in November of that year – as the zoological park did not have the proper facilities to house large reptiles in a climate that was transitioning from autumn into winter. The two lizards were quickly presented to the American Museum of Natural History, where they were stuffed and put on display in a glass case that created a facsimile of their original environment (Barnard 2011: 2, 97–8). Visitors could now view them up close, and can still do so today: static reminders of an earlier era. Alongside the display the museum ran never-released film footage taken on the expedition that led to the capture of the dragons to provide a vivid depiction of their original environment. The film provided a more active viewing experience, taking the viewer into the exotic world of South-East Asian fauna.

The footage is twelve minutes in length and focuses on Burden and his wife Katherine and their time on the remote Indonesian island of Komodo. Following a series of establishing shots – of the museum, the Komodo display, a variety of animals on the actual island and the construction of the expedition camp – in the first five minutes of the film, three scenes make up the rest of the footage. The first depicts the shooting of a water buffalo, which will serve as food for the camp as well as bait for lizards. The second extended scene features a series of quick clips that begins with Katherine shooting a Komodo dragon that was feasting on the water buffalo carcass. This quickly transitions into the construction of a trap, the shooting and placement of a deer in the trap, and then the capture of a lizard lured into it. The final scene focuses on two dragons ripping and tearing apart the carcass of an animal. Douglas Burden then shoots a dragon, which is carried back to the camp to await transport to a museum in the United States or Europe.

While of interest, the footage Douglas Burden shot on Komodo is crude. It provides basic information about the geography and fauna of the island as well as the arrival of the American expedition. The animals are shown in their natural environment, while some are shot or captured. The human visitors are never in danger and their time is spent collecting specimens for museums and zoological gardens. Basically, there is minimal narrative structure. The film ultimately holds little significance, except for those interested in the appearance of the island in the 1920s or the history of the specific expedition. The footage shot on Komodo Island in 1926, however, has been the subject of analysis in several texts, including Fatimah Tobing Rony's *The Third Eye* and Gregg Mitman's *Reel Nature* (Rony 1996; Mitman 1999). The authors describe the footage as being related to the amalgamation of both ethnographic and horror footage in Rony's interpretation or romantic primitivism for Mitman.

While the footage shot on Komodo has merited comment from scholars, the expedition, not the film, had more significant influence on cinema. Burden was not able to find a commercial distributor for the film. He did profit from the journey, nevertheless, through the publication of a book depicting his time in the Netherlands East Indies (Burden 1927). The text describes an American expedition that metaphorically moves back in time from modern civilisation to an antediluvian island where huge primitive beasts dominate. The brave Americans ultimately are able to secure some of these beasts and take them back to New York. The magnificent animals, however, are unable to live in the concrete jungle of the city. The tale Burden wove became popular throughout late 1920s' America, often finding its way into advertisements and other aspects of popular culture. With regard to cinema culture, Burden's tale ultimately became an inspiration for other film-makers and adventurers; it was one of the key influences in the development of the film *King Kong* (Merian C. Cooper and Ernest B. Schoedsack, 1933) (Barnard 2011: 52–3). The footage of Komodo dragons that Douglas Burden shot thus represents a stuttering attempt to present realistic images of animals that ironically led to one of the most fantastical depictions of animals on film.

South-East Asia was a popular site for film-makers from the West searching for the exotic and fantastic, whether it was the jungles of Borneo or the religion and cultures of Bali. Cinema at this time was expanding alongside America and its own imperial enterprise. The lure of the jungle – animals, exotic and unknown – played a key role in this. As Kelly Enright argues in her monograph *The Maximum of Wilderness*, the jungle took on new aspects of conception in the Western imagination during this period. It was 'a landscape that defied Western culture, with its technology and consumerism' (Enright 2012: 3). It became a place where Western desires could be projected. Film played an important role in this process. As scientific expeditions, often accompanied by film-makers, began to enter the tropics, they sought not only scientific information but also cultural narratives in which common tropes could be conveyed to the public. This chapter will trace the role that such footage played in creating an image of animals in the wild and how this was located in the ambiguous space that separated documentary from narrative film at the time. It was during this period that the entertainment industry influenced nature films by introducing staged performances, thus transforming them to the point where they became questionable in their authenticity (Burt 2002: 8). Such introductions reveal broader cultural tensions and anxieties about the perceived savagery and violence outside of Western civilisation. Animal documentaries shot in South-East Asia in the 1920s and the 1930s also played an important role in the development not only of documentary cinema, but also narrative cinema in general.

ANIMALS IN EARLY WILDLIFE FILMS

The concept of a 'wildlife film' only became well known in the mid-twentieth century, although the term 'natural history film' appears to have been common as early as the 1910s. Palle B. Petterson has compiled a list of at least 715 non-fiction films about animals that were made between 1895 and 1928 around the world (Petterson 2011). The vast majority (over 500) of these films were made in the 1910s and 1920s. Initially, the footage contained shots of animals in their natural environment. By the middle of the century, the wildlife film shifted into a more coherent form of film that fitted many of the principles of the Griersonian documentary tradition. While these films often involved the use of real animals and people from communities that had to interact with these animals, they creatively reconstructed this to appeal to a mass audience. This process changed the way animals would be depicted in such films, led to the further development of the wildlife or nature documentary film and also influenced the ways in which animals were depicted in conventional narrative films.

In his book *Wildlife Films*, Derek Bousé argues that wildlife films are underrated as an area of filmic creativity, yet overrated as a tool for science education and nature conservation, as they owe a greater debt to Hollywood than documentaries from the Griersonian tradition, which attempted to present a detailed and broad contextual understanding of their subjects. Fundamentally, Bousé argues that wildlife films are used to tell stories, not reveal scientific facts, and this has led to a 'tyranny of formula' (Bousé 2000: back cover). Ultimately films subject to such tyranny make nature seem dynamic and exciting, when in reality there is often silence and quietude. While they portray things that can happen occasionally in nature, they make it appear as if these occur constantly. A similar theme is at the core of the argument Stephen Mills – a film-maker and naturalist – makes with regard to wildlife films. Mills argues that such documents are a 'fantasy' of the natural world. They focus on megafauna, spectacular backgrounds, a compelling narrative, and exclude 'the real world' of politics, science, history and, most importantly, humans. While scholarly observers such as Mills and Bousé bemoan the presence of Griersonian-style advocacy on behalf of the animals as departing too far from scientific principles (Mills 1997: 6; Bousé 2000: 15), these artistic beginnings, and much of their staged approach, were greatly influenced by films made in South-East Asia, and represented a combination of the forces that cinema exerted on both documentary and narrative film.

Two of the leading producers of early wildlife films, and representatives of these influences and developments, were Martin and Osa Johnson. Martin Johnson began his career in the Pacific travelling with the novelist Jack London. After marrying the teenage Osa, Martin – who was fundamentally a vaudeville showman from Kansas – began to seek out new ways to make money. The Johnsons, as Bousé points out, expressed admiration for Paul J. Rainey, a sensationalistic film-maker who focused on safari films and became well known for *Rainey's African Hunt* (Paul J. Rainey, 1914) (Bousé 2000: 50). Realising that films based on footage of wild animals were marketable in the United States, Martin took his young wife to the Solomon Islands, where they created an ethnographic spectacle entitled *Cannibal in the South Seas* (Martin Johnson, 1918). Upon their return, the Johnsons toured the United States showing the film, and quickly became a popular attraction.

The Johnsons then travelled to Borneo, where they made *Jungle Adventures* (Martin Johnson, 1921), as they believed that footage of orang-utans and other wildlife would enhance the experience they provided their audiences, a decision that proved to be accurate. By attempting to make a film in Borneo, the Johnsons played into understandings of the exotic wilderness of South-East Asia as a location of savagery and violence. Several decades later this theme continued to appear in their writings. In her autobiography, for example, Osa Johnson mentions that the various tribulations – beyond any issues with film-making – she faced in Borneo included leeches and crocodiles along with the occasional charging buffalo (Johnson 1940: 165–7). Shooting a film in Borneo proved to be difficult, particularly filming the animals in their natural environment. As Osa recalled, 'The jungles on either side of the river were teeming with wild life, but how to photograph it was the problem' (Johnson 1940: 172). Such conditions frustrated Martin Johnson, as bulky camera equipment would not allow him to get footage of the animals under natural conditions, rendering most shots of orang-utans and elephants unusable. Osa went on to add that Martin faced 'an honest awareness of his inexperience of photographing animals. The jungle and its problems of light baffled him' (Johnson 1940: 179).

While technical issues with filming befuddled Martin Johnson, getting the animals to react in a manner that could later be used in the film narrative proved equally difficult. This was particularly true because he wanted to combine footage of wild animals and 'wild men' to create a film that echoed the vaudevillian origins of their entertainment-based approach (Ahrens et al. 2013: 63–4). Martin told his wife, 'I've shot over fifty-thousand feet of film on this Borneo trip, and I've seen that instead of making it a headhunters' picture, we ought to put it together as a sort of study of Borneo, natives, animals, and all' (Johnson 1940: 184–5). The solution was to create the desired scenes for the camera, along with the requisite action, resulting in very little in the film being 'natural'. The inclusion of the more ethnographic material was also an outcome of the difficulty of obtaining shots of the animals in the dense jungle. This can perhaps be most easily seen when a herd of elephants moves directly towards the camera. Johnson had assistants in native costume drive the pachyderms towards the camera and then included them as part of the narrative of the film.

By the late 1910s, the Johnsons were well known throughout America for their ethnographic films. The inclusion of animals in *Jungle Adventures*, their third film, enhanced that status. They had proven that they could create an effective narrative combining both humans and animals. This gained the attention of Carl Akeley, the chief taxidermist at the American Museum of Natural History, who asked the couple to travel to Africa, where they would help capture images of the wildlife in their natural environment using a lightweight camera Akeley had developed. The Johnsons quickly agreed, as Akeley and the Museum would lend legitimacy to their endeavours, which up to that point had given them some fame and fortune but little respect (Kirk 2010). The subsequent film, *Trailing African Wild Animals* (Martin Johnson and Osa Johnson, 1923), was a success and reflected a more fauna-centric approach to film-making. Although the Johnsons had shifted their attention to Africa, the sensationalistic and entertaining film-making techniques they had developed while filming the 'natural' in South-East Asia brought focus on the interaction of animals and local human societies that could be tied into a narrative of savage animals threatening human communities.

TRANSITIONS TO NARRATIVE FILMS

The trope of animal–human violence developed along with the documentary film although other such films adopted its approaches with far less sensationalism than was the case with the Johnsons. Robert Flaherty's *Nanook of the North* (Robert Flaherty, 1922) is usually considered to be one of the key films in the development of the documentary. The film also reflected a change in how animals were depicted. Although the film focused on the struggle of an Inuk man in the wilderness, the animals he encountered were larger metaphors for uncivilised nature (Petterson 2011: 160). Although it also contained staged scenes, there was far less emphasis on the danger that animals held for such societies (the enemy was often the harsh climate). Along with the documentaries that were being distributed throughout the world, such as the Dutch-made films from the Netherlands East Indies that Sandeep Ray discusses in this collection, *Nanook of the North* changed what a documentary film was to depict and how it was to tell the story. Such films were made in South-East Asia from the late 1920s, thus making the straightforward animal footage that Burden obtained in 1926 archaic in its approach.

While Burden may have been trying to capture some of the vivid action of *Trailing African Wild Animals*, he was falling behind developments in technology and storytelling, although he did try to present such action in a manner that would appeal to the viewer. *The Lost World* (Harry O. Hoyt, 1925) had been released the year before he travelled to the Netherlands East Indies and it contained depictions that were even more fraught with cultural anxieties and the need for spectacle. Based on Arthur Conan Doyle's novel, the film depicted ferocious dinosaurs clashing, and quickly became one of the most popular spectacles of the year. Mitman argues that this played a role in how Burden presented his footage of Komodo dragons (Mitman 1999: 24–5). Instead of making it appealing, however, Burden's Komodo footage was hopelessly out of date. Pathé executives in New York who wrote to Burden in January 1927 would only consider the possibility of the footage being of use in a newsreel. As 'dragon fever' dissipated in New York following the deaths of the two lizards in the Bronx Zoo, however, even the possibility of inclusion in newsreels was quickly withdrawn shortly thereafter.[1] There was little danger or drama in Burden's depiction of Komodo, and thus it was never shown in a commercial venue. Burden had made a film that was – in the words of a potential distributor to American cinemas – 'too educational and without sufficient dramatic or adventure interest to make a good theatrical release'.[2] As it could not secure a theatrical release, the footage of Komodo dragons simply became background for their display at the American Museum of Natural History.

The directors of *King Kong*, Merian C. Cooper and Ernest B. Schoedsack, learned the same lesson during this period. In 1925, they accompanied Bakhtiari nomads on their annual migration from plains on the Persian Gulf to summer pasture lands on the central Persian plateau. The subsequent 'nature drama', *Grass: A Nation's Battle for Life* (Cooper and Schoedsack, 1925), was not well received. Their next film, *Chang: A Drama of the Wilderness* (Cooper and Schoedsack, 1927) addressed criticisms that film needed more than simple nature footage; film needed action and this action should involve violent animals. The film focused on a Lao village in northern Siam (Thailand) where residents had to deal with numerous animal attacks, particularly from a tiger, on their domestic livestock. The film follows the construction of various devices to capture the various predators, and there is even a close encounter between a tiger and the main character, Kru. Any tranquillity the villagers achieve following these events, however, is temporary, as a herd of elephants stampedes through the village, destroying everything in its wake. This motivates Kru and the other villagers to participate in an elephant drive in which they enter the jungle and eventually herd them into a pen. Having tamed nature, Kru and the other villagers remain content in their peaceful village. Unlike *Grass*, *Chang* was one of the most successful films financially the year it was released, and even earned Academy Award nominations in the first year the awards were offered (Mitman 1999: 38–40).

Staged depiction of animals, and particularly animal – as well as animal–human – confrontations, had become a mainstay in popular films by this time. This was further emphasised when the Johnsons released *Simba: King of the Beasts* (Martin Johnson, Pomeroy, 1928) the next year. Made from footage shot in Africa in 1924 and 1927, the film incorporated a greater sense of narrative, as the animals were given motivations the audience could follow. More importantly, the film shows the Johnsons killing a variety of African wildlife, evading an elephant stampede and in the most famous sequence Osa apparently shooting a rhinoceros with one shot. While similar activities appeared in Burden's footage of Komodo, the element of danger present for the intrepid American couple lent the film respectability as well as an audience. The resulting film was able, some thought, 'to bridge the gulf separating science from showmanship' (Mitman 1999: 35).

Burden tried a similar approach with *The Silent Enemy* (H. P. Carver, 1930), a film that focuses on the Ojibwa of Canada and their hunting expeditions, which coincide with the migration of caribou. But once again, this raised the issue of authenticity. Burden's film did capture much of the wilderness of the Canadian plains. Nevertheless, the spectacular conclusion, among other scenes, was staged. The film-makers had missed the annual caribou migration by several hundred kilometres. To compensate for footage that needed to be as spectacular as that in *Chang*, Burden arranged for reindeer to be filmed in large pens – to maintain the illusion of freedom – to depict the migration. This was not the only staged event in *The Silent Enemy*. Such footage included a confrontation between a mountain lion and a bear. The two animals had been kept in the same enclosure and starved. After a few days, a deer carcass was thrown into the enclosure and the two animals filmed. That the two animals were not from the same environment – the mountain lion was from the American southwest – seemed to be irrelevant. More importantly, Burden had captured 'interesting pictures of animals'.[3] *The Silent Enemy* was not a success and left Burden a bankrupt. It is doubtful that the supposed 'authenticity' in the film played a role in its lack of success. After all, Cooper and Schoedsack had staged much of the tiger footage, as well as the elephant stampede in *Chang*. The advent of talkies in the late 1920s had shifted the focus of films featuring animal footage. Film-makers had to make a decision and this decision was rarely whether the film was 'authentic' or not. More importantly, the scenes featuring animals needed to be filled with action and movement, with an emphasis on violence and conflict. While Burden withdrew from film-making following the failure of *The Silent Enemy* to gain an audience, Cooper and Schoedsack moved into commercial cinema, making *King Kong*.

THE DECADENCE OF VIOLENCE

With the advent of the talkies, humans would now be the stars, thus transforming the language and style of animal-based films. Silent animals would have to be presented in a new manner. Hyperbolic voice-over narration and the accompanying violence would now come to dominate documentary films. An example is *Ingagi* (William Campbell, 1930), a popular film that takes place in Africa. Although the film is perhaps best known for implying a sexual relationship between a woman and a gorilla, it features the slaughter of animals in a variety of situations, at times due to confrontations among themselves and at other times due to shots of a hunter protecting a native village (Bousé 2000: 52–4). Such luridness found its greatest purveyor in Frank Buck, a collector of wild animals for zoos and circuses who was based in Singapore in the 1920s and 1930s. Buck became well known in America after *Colliers* magazine published a series of articles titled 'Bring 'em back alive', which focused on his adventures in Singapore and Malaya during the 1910s and 1920s. When a film based on the articles was released as *Bring 'em Back Alive* (Elliot, 1932) it became one of the most popular releases in the United States and Buck became a renowned film star. Buck then followed up his initial success with a series of popular capture films such as *Wild Cargo* (Armand Denis, 1934) and *Fang and Claw* (Frank Buck, 1935) that featured the same formula of numerous scenes of inter-species conflict, all clearly staged. Bousé describes these films as the 'worst kind of voyeuristic animal pornography', as they featured staged, gruesome fights to the death (Bousé 2000: 55). Buck would place the animals in small enclosures and goad them to attack each other. These scenes appeared at regular intervals throughout the film. For example, the first in the series *Bring 'em Back Alive* features at least eight such encounters, including a leopard versus a python, a tiger versus a crocodile and a bear cub versus a python. These scenes were filmed at Buck's camp, which was located in the Katong area of Singapore. When the director of *Wild Cargo*, Armand Denis, first asked Buck about the difficulties of living and filming in the jungle, Buck replied 'Jungle?. . . I intend to stay at the Raffles Hotel in Singapore and I think they'll have most of the equipment I need there already' (Denis 1963: 57). The camp where scenes of animals confronting each other were shot was only a few hundred metres off a main road, not deep in the jungle. 'It consisted mainly of a few cages containing a variety of despondent-looking animals, and of a number of enclosures more or less ingeniously camouflaged and in which obviously the animals were to be placed for various scenes to be photographed' (Denis 1963: 61). The animals were often bought or borrowed from Singaporean residents and were filmed without sound, which Buck and the director added afterward.

The staged manner of these confrontations reflects the unnatural approach in which most wildlife footage was obtained during this period. When Buck wanted to dramatise a confrontation between an orang-utan and a tiger, the director responded that such an encounter was 'inconceivable' as in the wild they would just avoid each other and animals would not 'normally fight to death for nothing'. Buck responded, 'When I'm around they do' (Denis 1963: 60–1). The absurdity of the confrontations reached a high point in *Wild Cargo*, when Buck is shown wrestling a tiger. The animal had actually drowned in a pit where it was kept. According to Denis: It was quite a scene and Frank Buck was at his most impressive. He advanced towards his adversary, and for breathless minutes he did battle with the corpse of the drowned tiger. Denis summarised the experience in his later autobiography as bordering on the satirical. It was 'as if I was working on a Marx Brothers comedy, instead of what was supposed to be a deadly serious film about the wild' (Denis 1963: 63).

Confrontations, action and excitement were the goals of the popular Buck wildlife films in the 1930s. This reached a point in which Buck would even reject any scenes that did not fulfil his vaudevillian understanding of what the audience wanted. This can be most easily seen through the eyes of Denis, who became an advocate of nature films that filled television screens in the 1950s and 1960s. Denis filmed several scenes involving elephant herds and processions in Ceylon (modern-day Sri Lanka) when he was on his way to Singapore. Although Denis was impressed with the results, Buck rejected their inclusion in the final film after he saw them in Singapore as he found them far too tame. This was because, in Buck's words, 'There's just no kick in this stuff. It's not what folks pay their money at the cinema to see' (Denis 1963: 60). The animal confrontations in Frank Buck films, despite their lack of authenticity, were highly effective and popular. They did not transform the nature film, they simply gave the audience what they craved: constant violence and action in the natural world. While Buck popularised this format to a great extent, it had been a common practice long before.

The popularity of the Frank Buck films lured Martin and Osa Johnson back to South-East Asia, and they spent fourteen months in Borneo in 1935–36. The Johnsons, after all, had been early purveyors of this approach to cinema, as they often provoked animals into reaction, creating a sense of movement and drama (Bousé 2000: 51). The resulting film was *Borneo* (Truman Talley, 1937), which was released only after Martin's death. With new cameras and equipment, the problems they had encountered with regard to filming the animals were greatly lessened. This time, for example, they captured an elephant herd more naturally, by setting up the camera along a trail and waiting for hours (Johnson 1940: 360). However, special techniques to obtain the desired reactions from animals were not totally abandoned. Martin Johnson, for example, used buzzing planes and tear gas to move an orang-utan into position (Johnson 1967: 124, 131 360).

CONCLUSIONS: STAGING VIOLENCE

The 1920s and 1930s were a period in which film was developing, as directors created new techniques for conveying basic stories. Animals had been common subjects in the era of the silent film. Prior to the development of the modern, fictional narrative film, or even the documentary, footage featuring exotic megafauna was popular with audiences. Newsreels regularly featured images of exotic South-East Asian fauna such as Komodo dragons. These large lizards played an important role in films ranging from the Dutch documentary *Flores Film* (Johannes Bouma, Simon Buis, Johannes van Cleef and H. Limbrock, 1926), which Sandeep Ray discusses in greater detail in his chapter in this collection, to a British Pathé news story on the transportation of the animals to Europe in the mid-1930s (Barnard 2011: 118). While the connection between the animal footage from Komodo and the stop-motion animation of

King Kong represent one of the clearest examples of how these tropic depictions of animals and their role in film shifted over time, they also reflect the emphasis on wild fauna in early film, particularly those shot outside of North America and Europe, and how it became even more fantastic and violent.

Martin and Osa Johnson (as well as Frank Buck, who continued to make films well into the 1950s) presented a fixation on animal violence that became a cornerstone of documenting fauna. The modern successor to these films can be seen in recent documentaries that are filmed – once again – on Komodo, or any other place in South-East Asia, which emphasise wildlife. In these depictions, which appear in films that range from award-winning, 'respectable' documentaries on the BBC narrated by David Attenborough to the various shows on the television channel Animal Planet, animals are active and vicious. Each of these films focuses on the ferocity of the animals, on Komodo showing a dragon or a group of dragons attacking water buffalo or other animals. They live in contrast to modern civilisation and play a metaphorical role in terms of the division between humans and animals.

Such events, however, are rare. When visiting Komodo, visitors are often shocked to see the large lizards sunning themselves and rarely moving during the day. They only need to eat every few months. Yet, this lack of 'action' is the crux of the issue. Viewers want excitement and action, and films have become transformed to provide an unrealistic depiction of nature on account of this. Authenticity becomes one of the key issues in such films, as getting shots of animals in the wild – particularly the dense jungle – proves difficult for any film-maker, particularly during the pre-Second World War era. Douglas Burden had not placed himself in any real danger, or at least captured it on film, and from the beginning this doomed the 'scientific' footage he tried to distribute to audiences. It had neither sufficient drama nor enough adventure to merit palpable interest from the viewing public.

NOTES

1. 'Letter from Pathé Exchange', 27 January 1927, American Museum of Natural History Archives, William Burden Papers (Komodo Expedition: E. R. Dunn papers), Box II, folder 9.
2. 'Letter from The Bray Productions, Inc', 15 May 1928, American Museum of Natural History Archives, William Burden Papers (Komodo Expedition: E. R. Dunn papers), Box II, folder 9.
3. 'Letter from Burden to Osborn', 26 June 1928, American Museum of Natural History Archives, William Burden Papers, Box 1, Folder 5; Mitman, *Reel Nature*, p. 47.

REFERENCES

Ahrens, Prue, L. Lindstrom and F. Paisley (2013), *Across the World with the Johnsons: Visual Culture and American Empire in the Twentieth Century*, Farnham: Ashgate.
Barnard, Timothy P. (2009), 'Chasing the dragon: an early expedition to Komodo Island', in Jan van der Putten and M. K. Cody (eds), *Lost Times and Untold Tales from the Malay World*, Singapore: NUS Press, pp. 41–53.
Barnard, Timothy P. (2011), 'Protecting the dragon: Dutch attempts at limiting access to Komodo Lizards in the 1920s and 1930s', *Indonesia*, 92, 97–123.
Bousé, Derek (2000), *Wildlife Films*, Philadelphia: University of Pennsylvania Press.
Burden, W. Douglas (1927), *Dragon Lizards of Komodo: An Expedition to the Lost World of the Dutch East Indies*, New York: G. P. Putnam's Sons.
Burt, Jonathan (2002), *Animals on Film*, London: Reaktion.
Denis, Armand (1963), *On Safari: The Story of My Life*, London: Collins.
Enright, Kelly (2012), *The Maximum of Wilderness: The Jungle in the American Imagination*, Charlottesville: University of Virginia Press.
Johnson, Osa (1940), *I Married Adventure: The Lives and Adventures of Martin and Osa Johnson*, London: Hutchinson.
Johnson, Osa (1967), *Last Adventure: The Martin Johnsons in Borneo*, London: Jarrolds.
Kirk, Jay (2010), *Kingdom under Glass: A Tale of Obsession, Adventure, and One Man's Quest to Preserve the World's Great Animals*, New York: Picador.
Mills, Stephen (1997), 'Pocket tigers: the sad unseen reality behind the wildlife film', in *Times Literary Supplement*, 21 February, p. 6.
Mitman, Gregg (1999), *Reel Nature: America's Romance with Wildlife and Film*, London: Harvard University Press.
Petterson, Palle B. (2011), *Cameras into the Wild: A History of Early Wildlife and Expedition Filmmaking, 1895–1928*, London: McFarland.
Rony, Fatimah Tobing (1996), *The Third Eye: Race, Cinema, and Ethnographic Spectacle*, London: Duke University Press.

Notes on the Contributors

Ian Aitken is Professor of Film Studies at the School of Communication, Hong Kong Baptist University. Amongst other book publications, he is the author of *Hong Kong Documentary Film* (Edinburgh University Press, 2014), *Lukácsian Film Theory and Cinema: An Analysis of Georg Lukács' Writings on Film 1913–1971* (2012), *Realist Film Theory and Cinema: The Nineteenth-Century Lukácsian and Intuitionist Realist Traditions* (2006), *Encyclopedia of the Documentary Film* (ed.) (2006, 2012), *Alberto Cavalcanti: Realism, Surrealism and National Cinemas* (2001), *European Film Theory and Cinema* (Edinburgh University Press, 2001), *The Documentary Film Movement: An Anthology* (ed.) (Edinburgh University Press, 1998) and *Film and Reform: John Grierson and the Documentary Film Movement* (1990, 1992, 2013).

Timothy P. Barnard is an Associate Professor in the Department of History at the National University of Singapore, where he specialises in the environmental and cultural history of Island South-East Asia. His research has focused on a range of topics including state formation in the eighteenth-century Straits of Melaka, Malay identity throughout history and the environmental history of Singapore and Malay film in the 1950s and 1960s. His studies of South-East Asian film include '*Film Melayu*: Nationalism, modernity and film in a pre-world war two Malay magazine', *Journal of Southeast Asian Studies* (2010) and 'Decolonization and the nation in malay film, 1955–1965', *South East Asia Research* (2009). His monographs include *Multiple Centres of Authority* (2003) and *Nature's Colony* (2016), as well as the edited volumes *Contesting Malayness* (2004) and *Nature Contained* (2014).

Peter J. Bloom is Associate Professor of Film and Media Studies at the University of California, Santa Barbara. He is the author of *French Colonial Documentary: Mythologies of Humanitarianism* (2008), which was awarded the Lawrence Wylie Prize in French Cultural Studies for books published in English between 2008 and 2009. He is also the co-editor of *Frenchness and the African Diaspora* (2009) and *Modernization as Spectacle in Africa* (2014). He is currently working on a manuscript entitled *The Curse of Minimal Difference: Sounding out Late Colonial Film and Radio*, among other projects.

THE CONTRIBUTORS 237

José B. Capino is Associate Professor of English and Cinema and Media Studies at the University of Illinois, Urbana-Champaign. He is the author of *Dream Factories of a Former Colony: American Fantasies, Philippine Cinema* (2010), winner of the 2012 Cultural Studies book prize from the Association for Asian American Studies. His contribution to this anthology is based on 'Cinema and the spectacle of colonialism', which received the dissertation award from the Society for Cinema and Media Studies in 2003. He is currently working on two monographs: *Martial Law Melodrama*, about popular film during the Marcos dictatorship, and *Projections of Empire: Documentary and US Imperialism in the Philippines*.

Camille Deprez studied at Sorbonne University and National Institute of Oriental Languages and Civilisations (INALCO) in Paris. She is a Research Assistant Professor in the Academy of Film of Hong Kong Baptist University (2011–16). Her initial research areas were the Indian mainstream film – or Bollywood – and television industries. Two single-authored books, *La télévision indienne: Un modèle d'appropriation culturelle* (2006) and *Bollywood: Cinéma et mondialisation* (2010), academic articles and book chapters came out of these two long-term research projects. More recently, her research has focused on the history of Indian documentary film and French colonial documentary film in Asia. She is the co-editor of *Post-1990 Documentary: Reconfiguring Independence* (Edinburgh University Press, 2015).

Annamaria Motrescu-Mayes is a Research Fellow at Clare Hall and an Affiliated Lecturer and Research Associate at the Centre of South Asian Studies, University of Cambridge. While her research centres on British imperial studies, her primary intellectual work is as a visual and digital anthropologist. In collaboration with several higher education and research institutions in Europe, South Asia and China, and with colleagues from the Faculties of Education and History at the University of Cambridge, she explores new research and pedagogical methodologies that use theories of visual culture in advancing modern history programmes. Her scholarly work includes various publications and several outreach projects at universities and research institutes in the UK, Asia and Europe (http://bit.ly/1BHi73B). She is convenor of the annual seminar series 'Visual constructions of South Asia' (http://talks.cam.ac.uk/show/index/50675) and founder of the Amateur Cinema Studies Network, the first international project promoting amateur cinema/media studies (http://amateurcinemastudies.org). In 2015, she held a Research Fellowship at the Harry Ransom Centre, University of Texas at Austin, and has recently secured a publishing contract for the first volume of *Visual Histories of South Asia: India* (co-edited with Marcus Banks, forthcoming 2016).

Sandeep Ray received a PhD in History from the National University of Singapore in 2015 and is currently a Luce postdoctoral fellow at the Chao Centre for Asian Studies, Rice University, USA. In 2013, researching for his dissertation on early Dutch colonial propaganda films titled, *Celluloid*

Colony: Occluded Histories of the Netherlands East Indies from Moving Images (1912–30), he spent eight months at the exhaustive archives of Beeld en Geluid and the Eye Film Institute in the Netherlands analysing hundreds of films. His documentaries have been screened at several festivals and forums including Pusan, Taiwan, Sydney, Delhi, Iran Cinéma-Vérité, the Jean Rouch Ethnographic Festival, the Margaret Mead Film Festival and the Flaherty Seminar. Sandeep Ray frequently reviews films and is a juror of the Festival Film Dokumenter in Yogyakarta, Indonesia.

Tom Rice is a Lecturer in Film Studies at the University of Saint Andrews. He is the author of *White Robes, Silver Screens: Movies and the Making of the Ku Klux Klan* (2015). He previously worked as the senior researcher on a major archival project on Colonial Film (www.colonialfilm.org.uk), for which he wrote more than 200 historical essays. He has published extensively on British colonial, government and educational film, as well as non-theatrical film in America. His articles have featured in various edited collections, such as *Empire and Film* and *Film and the End of Empire* (2011), and in journals including *Film History*, *Journal of British Cinema and Television*, *Historical Journal of Film, Radio and Television* and *Journal of American Studies*.

Emma Sandon lectures in film and television at Birkbeck, University of London. Her research publications focus on British colonial film and photography, early British television history and South African film history. She was on the core management team of the *Colonial Film: Moving Images of the British Empire* project, http://www.colonialfilm.org.uk, and on the steering group of the Women's Film and Television History Network (UK), https://womensfilmandtelevisionhistory.wordpress.com. She is an Honorary Research Fellow of the Archive and Public Culture Research Initiative at the University of Cape Town and a Research Associate to the Chair of Social Change at the University of Johannesburg.

Dean Wilson received his PhD in French from the City University of New York Graduate Center, with the dissertation *Colonial Vietnam on Film: 1896–1926*. He designed and administered the Film Studies Programme at the University of Social Sciences and Humanities in Hanoi, Vietnam under a major grant from the Ford Foundation. He is currently a guest professor in the Department of Art History and Cinema Studies at the University of Montreal.

Thong Win is a PhD candidate in the Department of Film and Media Studies at the University of California, Santa Barbara. His research interests include transnational influences on Vietnamese revolutionary film-making and the local configurations between state authority, film production and distribution in post-colonial Vietnam

Index

.../014 India, 135, 137–9, 141–4, 145n9
1955: The Year in Malaya, 56

Abel, Richard, 7
Ackerman, Fred C., 81, 102n1
Advance of Kansas Volunteers at Caloocan, 81
Advance with Science, 40
Aitken, Ian, 2, 9, 16, 18–19, 36–7, 51, 67
Aitken, Ian and Ingham, Michael, 2
Akeley, Carl, 228
Aldrich, Robert, 3–4
Allégret, Marc, 8
Amad, Paula, 4, 206, 214, 217–18, 221n9
American documentary films made in Asia, 13–14, 95, 100–2
American imperialism and colonialism, 79, 82–3, 88–9, 100–2
American Museum of Natural History, 223, 228–9
Anderson, Warwick, 89
Antoine, Marthe, 211–12, 214
Appels, Eddy, 111–12, 119, 121, 125
Archives de la Planète/Archives of the Planet, 205, 210, 213, 217, 219–20
Aryeetey, Sam, 59
Atlantide, L', 8
Attenborough, David, 234
August Revolution of 1945, 173, 176, 184n3, 188, 193

Australia and Malaysia, 39
Australian National Film Board, 50
Avellana, Lamberto, 96

Bahadur, Jagatjit Singh (Maharaja of Kapurthala), 205, 207, 215–17
Baj, Jeannine and Lenk, Sabine, 7
Baldoz, Rick, 89–91
Ballantyne, James, 161
Bao Dai, 187–9, 192
Baroek, Alexander, 123
Barr, Michael D., 31, 35
Basket, Michael, 2
Battle for Peace, The, 100
Battle of Moc Hoa, 172
Battle of Tonkin, The, 9
BBC, 63–4, 72–3
BBC Listening Research Department, 65
Beamish, Tony, 76n15, 76n17
Beeld en Geluid, 125
Belmonte, L. A., 96, 99
Beltjens, Piet, 108, 117
Ben-Hur, 112–13
Benali, Abdelkader, 8
Berchmans, Brother, 108
Bergson, Henri, 218
Berita Singapura, 29, 32–42
  establishment of, 35–6
  opposition to, 37–8
  close of, 38
  categories of topics, 38
Bernarys, Edward L., 41
Better Man, The, 58
Blanchard, Nicolas, 4

Blanchard, Pascal, 2
Bloom, Peter, 3–4, 8
Bonaparte, Napoleon, 186
Booth, Herbert, 134
Bousé, Derek, 226, 231–2
Brendon, Piers, 57
Bretèque, François de la, 210, 221n9
British documentary film movement, 128–9, 139
British East India Company, 148
British Empire and Commonwealth Museum, 145n8
British Ministry of Information, 165n5
British Woman's Guild, 162
Brooklyn Institute of Arts and Science, 86
Brunhes, Jean, 206, 218–19
Buck, Frank, 231–4
Buddhism, 162
Buis, Simon, 13, 107–12, 114, 117, 119, 121–5
Burden, William Douglas, 114, 221, 223–5, 229–30, 234
Burns, James, 3

Capino, J. B. T., 13
Care of Abandoned Children, 39
Cargo from Jamaica, 141
Carruthers, Susan L., 3
Cathay Film Services, 35, 42
Celebration of New Housing, 40
Central Office of Information (COI), 5, 48
Chafer, Tony and Sackur, Amanda, 3
Chan, Nadine, 68
Chang: A Drama of the Wilderness, 229–31
Chapman, James, 64
Chevalier, Maurice, 129
Chowdhury, Prem, 3
Christianity, 4, 21, 100, 109, 110–11, 117–19, 121–3, 131, 133, 137, 148–51, 157–8, 160–4
    Catholicism, 9, 20, 97, 107–9, 112, 117, 119, 123, 125, 128, 130, 133, 135, 148
    evangelicalism, 12, 17, 20–1, 107–12, 117, 122, 124, 130, 133–4, 137–8, 140, 151, 154, 157, 159, 162–4
    Methodism, 154–9, 165nn10, 11

missionary activities, 4, 5, 9, 15–17, 20–1, 108–15, 117, 121, 123–6, 128–44, 148–64, 218
    Presbyterian (ism), 161
Christoffel, Hans, 109
Chronicle: A Magazine of World Enterprise, 159
Church Missionary Society (CMS), 150–1, 164, 166n20
Church of Scotland (CoS), 151, 160–4, 166n20
Church's Guide to Films for Religious Use, The, 160
Churchill, Winston, 74n2
Cinematographic Mission of 1918, 195
Cleaning up Operation, 39
Clifford, Hugh, 71
Clifford, James and Marcus, George, 73
Cold War propaganda, 96–7, 100–1
Colonial Cinema, 50
Colonial Film Unit (CFU), 7, 53, 165n5
Colonial Institute (Vereeniging Koloniaal Institute), 10
Colonial Office tradition, 6–7
Communism (or Communist Party), 5, 9, 10, 14, 20, 31, 64, 68–9, 95–9, 161
    Chinese, 34, 39, 162
    French, 189
    Indochina, 188–9
    Malaya, 5, 30, 36, 49–50, 55–7, 68, 72, 74, 75n11
    People's Committees of the Indochinese Communist Party (ICP), 188
    Philippines, 96–9
    Singapore, 30
    Vietnam, 21, 173, 177–8, 183, 189, 198
Congregationalist, 138
Conklin, Alice, L., 4
Cooper, Merian C., 229, 231
Cooper, Nicola, 2–3
Cornuel, Paul, 210
CoS Foreign Mission Committee, 160
Couvreur, A., 109
Cowans, Jon, 2
Cox, Jeffrey, 151
Creed, Barbara and Hoorn, Jeanette, 4
Criminal Tribes Acts of 1871 and 1911, 152

Crossman, Richard, 66
Crown Film Unit, 5
Cull, N. J., 96
Cullather, Nick, 92–3, 101

Đặng, Xuân Khu *see* Trường, Chinh
Daughton, James P. and White, Owen, 3
Davidson, Basil, 53
De Bussy, L. P. H., 11
De Tijd, 107, 110–11, 123
Deery, John, 66–7
Del Mundo, C. A., 13
Delgado, Anita, 216
Democracia, La, 87
Democratic Republic of Vietnam (DRV), 186, 188–90, 196, 198
Denis, Armand, 232
Dennery, Étienne, 211
Deocampo, N., 13
Department of Information (Federation of Malaya), 47, 50–1
Deprez, Camille, 2–3, 6
Depue, Oscar, 82–5
Dhakidae, Daniel, 122
Di Carmine, Roberta, 3
Diamond, Howard, 159
Dickason, Deane Henry, 150, 160
Docu-dramas, 96–7
Doyle, Arthur Conan, 229
Druick, Zoe and Williams, Deane, 4
Dumas, Roger, 205, 209–10, 212–19, 220n6, 221nn9–11
Dutch colonial documentary cinema, 10–13

Edison, Thomas, 81
Edwards, W. Le Cato, 155, 157, 160, 165n11
Ellis, John, 65
Elton, Ralph, 49, 67
Emergency Information Services, (EIS), 50
Empire Marketing Board (EMB), 5
Film Unit, 133, 140–1
Eye Film Institute, 125
Ezra, Elizabeth, 4, 8

Feyder, Jacques, 8
Fighting Leprosy in India: The Work at Dichpali, 158–9
Filipino Repatriation Act, 89–91
Films Division of India, 6

Films Division of the COI, 5
Films for Church and Youth, 133
First Indochina War, 172, 177, 186
First World War, 189, 191, 205, 210, 215
Five Faces, 49
Flaherty, Robert, 119, 228
Flores Film, 110–19, 122–3, 126n4, 233
Forging Closer Ties, 40
Fouchard, Serge, 220
Fox, Jo, 65
Franco-Prussian War, 218
Free Church of Scotland, 160–1
Freedom for Ghana, 53–5
French colonial documentary cinema, 8–10
French early film pioneers, 7–8
French Fourth Republic, 190
French Military Film Services, 9
French National Film Archives, 201n10
French Popular Front, 195
From India's Coral Strand, 152–3
From Mindanao to Milly Martin, 99
From Savages to Civilization, 86
Frykenburg, Robert E., 165n3
Furhmann, Wolfgang, 3

Gan, Cheong Soon, 55
Gandhi, Mahatma, 211, 213, 217, 219
Gao Rang/Grilled Rice, 179
Gaulle, Charles de, 187
Ghana Film Unit (Gold Coast Film Unit), 52–5, 59–60
Ghanaian independence, 53–4
Girardet, Raoul, 4
Gleeck, Lewis, 101
Golay, F. H., 82
Gooding, Francis, 150, 159–60
Govan, Harry, 67
Graham, Sean, 53, 59
Greater East Asian Co-Prosperity Sphere, 193
Greene, Hugh C., 66, 75n7
grey propaganda and unattributed materials, 96–9
Grierson, John, 51, 65, 128, 130–3, 137–44
Griersonian influence and tradition, 6–7, 18, 51, 53, 226
Grieveson, Lee and MacCabe, Colin, 4
Grossupova, Maria, 216
Grunspan, Claude, 179
Guerrilla cinema, 174, 180–1

Ha, Marie-Paule, 3
Habermas, Jürgen, 41
Hack, Karl, 66, 69
Hamilton, Roy, 122
Hardiman, David, 157
Hargreaves, Alec, 3
Harper, T. N., 47, 57, 69
Hawes, Stanley, 50
Hawes report, 67, 75n10
headhunters, depictions of, 87
Headhunters, The, 86
Health for India, 160
Higgins, Edward, 151
Higson, Andrew, 64
Hilsman, Roger, 88
Ho, Chi Minh, 10, 173–4, 176, 180, 182, 186, 188–9, 192, 197–9, 200n1
Ho Chi Minh in France, 188–90, 194, 196–9
Hodge, Tom, 35–8, 40, 42, 48–52, 58–9
Hogenkamp, 12
Holland Neutral: The Army and Fleet, 12
Holmes, B., 82
Holmes, Elias Burton, 82–5
Home Organisation Department (HOD), 154
Hong Kong Shanghai Bank Corporation (HSBC), 128–9, 132, 134–8, 140–2, 144
Howse, Henry, 150
Huk in a New Life, The, 96
Huk rebellion, 96
Hussain, Mohammed Zain, 59, 71

Imperial Japanese Army (IJA), 187–9, 193–4
In Old and New Manila with Burton Holmes, 82
India, 131–3, 135, 137–9, 141–4
India Mission, 160
Indian Nationalist Movement, 217
Indigenous Work-force section (Main-d'œuvre indigène, MOI), 197
Indonesian Balai Pustaka/ Bureau of Literature, 122
Infantry Regiment, The, 39
Information Research Department (IRD), 66, 75n8
Ingagi, 231
International Athletics Competition, 40

International Exposition of Art and Technology in Modern Life, 195
Islam (Muslims), 21, 100, 108–10, 116–17, 119, 121, 123, 166n14, 209, 211–12, 219
Islamic Sultan of Bima, 109
Israel, Milton, 3

Jacobson, Matthew Frye, 79
Jaikumar, Priya, 3
Jakobson, Roman, 74
Japan–Russo War, 188, 190
Japanese Minister of Foreign Affairs, 193
Jassen, Arnold, 107
Jesuits, 109
Johnson, Martin, 226–8, 230, 233–4
Johnson, Osa, 226–8, 230, 233–4
Jungle Adventures, 227–8
jungle sound effect, 71

Kahn, Albert, 205–6, 208–20, 220n5
Karnow, Stanley, 101
Katholieke Missien, De, 109
Kaur, Raminder and Mazarella, William, 3
Kerkvliet, B. J., 96
Kerr, Isabel, 158, 166n14
Khai Dinh, 192
Khương, Mễ, 171, 176
Kim, N. B. Ninh, 177
Kim Van Kieu, 192
Kinematograph Weekly, 50
King Kong, 225, 229, 231, 234
Kinta Story, The, 59
Knife, The, 50, 68
Koerier, Limburger, 112–13, 126n2
Kramer, P. A., 81

Lakshini the Santal Girl, 155
Lamster, J. C., 10
Landau, Paul and Kaspin, Deborah, 3
Larkin, Brian, 3
Lashmar, Paul and Oliver, James, 3
Latham, Robert O., 160
Law, Ow Kheng, 49–51, 56, 59
League for the Independence of Vietnam (Viet Minh), 188–90, 194, 199, 202n26
League of Nations, 191, 215
Lee Kong Chong, 37–8
Lee Kuan Yew, 30–3, 37, 41

Lemon Grove, 128–9, 131–8, 140–4
Leprosy, 88–9
Letter, The, 58
Limbrock, H., 119, 125, 233
Lingle, Christopher, 32
London Missionary Society (LMS), 149–51, 155, 159–60, 163–4, 166n17, 166n20
Lord Irwin (Edward Frederick Lindley Wood), 208, 210, 216
Lord Irwin at the Maharaja of Kapurthala Palace, 209, 218
Lost World, The, 229
Lowe, John, 158

MacFarlane, William, 161
MacGillivray, Sir Donald, 51, 57
McKinney, Marc, 4
Maharaja of Patiala, 215–17
Mai, Lộc, 171–2, 176, 182
Mai, Thu, 186, 196–7
Mai, Trung Thu, 195–6, 200n1
Maid in India, 133
Maintaining Cleanliness, 39, 42
Making Candles, 40
Malaya Celebrates, 51–2
Malayan Communist Party, 85n11
Malayan Emergency, 49, 50, 57, 63, 65–71, 73–4
Malayan Film Unit (MFU), 36, 45–60, 67, 69, 71
Malayan independence, 45, 55
Malcolm, G. A., 92
Marcel, Alexandre, 218
Margolin, Jean-Louis, 32–3
Marker, Chris and Resnais, Alain, 10
Marshall, Alex, 55
Martin, Charles, 86
Mauzy, Diane and Milne, R. S., 31–4
Maximum of Wilderness, The, 225
Meiji Restoration, 188, 200n5
Merdeka for Malaya, 45–60
Methodist Missionary Society (MMS), 149–51, 154–9, 163–4, 165n13
Milner, Anthony, 69
Mindanao, 99–100
Ministry of Information (MOI), British, 6, 64
Ministry of Information and Propaganda (Vietnam), 183

Miracle of Jurong, 39
Mission Cinématographique/ Cinematographic Mission, 191
Missionary Film Committee (MFC), 150, 164
Mitman, Gregg, 224, 229
Monnikendam, Vincent, 12
Monsaingeon, Eglantine, 7
Mother Dao, 12
Moving Picture World, The, 87
Mullens, Willy, 12
Murray-Levine, Alison, 3–4, 9
Musée Albert-Kahn in Boulogne, 206
Musser, Charles, 82
Muthalib, Hassan, 58, 67

Nanook of the North, 119, 228–9
Nasruddin, M. R. and bin Zulkhurnain, Z. N., 55
National Archives of Singapore (NAS), 38
National Day, 40
National Social Purity Crusade (renamed National Council of Public Morals in 1910), 151–2
Native Life in the Philippines, 86
Nehru, Jawaharlal, 213, 219, 220n2
New Development and Housing Week, 40
New Look at Housing, A, 33, 40, 42
New Police Recruits, 39
New Schools, 40
New Town Secondary School, 40
New University Chancellor, 40
New York Institute of Photography, 117
New Zealand, Friendly Ally, 38–9
Newman, Andrea, 136
Ngee Ann College, 40
Nguyen Ai Quoc *see* Ho, Chi Minh
Nguyen Du, 192
Nguyễn, Đức Dương, 174
Nguyen, Kim Chuong, 202n28
Nguyen, Lan Huong, 192
Nguyễn, Van Ky, 184n3
Nguyen, Van Vinh, 192
Những người mang ánh sang/People Who Bring the Light, 179–80
Nicholas, Sîan, 65
Nichols, Bill, 96
Nkrumah, Kwame, 53, 59
No Tears for Ananse, 59

Non-specialised Workers programme (Ouvriers non spécialisés, ONS), 196–7
Noone, Dick, 72
Noone, Herbert Deane 'Pat', 71–4
Norindr, Panivong, 3
North Atlantic Treaty Organization (NATO), 186

Ochse, Isidor Arras, 12
Office of War Information, 14
Olsen, Ellen, 153–4
Orang Asli, 63, 70–4

Pacific War, 193–4
Pathé, 7
Peace Corps, 99
People Who Bring the Light, 180
People's Action Party (PAP), 30–42
  and education, 33, 40
  and housing, 33, 40, 42
  and race relations, 34–5
People's Singapore, 35
Perang Pasifikasi/War of Pacification, 109
Perfume Factory, 40
Pétain, Marshal Philippe, 187
Peterson, Alec D. C., 67
Petterson, Palle B., 225
Pham, Van Dong, 197
Pham, Van Nhan, 196–7, 200n1, 202n25
Pham Quynh, 192
Phan, Boi Chau, 188, 191
Philippine Civic Action Group (PHILCAG), 100
Philippine Republic, The, 93
Philippine Troops in Korea, 100
Philippines, The
  American colonial documentaries in, 79–102
  at the end of Second World War, 92
  colonisation of, 92–3
  decolonisation of, 91, 93, 101
  independence, 91, 93–4
  post-colonisation, 93–4
  Spanish colonisation of, 93
Pine, Diana, 48
Pinoteau, Pascal, 8
Police Women, 39
Potato Chips Factory, 40

Potter, R. E. D., 67
Prime Minister Lee Kuan Yew in Brussels and London, 41
Proletarian Film League of Japan (Prokino), 201n18
Pronay, Nicholas, 64
Public Relations Department (Ghana), 60

Queen Elizabeth II, 51–2

Rach, Willy, 13, 108, 111–12, 119, 125
racism, 8, 34, 41–2, 49, 50, 52, 54, 69, 82, 86, 128–9, 131, 135, 140–4, 145n17, 216
Radio Malaya, 70–4
Rahman, Lisabona, 121–2
Rahman, Tunku Abdul, 57–8
Rainey, Paul J., 227
Raju, Zakir, Hossain, 3
Ramakrishna, 50, 67
Rathbone, Richard, 46, 58
Ray, Sandeep, 233
Rebuilding Houses, 40
Reception at the Parliament in New-Delhi, 210
Reith, John, 65
Report of the Department of Broadcasting (Singapore), 75n12–14
Revolution (Vietnam), 21–2, 171–4, 179–83, 183n1, 199
revolutionary cinema, 172, 174–6, 178–81, 183
Revue militaire, 209
Reynolds, Glenn, 3
Ria Rago, 119, 122–3
Rice, M., 86–7
Rice, Tom, 3–4, 67, 151, 165nn7, 8
Richards, Jeffrey, 63–5
Roan, J., 82
Robertson, Eric, 74, 76n19
Rony, F. T., 8, 9, 86
Rony, Tobing, 224
Roseman, Marina, 71, 73
Rotha, Paul, 133
Rouch, Jean, 10
Roussel, Lieutenant Colonel, 150–1
Russell, Patrick and Taylor, James Piers, 74n1

Saint Joseph's Missionary Society, 21, 128, 131–4, 138–9, 141, 143, 151, 165n6
Salvation Army (SA), 150–4, 157, 159, 163, 165nn7, 8, 197
Salvation Army Work in India, Burma and Ceylon (aka *From India's Coral Strand*), 152
Samaj, Brahmo, 218
Sang Nila Utama Secondary School, 34, 40
Sanyal, Shukla, 3
Sarkar, Bhaskar, 3
Sarraut, Albert, 8
Schoedsack, Ernest B., 229, 231
Second World War, 196, 234
Sellers, William, 53
Shalom, S. R., 96
Shaw, Alexander, 49
Sheppard, Mervyn (Adbul Mubin), 67
Sherzer, Dina, 2
Silent Enemy, The, 230–1
Simba: King of the Beasts, 230
Singapore Anti-Tuberculosis Association, 39
Singapore's Help to Malaysia, 39–40
Singaporean independence, 30–1
Singing Trio, 40
Sioh, Maureen, 71
Skilled Tradesmen in Peace Corps, 99
Slavin, David, 3, 8
Smyth, Rosaleen, 3
Societas Verbi Divini (SVD), 12, 107–8, 110–12, 116, 119, 124–5, 127
Société Autour du monde, 210, 220n3
Société Indochine Films et Cinémas, 184n3
Song of Ceylon, The, 5
South and South-East Asia Documentary Film Research programme and website, 1
Southern Resistance Cinema, 182
Soverdi, 121, 125
Soviet Cinema, 201n16
Spotlight on the Colonies, 48
Spurr, Norman, 150
Statues Also Die, 10
Steenbrink, Karel, 109, 116–17
Stockwell, A. J., 46, 69
Stollery, Martin, 4

Straits Times, The, 48, 51, 56, 59
Sullivan, Rodney, J., 86

Tagore, Rabindranath, 211–13, 215, 218–19, 220n5
Tan Tai Yong, 30
Taylor, Philip M., 3, 64
Templer, Gerald, 67, 76n17
Third French Republic, 187
This Is My Home, 96–9
This is the Philippines, 91–2
Thomas, Martin, 3
Thongchai, Winichakul, 172–3
Through Fires of Persecution, 157
Timeless Temiar, 71
Toh Weng Kai, 36, 38
Touch and Go, 58
Trailing African Wild Animals, 228–9
Tran, Van Tra, 182
Trans-Vietnam Railway, 199
travelogue, 83–4, 86
Treaty of Versailles, 215
Trial and Triumph: The Story of Vekata Rao of Hyderabad, South India, 157
Trường, Chinh, 177, 179–81, 183, 184n4
Truyen Kieu, 192
Turnbull, C. M., 30–2, 34

UCLA Film and Television Archive, 91
Unattributed materials and grey propaganda, 96
United Church of Northern India, 161–2
United States Information Agency (USIA), 95, 100–1
Universal Exposition of 1900, 195
Unloading Lighters, Manila, 81
US Signal Corps, 14

Van Dijk, Janekke, 11
Verstraelen, Arnold, 108
Viet Minh *see* League for the Independence of Vietnam
Viet Nam Feature Film Studios, 174
Viet Nam Film Institute (VFI), 184n5
Visiting New Flats, 40
Vocational School, 40
Voices of Malaya, 49, 69
Voyage au Congo, 8

Wadiyar, Kanteerava Narasimharaja (Maharaja of Mysore), 217
Warwick Trading Company, 5
Wavell, Stewart, 73, 76n17
Welch, Richard, 90–1
Wesleyan Methodist Missionary Society (WMMS), 154, 166n20
White, Nicholas, 67
Wild Cargo, 232
Williams, William Appleman, 101
Wilson, Woodrow, 82
Wintle, P. and Homiak, J. P., 89
Woods, Philip, 3
Worcester, Dean, 85–7
Worry Free, 58
Wright, Basil, 5, 131–3
Wright, Noni, 37–8, 43n6
Wurfel, D., 100

Young Men's Guild Mission, 162

EU representative:
Easy Access System Europe
Mustamäe tee 50, 10621 Tallinn Estonia
Gpsr.requests@easproject.com

www.ingramcontent.com/pod-product-compliance
Lightning Source LLC
Chambersburg PA
CBHW050850230426
43667CB00012B/2234